I0143049

Surrender

Surrender

Book 4 of the Raptor Castle Series

SOPHIA JOHNSON

Surrender
Copyright © 2012 by June J. Ulrich

All rights reserved. No part of this book may be reproduced in any form or by any means without the prior written consent of the Author, excepting brief quotes used in reviews.

The book is a work of fiction. Names, characters, places and incidents are the product of the author's imagination or are used fictitiously. Any resemblance to actual events, localities, or persons, living or dead, is purely coincidental.

Cover design by Delle Jacobs
http://www.dellejacobs.blogspot.com

Typesetting by Hale Author Services
www.haleauthorservices.com

Visit the author's website at www.sophiajohnson.net

Acknowledgements

For my wonderful husband Gil who continues to feed me every night. Sometimes he has to whistle loud and shrill when I get too engrossed in what I'm doing to think of being hungry!

My daughters, Val and Lorrie, are my biggest fans. They don't mind telling their friends that their mother is a sensual historical romance writer. I wonder if they'll tell their grandchildren.

Chapter 1

Raptor Castle, Scottish Border to Northumbria.

Why in Hades was she sitting bare-arsed on the cold ground when she should still be curled up in her warm, comfortable bed?

Elyne startled, chasing all remnants of sleep from her mind. She shivered and rubbed her arms, dew-wet where the thin, yellow smock had drooped and exposed her flesh. Wondering what might be in the wet grass beneath her bottom didn't help. For truth, her fear of spiders caused her shivers to turn to shudders. She sprang to her feet, quickly brushing her hands over her hips and legs.

She frowned. Shook her head as she looked around. Why *was* she beneath an apple tree in the middle bailey? In the dead of night? Something fell from her lap when she stood. She retrieved a small handful of greens and held it to her nose.

Hm. Herbs, but not those she generally picked.... Had she been dreaming?

An elusive memory teased her as it swirled in a dark, gray haze. She squeezed her eyes tight and wrinkled her nose. Her brows met in a fierce frown as she willed her mind to recall it. Surely, it would come to her why she was outside the keep at such an odd time of night.

Bright colored streaks shot behind her closed lids then changed to flashing images as she coaxed them into her mind's light, piecing them together. As the images formed, she shuddered and groaned.

A black wolf. Leaping from atop a boulder, his eyes

gleaming, his teeth bared in a throaty snarl. For nigh on to two years, the beast had haunted her dreams. In the past nine months, the wolf had slowly evolved into the form of a man.

Had she seen his face this time? Nay. Shadows still hid him as they had done in all the other visions. For certs, she wouldn't share them with her father. He'd had cause enough for mirth over her dafty tales — as he called them — in the past years.

But not last eve! When the gatekeeper appeared to ask permission before allowing a Highlander and his two men to enter, his frown had changed to surprise. They had ridden up to the drawbridge after the guards had lowered the portcullis for the night. Bleh! Her father sent her to bed without allowing her to see who came at such a late hour. She had the right to. After all, a sennight ago it was she who dreamed a Highland warrior would come in the very same way.

With a father like Chief Broccin, 'twas no wonder she dreamt such… such what? She scowled and thought. But not for long. The sound of a man's boots striking the cobblestones reminded her of her present predicament. She dropped the wilted herbs, grabbed the nearest branch of the apple tree and scrambled upward. Afore the man rounded the corner, she was perched mid-tree facing the well, her left arm hugging the trunk.

Drats. Her heart pounded. Had she some spell which called the man-beast of her dreams into the world? She took a shaky breath and peered below.

Ah. No wolf. Only a man carrying a helmet in the crook of his arm. She tilted her head and studied him. 'Twas a shame there was not more moonlight. From his height and the breadth of his shoulders, he was most impressive. He observed the well then apparently made up his mind. With the sinuous grace of a sleek animal, he prowled around the small area and studied it. He hesitated for a heartbeat or two before he placed the helmet on the huge boulder standing nearby.

From the depth of his hair coloring, it must be black or a very deep brown. Shaggy, it hung down the back of his neck past his shoulders. A hank slid over the left side of his forehead teasing his eye, annoying him, for he shoved it back. Because of its unruliness, 'twas probable he'd cut it himself.

Elyne pressed her fingers to her lips to stifle a giggle, for the man disrobed as quickly as a loose slattern tempted by gleaming coins. Though, truth to tell, he had on less clothing than any whore. Naught but a woolen kilt carelessly draped around his body and over his shoulder, held in place by a leather sword belt strapped around his slender waist.

The belt and cloth he tossed atop the bolder, near knocking his helmet to the ground. His sword received gentler treatment for he carefully balanced it against the well near to his hands.

But it wasna the sword which drew her attention. His bare body did. His, um, strong, muscular arms. Wide, impressive shoulders. His bared back. Oh, my. When he bent to rid himself of his boots, his fine arse caught her gaze. Muscles played over taut flesh when he faced the well to lower the bucket and pull it up again, filling both wooden pails set beside the well for washing. When he shifted, the movement highlighted strong, sturdy legs.

For certs, those legs were covered in black hair? Would it be wiry or perchance soft? She wasn't sure. One summer when her friend Catalin came to visit, she'd brushed against her brother and cousin's legs the day they all stole away to the lake to teach her to swim. Their hair was neither wiry nor soft. Mayhap coarse? She'd never stroked her hands over a man's legs. Or anyone else's. Had never felt the urge to.

Until tonight.

Ack! Could a person hear another's thoughts? The man turned and scowled, studying everything around him. Thank the good saints he didn't look upward — except at the nearest window openings.

She barely dared to breathe. She must stay hidden.

He was nekid. She was close to the same state of undress.

Her smock was so thin anyone could see through it. She should have discarded it years ago, but it was soft from wear and perfect for balmy nights.

She must stop thinking. He'd stilled again. Did he sense someone watched him? Nay. He shrugged his shoulders, took the first pail and held it high, letting the water cascade over his body. She fancied she could see the chill bumps on his skin. Only a Highlander could stand such cold water of a night. Or her brother Ranald. Even in winter, monks never had heated water to bathe.

She stilled her thoughts again. He hooked his fingers in the soap tub, took out a goodly amount and began rubbing it briskly over his body. He backed up to give his arms room to scour his chest. His body was finely honed, the flesh separated by bunching muscles across his breast. His hair-encircled nipples must surely be hard from all the friction. She lost interest in trying to spy them. Her sight had locked onto the dimly lit rippling muscles leading down to divide the hard slab of his stomach, belly and narrow hips.

When his hands lathered from his waist, over his belly and ruffled the hair leading an interesting line to his maleness, her mouth was so dry she may as well have stuffed it with wool from a shorn sheep.

Mayhap it was a good thing she could not see him in the light of day. She would have fallen from the tree by now.

Graemme, a Morgan of Clibrick Castle, knew someone watched him with such intensity that he edged closer to his sword. He continued to cleanse himself as if unaware. Should he see the slightest advance or shift that gave away the person's position, they would find his sword at their throat.

He took slow, measured breaths as his eyes beneath hooded lids probed the shadows. He splashed his right hand in the second pail of clear water. Soapy fingers couldna grip a sword steadily without a waver. His best defense was to appear unwary of danger and take an attacker by surprise. He didna want to kill needlessly. The chief here was neither a Morgan nor a Gunn but, by looks and reputation, he was fully as warlike as both families.

When his left hand lathered his cock, it took his full concentration not to hesitate on hearing a soft gasp. He slightly tilted his head to the side and his gaze followed where his ears picked up the sound. Ha!

No assailant would wear such light-colored cloth.

No assailant would perch in a tree in the dead of night.

Had a serving maid come to steal apples when no one was about? Mayhap he would have someone to warm his pallet. It had been near a month since he swived a woman. Just the thought set his cock to swell and stand upright to stare at him.

Eager.

Ready.

Begging.

He stroked the soap over the head, down the shaft and between his legs, hefting his hardening sacks.

"Dinna worry, lads," he crooned. "Soon ye'll have a hot, wet sheath and warm buttocks to comfort ye after pounding against naught but a leather saddle so many days."

His keen ears picked up another gasp. He grinned.

"Is it my cock ye wished to spy, lass?" His voice was near a harsh growl with his need.

His flesh was so hard, so eager he didn't think he could last until he entered the lass. Best to take the edge off aforehand. He stroked his engorged flesh. Slowly at first. Then faster. But not too fast. Not until that special feeling that told him he was about to spend. His head raised and arched backward as the sky cleared. Moonlight streamed down on the apple tree.

His face tensed, anticipating his release. His gaze fastened on startled eyes opened wide and gleaming in the moonlight. They belonged to the most comely face he had ever seen. If he did not know better, he would deem 'twas the face of an innocent angel. But no innocent angel hid in a tree to spy on a man.

"Come down, pretty lass. If 'tis bed sport ye crave, I'll be happy to swive with ye." He waggled his brows and grinned.

The girl drew up her legs trying to fold into a ball and hide herself, but the branch was too small. He laughed outright.

"Come, lass, ye are well and truly caught spyin'. And ye were all but droolin' enough to rinse me."

He lifted the bucket and upended the water over his head.

His cockstand wilted.

Deflated. Like a soap bubble touched with a warm fingertip.

Cold water ran in rivulets down his body to disappear between the cobblestones surrounding the well. He shook himself like a huge dog, causing his sex to sway and bounce against his thighs then walked over to stand beneath her.

His hand flashed up and snared a creamy ankle. When she kicked out at him, he laughed, deep and throaty.

Elyne held tight to the tree while he tugged at her leg. The branches swayed and creaked, and knowing the limb was about to break, she shrieked.

Loud.

"Halt! Who goes below?"

Bleh! No way to hide, now. She was done for.

The hand grasping her ankle jerked as if in surprise.

The guard atop the wall-walk made enough noise to alert the dead as he shouted an alarm. From the sounds of men's voices and boots running, likely half the guards on the wall were scrambling to the stairway leading below.

Whoever would have thought so many things could go wrong all at once?

Something had to occur first. She'd heard the loud crack of the branch when it tore from the tree and she hurtled down. At the same time, she'd cracked her head against his and knocked the man to the ground.

The very nekid man.

She was atop him. Her smock had twisted around her waist. She knew it was so because cold air felt like ice on her nether cheeks. She tried to rise. 'Twas awkward. Who knew a man's body could be so wide? She rocked and tried to get her right knee off his, um, precious parts. He grunted with pain. He tried to help. His hands were on her bare arse seeking to lift her.

Her father's shouts rent the air. Afore she could count five breaths, it sounded as if everyone in the keep had swarmed into the bailey.

She frowned. Why was the first thing she saw — after the painful stars cleared from her eyes — the sight of her father's very large, bare feet?

She gulped.

The earth shifted.

"Ack! Merciful saints!"

She threw out her hands to steady herself. They landed on thick, wet hair. She looked down to find her fingers gripped the hair at the man's temples and pinned his head to the ground. Her gaze locked on deep brown eyes squinted nearly closed in fury and lips pulled back in a silent snarl.

She was near pulling the hair from his head. She balanced on one hand and lifted the other. It didn't help. In fact, it made it worse for her hand slipped, yanking his hair even more.

"Shite!"

She scowled back at him and spread her legs to steady herself. It caused her to reconsider her position. She was sprawled atop him. Every move she made pressed her feminine parts more intimately against his sex. Two very hard ballocks warmed her thighs, and above them his rampant tarse, stiff as an ax handle, pressed against her stomach.

"Lass! Be still!"

"Tsk. No need to yell, sir. I was trying to help."

She sought to lift herself from his wet body but should have saved herself the effort.

She yelped, for a hard arm snaked around her waist and lifted her like a floppy bag of grain.

"Hist! Elyne." Her father's commander Domnall whispered the caution as he settled her on her feet.

The Chief growled with anger, his scowl ferocious, when his gaze raked her from head to toe. She glanced down and bit her lips. For truth, she looked near nekid. Her smock had acted as a fine drying cloth. Unfortunately, it became near invisible when wet. As it now was.

"Cover her," Chief Broccin thundered.

Spying the kilt laying on the boulder, the commander whipped it out and around her, giving her back a pat. Her aunt stepped around her father and came to put her arm across Elyne's shoulders. She thanked all the Saints above that her aunt happened to be paying them a long visit.

Elyne hugged the wool close under her chin and tried to still her trembling. She'd been in trouble before. Once, someone had even kidnapped her. But now when she saw her father's broadsword pricking the hollow in the man's neck causing blood to trickle down his flesh, her knees near buckled under her.

"Broccin, mayhap you should ask what has happened afore you skewer the man?" Her aunt's hand patted Elyne's shoulder as she spoke.

"Ask? I have eyes to see, sister. Is he not nekid? Was she not atop him, her smock hiked around her hips?" He stopped, drew in a breath then bellowed, "*Swiving*?"

When all eyes turned toward her, Elyne felt her face flush. Even so, she lifted her chin high.

"I was *not* swiving."

"Dinna dare call yer father a liar!"

CHAPTER 2

THE CHIEF'S SHOUT CAUSED his hand to move, digging the broadsword's tip even deeper into Graemme's vulnerable neck.

What hurt even more was the words "yer father" careening off the walls of his skull.

No scullery maid.

No goose girl.

Not even the baker's daughter!

He had exposed himself. Had.... The thought of what he *had* been doing to entice what he knew now was the chief's daughter, made him groan and squeeze his eyelids shut. He swallowed. Uh! Wrong move. If he wasn't more careful, he would lose that bobbing lump that marked his throat as male.

Hearing shouts and grappling between men, he opened his eyes and knew it was his friends, Brian and Colyne, restrained by Raptor knights.

"Guard them in the stables until I deal with this," Broccin ordered. "Take Elyne out of my sight. She isna to leave her room, do ye ken? If I see her afore I command it, I'll take a whip to her!"

Graemme didn't dare move. So. Her name is Elyne. Judging from her father's voice, she had best listen to him. The wind turned brisk, ruffling his body hair as it swept over him. A good thing he wasn't modest, else he'd have turned scarlet by now. He glared at two women near stumbling over their bare toes so intent were they on staring between his sprawled legs. Though his cock was a lifeless fellow right now, he was still a long one. He didn't attempt to close his legs. The movement would pinch his witless cock and his balls if he couldna lift them out of the way.

Broccin must have seen where the women stared, judging from his snarls.

"Get back to yer beds else ye'll be set to scrubbing floors afore day's light. Ye men! Return to yer duties." He turned to the last man. "Domnall, get this rutting eejit up and bring him to my solar." He whirled and stamped away, the sound of furious bare feet slapping the cobblestones followed him.

Graemme took a deep breath and dared to swallow once the sword left his neck. The man named Domnall was the one who had lifted the squirming bundle of flesh off him. At least the fear of having his head loped off had kept his cock from springing to life at her movements. Had it done so, likely the sword would have been at that part of his body instead. Domnall leaned down and offered a helping hand. Graemme shook his head and hoped his legs didn't wobble when he sprang to his feet.

Two men stood nearby with their swords drawn. Did they think him foolish enough to run? Huh. They were grinning.

" 'Twas a foolish choice for bed sport, lad," Domnall said, the corners of his lips quivering.

"Do ye think me daft? Had I known 'twas the chief's daughter, I would have jumped *in* the well, not stood *by* it."

"Too bad you already bathed. You're in deep shite now." The man chuckled and shook his head.

He sent one of the grinning guards to fetch something to cover Graemme then tossed Graemme's boots and helmet to him. Walking over to the well, Domnall retrieved the sheathed sword waiting there, slowly pulled it out and hefted the steel, testing it for his own strength. When he slid it back in, he tilted his head to the side, listening to the metal sing. He studied the scabbard and ran his fingers over the snarling, black wolves burnt into the leather. He raised a brow at Graemme.

"Shame. You made an excellent choice of a sheath for your killing sword but not where you thrust your lusty cock. I'll carry this for now."

Graemme quickly shoved on his boots. After stomping

them into place, he heaved a deep sigh of resignation. The soldier returned on the run and handed a drying cloth over with a snicker. "I couldna find a kilt; all the men were sleeping in them. 'Twas the biggest cloth that wasna wet."

Graemme looked at it in disbelief then shrugged. "Was it meant for a child?"

He stretched it around himself and it met at his left side, though barely. Once he'd donned his sword belt, the several layers of leather held the cloth in place. Satisfied, he buckled it low on his waist. Carrying his helmet in the crook of his arm, he looked down and saw how little the cloth covered his bulging sex. Feigning unconcern in his disarray, he moved his helm before him in hopes of covering more of his private parts.

"Where to?"

He rolled his head to relieve his stiff neck. His forehead ached and pulled, likely swelling the size of a fat goose egg from the way it felt. He didn't bother wiping away the blood that had welled in the little valley at the base of his neck. 'Twas probable he'd be spilling a lot more afore this night passed.

Elyne stood beside her bedside table, undecided whether to sit on the ample ledge at the window opening or climb on the bed. She eyed Aunt Joneta, and Ada, the servant who was more friend than maid.

"I fell out of the tree," she said for the third time since they had walked back with her to her bed chamber. She scowled when her aunt grinned.

"Did you fall or did you jump, love. It has been many a year since I have seen such a splendidly naked man," Lady Joneta said.

"He pulled my leg and I fell!"

"Maybe we're going about this in a backward way? Instead of starting from what we saw, tell me why you were not here in your bed?"

Elyne groaned and tried to kick the wet clothing crumpled

on the floor, but Ada snatched it away in time. Though she now wore a dry smock and gown, she had pulled the man's green, black and blue kilt across the small of her back and draped it over her arms.

Lady Joneta studied Elyne, making her want to squirm.

"Come, love, we had best prepare a good excuse for your father."

Ada tilted her head, her eyes alight with curiosity. She nodded, guessing the reason.

"Ye had a walking dream, again, eh?"

Elyne sighed and climbed up on the bed to sit, legs crossed in front of her. Mayhap they would believe her. They had not made fun of Elyne's dreams near as much as others had.

"Aye. I woke in the bailey, sitting beneath the apple tree. The dream had startled me awake. I did not go there to meet that man."

Now and then, she lifted the kilt to her face and inhaled. An enticing scent. Pine and sandalwood blended together.

"Ah." Joneta's eyes smiled at her. "At least you were not kneeling in the muck of the pigs' sty."

"Or sitting on cow pies in the middle of the pasture like last summer." Ada's grin spread from ear to ear.

"True, but snuggling atop a naked man brings a lot more trouble than needing a hot bath," Joneta said as she shook her head.

"I dreamt about the black wolf again. Only this time, he turned into a man." She stopped and shrugged. "Almost a man. All but his head."

"How did you go from sitting under the tree to being atop him?"

Ada looked eager to learn it all.

Elyne shrugged her shoulders and spread her hands wide.

"I heard his boots striking the stones and did not want anyone to see me. So, I climbed the tree."

"He didn't have boots on when we got there." Joneta looked at her, and seeing her blush, nodded. "You watched him bathe? Your brother Ranald has told you many times that your curiosity was going to get you in trouble."

Elyne sighed. She rubbed the kilt across her nose again, pretending she scratched an itch, and took a deep breath. Likely, he slept beneath the stars and traveled through forests for many days to have such a fresh, exciting scent.

"You think I meant to spy on him? I couldna very well tell him I was in the tree near nekid, now, could I?"

She blurted out the rest of what happened after the man undressed. But not all of it. Why, he had taken delight in handling his secret parts until he spent himself on the ground! She couldn't tell anyone about *that*. She cleared her throat.

"I truly did not expect him to strip and bathe. No man but Ranald would wash at the well when the water is near ice," she added, knowing her face flushed. "He, um, looked up at the night sky when he scrubbed, his, uh, stomach. That's when he spotted me. He believed I was a servant girl seeking a bed partner and grabbed my foot."

"Ah. The limb broke." Joneta looked down at her hands, then back up to study Elyne's face. "Did he take advantage of your inexperience and mayhap, um,..."

"Nay!"

Joneta's eyes sparkled. "Well, now, if I were many years younger, I would gladly change places with you."

Ada giggled. "Mayhap we could lure him to the well again?"

"Not if he looked at you as if he wanted to slit your throat, you wouldn't." Elyne huffed in annoyance.

"Hm. There is that." Lady Joneta sighed and nodded.

"Father won't kill him, will he?"

"Nooo. If that was my brother's intention, he would have done it right away."

Elyne had to agree. Unfortunately. Not that she wanted the man dead. But she didn't like the other solution, either.

If her aunt had not been visiting Raptor Castle, Elyne would be below listening at the door to her father's solar. With Ada beside her. When she was alone again, perchance she should gather supplies together in case she had to flee in the middle of the night.

Her stomach gurgled at the thought.

This time, it seemed unlikely she'd find an easy way out of her problem.

CHAPTER 3

GRAEMME STOOD IN THE dim solar, a guard on either side, and eyed the large, heavy man sitting in near-shadow across from him. A brace of candles stood no more than five paces behind the chief. Their weak light accented the stubborn set of the lord's jaw on the right side of his face. Graemme knew from earlier this eve when he had entered the keep, that the man's hair was dark brown or near-black like his eyes. For certs, his neck looked strong enough to support the head of a bull.

This angry Scot was not unlike Graemme's own father in coloring. Huh. Not unlike in body build, either. They both could be mistaken for Zeus in human form.

"Ye'd best tell me how ye lured my daughter to swive with ye right out in the open where any randy bastard could watch!"

Chief Broccin slammed his fist down on the table, causing the pewter cup to tilt and splash near half the ale onto the wood.

"I have told ye times aplenty that we *were not swiving*. She fell out of the tree and landed atop me." Graemme's jaw snapped together.

Just mentioning it, Graemme remembered the feel of her soft body stretched atop his own hard flesh. With little thought, he could also see her wet smock revealing ivory skin and small, beautiful breasts — and the dark triangle guarding that honey-eyed place when Domnall snatched her away. Feeling his shaft stirring, he shifted the helmet over his sex.

"Ye expect me to believe ye walked up to the well, got yerself nekid and a beautiful young woman fell from the tree like a ripe apple and splattered on ye?" Broccin's glare at Graemme showed he wanted to sever his cock and stick it on a spear as a warning to all men.

Shite! He'd best keep to the edge of truth in case the girl lacked sense and told him all. Agh! Hopefully, not *all*.

"Not quite fell. A foot dangled near in front of my eyes. I grabbed it, thinking to prevent having my throat slit in the dark. I didn't know it was your daughter until you called her such."

Broccin snorted in disgust.

"That's just rat-brained enough to be true. What think ye, Domnall?"

"We have found the lady in far stranger places, my lord. She didn't look to be too distressed. Not enough for you to maim or disfigure a man."

"Distressed? Humph. Looked to be enjoying herself, to my eye." He scowled at his commander. "What think ye to twenty lashes?"

"Ye canna thrash yer own daughter!" Graemme was sick at the thought.

"Not her, dumb wit. Ye."

He swallowed and tried not to flinch.

"I dinna think yer son Ranald would forgive ye if that were to happen. He's sensitive to that, ye know," Domnall said.

"Mayhap take a finger or two? Or the toes on one foot?"

"Nay. No maiming. The lasses dinna take kindly to men leaving trails of blood when they run from the keep."

"Well, then. I'll think of something that will satisfy me in another way." He snorted and jutted his chin at Graemme's bare sex peeping below the helmet. "And get him a kilt out of the chest!

Domnall jerked open the wooden chest beside the fireplace and tossed Graemme a wide length of wool cloth.

Keeping his back to the Chief, Graemme quickly changed his clothing. Once he'd draped the kilt over his shoulder, he tucked the end beneath the belt. He didn't know whether he was over the worst of it or not.

Eying his sword, he could forget about asking for its return. For now.

Broccin motioned for him to sit in a chair opposite him and

spoke again as if he had not stopped before. "But I'll not have Ranald's temper disrupting things if he finds a new bastard at Raptor next summer."

'Twas *not* the end of it. The worst was coming.

"He'll wed her."

"What?' Graemme sprang upright. Suddenly the thought that mayhap twenty lashes would have been easier, entered his mind.

"Dinna play like ye have no ears. Ye heard me aright. Sit!"

He stood as still as stone until Domnall shoved the chair to brush the back of Graemme's legs. He sat.

"You may go," Domnall said to the two guards patiently waiting, and grinning, behind Graemme. "Check on his men in the stable. Make sure they have pallets for the remainder of the night."

After the door closed behind them, Chief Broccin poured three cups with ale, slapped one down in front of Graemme then pulled his seat closer to the table opposite him.

"Give me yer family name and holdings."

"I am Graemme, the youngest son of Angus, The Morgan of Clibrick Castle in the Highlands."

Broccin nodded, looking satisfied.

Shock began to leave Graemme, replaced by cold anger. Had they been playing with him this entire time? He scraped the chair sideways and stretched out on it. Slowly sprawling his legs in a comfortable way, he swigged the ale pretending he had known they bluffed about the whipping and the maiming.

He had no recourse but to marry. No one would believe he had not been ramming his cock into her when they had witnesses aplenty that he was nekid beneath her. With his hands on her bare arse as further proof.

"Ye wish me to marry yer only daughter when ye know nothing about me?"

"Aye. I wish it. I know enough. Ye are sprung from the loins of The Morgan of Clibrick."

"Huh! Being The Morgan's son makes me a worthy husband for yer daughter?"

"Nay. Dinna be a gowk. Ye are the first man she canna refuse to wed for her usual silly reasons."

He thought Graemme a fool? Was the man dafty? From the sounds of it, this Elyne had suitors aplenty. He wondered what those *silly* reasons were. Mayhap he could use one of them himself.

Graemme had no wish to wed. Had no time for it, either. If not for his brother Magnus' inflexible quest for revenge, Gramme would never have stopped at Raptor. He should have paid heed to the tales of strange happenings at the castle. Huh! He'd thought it naught but fanciful thinking. What man could turn into a black raptor at will? Nor did he believe if the lass didn't favor a suitor, she called on a frightful crone to roam the halls at the midnight hour to protect her.

He cleared his throat, hoping to clear his mind.

"When yer daughter has naught but foolish dreams, how can she refuse to wed where ye wish?"

"Did ye not talk to my daughter afore ye swived her?"

"I did not…"

He groaned hearing Domnall smother a laugh with a cough. Seeing the rage build in Broccin's face, he sought to cool it.

"I meant to deny that I took advantage of yer dear daughter. It was a strange accident and nothing more."

"Still, ye have ruined the girl. She must wed and even she canna deny that." Chief Broccin turned to Domnall and scowled. "Send for the little fool afore she has time to make up some ridiculous dream to get herself out of this scrape."

Domnall was up and lifting the latch before he finished speaking. Graemme rolled his shoulders, wishing he was any-where but here. A cold draft of air from the opening door blew between his bare legs and up beneath his kilt, tickling the hairs on his stones. He'd always thought Lowland Scots were soft as their neighbors in Northumbria. Not so this family. The window shutters stood open letting the cold night air gust into the room. The candlelight flickered and all but two lost their flames as Domnall returned.

"Relight the cursed things. Too bad Ranald isna here to

see to it properly."

A strange thing to say. Domnall frowned at his lord and gave a slight shake of his head at the chief then bent to light a twig.

The room was large, even compared to Clibrick Castle. They sat at a sturdy table, centered in the room. A vivid tapestry warmed the long wall behind Chief Broccin. It caught him up in it. It was so vivid he felt he was standing atop a hill gazing across a lush, green valley where an abbey or convent stood in the distance. He could not tell which, but the stone cross above the entrance signaled it was either one or the other.

The wall opposite held naught but several battle weapons. A mace, a war hammer, a much-used bow and a broadsword flanked a shield. Two shiny, black eagles flew on a field of yellow; a red bar, painted diagonally across, divided it. There were dents in the shield. A rusty stain...

He didn't ask about it.

He had walked by a small table when he'd entered and saw what looked to be maps or parchments of some kind. One lying open showed sketches of hills, trees, castles and such.

A man's room. He would relish hearing what went on within that room over the years. Huh! It would likely turn his straight, black hair to curly gray.

The door burst open and Elyne hurtled in, stirring the air in the room enough to snuff out more candles. The lady Joneta followed at a more dignified pace. The guard started to go toward the hearth, but Broccin threw up his hands and gave a disgusted look.

"Dinna bother. She'll flutter around and put them out faster than we can keep them alight."

Elyne took in the scene the minute she entered the room. The Highlander sat across from her father, his body relaxed as he leaned back in the chair, his long, hairy legs sprawled comfortably in front of him. A kilt covered his pertinent parts, but it left from his knees downward bare.

A soft repetitive sound drew her gaze to his left hand. 'Twas fisted until the knuckles were white, striking against his knee. Hm. The kilt slung over his shoulder sagged open and revealed the mat of crisp black curls that covered his chest. The pulse jumped in his neck, fast and strong.

Agitated.

His chin was far stronger than she remembered from her first glance of him. It was deeply shadowed as were his cheeks. His thick hair was a mess. Probably dealing with her father made him near pull it out in frustration.

He looked tired and irritated. More than irritated. He glared at her as if he blamed her for his dire straits.

She scowled back and rubbed her fingers over the soft kilt folded in her arms to keep herself from sniffing it one more time afore she returned it to him.

As she dropped the kilt unceremoniously onto his lap, she glanced aside at her father and held her head high.

"Ye suggested I flutter? I ne'er flutter."

"Next ye'll be sayin' ye are sure-footed as a barn owl walkin' the rafters."

"That I am."

Why did the Highlander stiffen?

Her father pounced on her answer quick as a hawk seizing a plump grouse.

"Ha! Then ye didna fall out of the tree like a rotten apple. 'Tis good ye took a fancy to Graemme here since ye'll be weddin' him once we settle the time."

Lady Joneta spoke quickly. "Brother, do not decide in haste. Perchance there is a good reason for what we saw this night?"

"Aye. I canna marry him! He will… he will…," she spluttered, not knowing what he would do to cause disaster in a marriage since she had not as yet had a final dream about him. Most revealed themselves sooner, but the dreams of the black wolf, though frequent, had not been complete enough to know the danger that awaited.

"He will what? Bring his leman to live with ye at his keep? Throw ye from the battlements when ye dinna produce an heir? Will he show himself to prefer young boys over ye after ye wed?" Broccin's brows lifted.

"They were all good reasons, Father!"

"Hm. Mayhap. But ye have no good reason not to wed Graemme here and a very good one for marrying."

"Pfft. What good reason could that be?" Elyne shrugged.

Lord Broccin's face hardened, his chin thrust forward.

"If ye dinna, I am tempted to relieve yer friend here of his stones...." His voice trailed off as he leaned back in his chair and waited for her reaction.

The Highlander bolted upright in his chair. Elyne tapped a finger on her chin and rolled her eyes upward to study the ceiling, wondering if she should consider defying him further.

Broccin's lids lowered. His back eyes smoldered with menace. In a slow, silky voice, he continued. "Now, then. Afore I am through cleanin' my blade, I will have Domnall here get coins aplenty from my money chest. He will use them to pay the good sisters at Mary Magdalen to keep ye there for the rest of yer hapless life."

Domnall, casually leaning one shoulder against the side of the fireplace, clamped his lips together so tightly they lost color. Lady Joneta gave a low cry of fear.

"For shame, brother. You canna mean such cruelty." Lady Joneta moved to stand between Elyne and the chief.

"Ye think not?" He snarled low in his throat. "Did no one learn from the last time a child of mine sought to thwart me?"

Terror filled Elyne. Her throat closed and her heart pumped as though she had raced up the stairwell clear to the top of the corner tower. She folded her arms across her chest, her hands clenching her forearms to hide their trembling.

She didn't doubt him, had good reason not to. Her sire had ordered Domnall to abandon her brother Ranald at Kelso Abbey. How could a father yell he didna care whether his son lived or died as long as he never returned to Raptor Castle?

One thing she knew full well. A man valued his sons far more than he did any daughter. Her only worth was in marrying well and providing him with a good alliance and extra land.

Graemme surged to his feet, spilling the carefully folded kilt to the floor. Never had he known a father to cause such fear equal to what he sensed in Elyne. Her face turned ashen, her eyes took on a hunted look and he had no doubt her knees quaked. But for all that, her chin lifted. For certs, the lass had a warrior's courage!

He rested a heavy hand on her shoulder and pressed her flesh in warning, hoping she would keep her tongue behind her teeth until her father's temper cooled.

"Ye have no need to threaten such dire events, my lord. The lass *will* marry me. Ye have my vow on it." His jaws hardened, for never did he make a vow he didn't intend keeping. Elyne tensed even more beneath his hand. His calloused fingers tightened on her shoulder and gave it a little shake. The fey girl was muddled enough to defy her father. He looked over at the older woman and nodded.

"Lady Joneta, please see my bride-to-be to her bedchamber whilst we decide what needs be done."

His face implacable, Graemme turned Elyne and forced her to meet his hardened eyes. "Go to yer room. Now," he ordered in his sternest voice. Elyne opened her mouth to object. "Enough! We will talk on the morrow." He spun her to face the doorway and gave her a slight shove.

"Come, Elyne. We can do no more here." Lady Joneta took a firm grip on her niece's elbow and urged her from the room.

The door had no sooner closed firmly behind them than Chief Broccin slammed his fist on the table so hard a lesser wood could not have withstood the blow.

"By Hades! Ye are more than all the mewling men put together who panted after my daughter."

"She has had ample suitors to judge, eh?"

"Aye. She became troublesome over her first suitor on fearin' he would house his leman in the keep."

"For certs, Broccin, the lass did dream true," Domnall put in. "Douglas brought his leman into the keep a moon after he wed the MacDonald's youngest lass.

"Women do take mislikes to that." Graemme nodded.

"Aye. Her fears of young Niall held worth, too," Domnall

added. "The lad couldna bring himself to break his bride's maidenhead until his father threw Niall's favored squire into the moat and drowned him."

Broccin made a disgusted face. "Huh! But she turned her nose up at a fine keep for the simple reason the man was twenty and two years her senior."

Domnall spoke up. "Perchance she feared she would be like Lady Letia and her bairn would be birthed after his sire died. The stress of swiving likely did Warin de Burgh in."

"Hm. My sire is much older than that with his current leman." Graemme thought of the young, red-haired lass who seemed to adore his father.

"Elyne also claimed she feared Aymer would toss her over the battlements if he couldna perform his marital duties and produce an heir," Chief Broccin said.

"I would expect more than one lass *fell* down a stairwell because of such." Domnall frowned and rubbed the stubble on his jaw. "'Tis too soon to tell if old Aymer's wife carries a much-wanted heir. She may yet be tumbled down one."

"Pfft! The twit could learn to make a cock swell for a man past his prime." The chief scowled, not caring it was his only daughter he talked about.

"Aye, but only slatterns know of such." Graemme hid a shudder of disgust. How could any father expect his innocent daughter to have knowledge of intimate things?

"A serving wench could use her mouth to prime a wilted cock to stand hard enough he could hump his wife."

Graemme cautioned himself not to roll his eyes. "'Twas kind of ye to turn the men away."

"Heh. Not me. They left like they feared Lucifer's crusty tarse was hot after them. The stable lads claimed the men babbled some tale about the ghost of an old crone comin' in the dead o' night and threatenin' to cast a spell on them."

"A ghost? What spirit's spell would be so fearful a man would willingly forfeit an alliance with Raptor Castle?"

"One I would heed! She foretold their stomach would spew forth vile green liquids, their arse would flow like a waterfall and their cock shrivel and rot if they didna leave at first light."

Graemme nodded gravely. "'Tis a curse I wouldna care to chance!" He had his suspicion of who played the old crone at Raptor Castle.

"Enough blather. We canna have the wedding until Father Martin returns from Hunter Castle. Still, I would have yer betrothal vows said on the morrow after we break our fast."

"Then we must decide what an alliance between our families will provide. I can see no obvious gain for either of us." Graemme settled back on his chair and accepted a fresh goblet of wine from Domnall.

"Keepin' yer stones hangin' in their rightful place isna gainful?" Broccin raised his brows.

"Ye are tellin' me that was not a threat to force the lass in line?"

"Huh! Ask Domnall."

Graemme looked at Raptor's commander who pressed his lips together and simply nodded. By Satan's fetid breath! This chief was as savage as the Morgan and Gunn clans combined. He shook his head, whether in admiration or disgust, he wasn't sure.

"Other than keepin' yer body parts together, ye will gain powerful alliances here on the border country. In yer travels, ye have heard of The Black Raptor, have ye not?"

"Aye. Near halfway from the Highlands, people tell of the fear this man brings. When in a rage, he causes fires to light, and strange winds and such occur. Some even say 'tis not man at all but a feathered raptor the size of one."

"Nay. 'Tis a man right enough."

"Truth to tell, was he once a pious monk? I canna believe any man used to wearing the cross could do the deeds said of him."

"'Twas no tall tale. Ask him some day." Broccin barked a short laugh.

"Ask?"

Broccin looked at him, a sly grin on his face.

"Aye. He will serve as witness to yer weddin' vows." Broccin belched and patted his stomach. A pleased smile spread across his face, and to Graemme's surprise, he winked.

"The day ye wed, ye gain the devil as yer brother-by-law."

Chapter 4

"I ALWAYS FEARED ONE day Father would turn on me. He seeks to discard me as he would offal in the moat." Elyne was so affrighted she could not stop the shivers coursing through her body. Trying hard not to spew her last meal, she swallowed the bitter fluids that surged to her throat.

"Discard? Nay, child. How can you think of marriage to a comely man in such a way?" Lady Joneta hugged Elyne's shoulders as they entered her bedchamber.

Ada stood waiting, a nervous smile on her lips. "I thought ye might need the comfort of yer furry friend."

Sharp yips and barks greeted Elyne as a scraggly dog launched himself at her and pawed her leg to demand attention. Its ears were unlike each other. One gray ear stood rigidly at attention while the other drooped like a small cabbage leaf left to brown in the sun for a sennight. Elyne nodded glumly at Ada then reached down to scratch the bumpy, gray head.

"They are savages in the north. 'Tis said they still wear animal furs and are so warlike women canna go into the villages for fear of being kidnapped." Elyne's hands began to tremble.

"I would think animal furs are warmer than woolen kilts," Ada suggested, "but why are ye speakin' about going north?" When Elyne's shoulders drooped even more, she had her answer. "Ye are to wed that braw nekid man, then?"

"Father said we are to repeat betrothal vows on the morrow." She gulped and blinked at her aunt. "If this Graemme is still here."

Ada nodded, understanding passing between them. "Well, now, ye need a good night's rest and things will look much better afore the next night comes."

Ada bustled over and opened the clothing trunk on the far wall. She near tumbled in when the dog gamboled over and nipped at her heels.

Elyne picked him up and hugged his squirmy body to her chest.

"I can see your thoughts, Elyne." Lady Joneta shook her head and rolled her eyes. "This man will not be easily fooled by your playing the ghost of an old crone. More likely, on the morrow's dawn, he will still be abed. With you beside him." She laughed when Elyne's eyes widened and Ada straightened as if someone had shot an arrow into her nether cheeks. "My brother may believe in ghosts and crones curses, but I am not so dim-witted."

"Yet ye never told?"

"Nay. Those men were not suitable for you. This one gives me a different feeling."

"Aye. With me, also." She went on when her aunt tilted her head at her. "When he stares at me, I am so fearful I have chill bumps and strange sensations low in... my body." She flushed not wanting to describe that exact spot. "'Tis a very strange feeling. Not rightly tremors. More like a heartbeat where there is no heart?"

"You are sure 'tis fear?" Joneta's smile seemed to hold a secret.

"Truly, it is."

She frowned when Ada snickered. Wanting to turn her aunt's attention from the Highlander, Elyne murmured and ruffled the fur on the dog's back as she put him on the floor.

"That must be the most ugsome dog in all of Scotland, Lass." Lady Joneta shook her head in wonder at the creature

"Ye think he is ugsome?" Elyne frowned and studied him. "He is such a happy lad that I ne'er thought him less than, um, plain?"

"Hah! He is beyond plain, Lovey. Everything about him is at odds from his ears to his paws. His front legs are firm and straight but barrel staves must have formed his rear."

Ada helped Elyne change into a sleeping garment, and as her head cleared the warm cotton smock, Elyne reached up to shove her tousled hair out of the way and studied the dog. As he scampered over to grab hold of a carelessly dropped ribbon, she looked at him from the rear. Seeing all four legs at once, she chuckled.

"For truth, they do. When my brother rescued him from Baron Rupert's forest, he thought perchance the evil man had caused him injury as a small pup."

The dog happily wagged his scrawny tail and raced back to grab the toe of Elyne's leather shoe. He pulled and tugged then growled and shook his head so fiercely he near upset her balance. She hopped up on the side of the bed to take them off.

"Um. We canna keep calling him *dog*. What think ye of Matin for his name?" Seeing their questioning expression, she explained, "The priest was singing the psalms for Matins when Ranald rode into the bailey with the wee, scrawny dog in his arms."

"Huh! Too much dignity in the name for the likes of him," Lady Joneta said.

As soon as Elyne untied the lacings around her ankle, he yanked the shoe from her foot and ran around with it in his mouth, happily growling and beating it against the floor.

"Foolish dog. Ye'll ruin my best shoes."

Elyne started to hop down to retrieve them, but Ada grabbed the shoes from the dog and set them atop the bedside table out of his reach.

"Ye had best take him to the stable for the rest of the night, Ada. He is in sad need of a bath."

Ada nodded and scooped the dog up in her arms. While Ada's back was turned from Lady Joneta, she quickly whispered. "I'll see to our guest. Mayhap a warning will be enough to send him on his way at midnight."

"Come, Lovey. Into bed with you. First light will be here afore you know it." Lady Joneta kissed Elyne's forehead and she and Ada quietly left the room.

Elyne's loving aunt had acted as mother to her brothers

and her when their own had died of fever many years before. Elyne did not know what she would do without her. Had she not resisted her other suitors, she would be married to one of the simpletons now and be living near Raptor Castle. At least she would be able to see her family and friends within a day's ride. But the Highlands? Once she left, would she ever see them again?

'Twas not likely.

There was but one way to insure the Highlander left Raptor and sped back from whence he came. She knew now why she awakened beneath the tree with a handful of herbs — because she would need them if Ada's warning didn't work.

She waited until there was utter silence in the keep. Reaching out, she grabbed her shoes off the table and quickly put them on. In a hurry now, she swung her cloak off a wall peg beside the door and draped it around her shoulders. She made herself slow down and eased the latch up.

She crept down the stairwell and near hugged the walls as she made her way through the great hall. Pallets covered much of the floor, and whenever a restless sleeper turned, she froze until they settled again. Between loud, grating snores and thunderous farts, her footfalls went unheard.

Once outside, she paid heed to the guards atop the wall-walks as she quickly went from shadow to shadow to the herbal garden. Carpenters had built a workshop against the outer wall there for her mother. She took the key from her cloak's pocket and gathered the heavy wool around the lock to make a cushion. As she cautiously turned the key, the cloth muffled the sound of the lock snapping open.

Even as a young girl, she had enjoyed preparing potions and such here with Aunt Joneta, using recipes her mother had recorded on old parchments too worn to use for carrying messages. Inside the warm interior and beneath the dried herbs hanging from the roof-beams, stood a long wooden table where she and her aunt had mixed elixirs, purgatives, prepared tinctures and stirred rubbing oils when their stocks were low. She took a deep breath, enjoying the smell of the drying herbs, knowing that when she lived, her mother had breathed the same scents.

Bottles, jars and flagons, some with oils and others with wine distilled with herbs, filled the shelves along the back wall. She pulled a three-legged stool over and stood atop it to retrieve a small vessel near out of sight on the top shelf.

Since her first worrisome suitor had pricked her ire, she had stored a bit of honeysuckle plant chopped so fine it was near powder in a jar and sealed it with a wax lid. It was ready for use in case a man was not sufficiently afeared of the old crone to leave her in peace. A small amount cured locked bowels; a larger amount also caused vomiting. She removed the correct amount for a man Graemme's size and funneled it into a vial.

On her way back out the door, she spied the drying racks where purple-black plums picked at the edge of ripeness and dried until they shrank and crystallized into gummy sweetness. Each Sunday, she gave some to the cook to spread on her father's porridge. It helped relieve his excesses in eating the sennight before. She grabbed a goodly portion of these and wrapped them in a small linen cloth. Storing everything in her pocket, she returned to her room.

When Graemme entered the bedchamber, the maid Ada was plumping his pillows. As she turned to leave the room, she had one hand on the door latch then hesitated, looking uneasy.

"Sir, my mistress is kind and wouldn't want to see you harmed. 'Twould be best if ye didn't sleep within the castle this night. 'Tis rumored amongst the villagers that a warlock has taken a fancy to the Chief's daughter."

"Oh? Would this warlock be the Black Raptor? I hardly think he would 'take a fancy' to his own sister."

"Nay!" Ada blushed at the thought. "'Tis an evil man my mistress refused. He wants no human to have her. If you sleep within, he will send his minion to lay a curse on you. I am sure you heard of the many men who fled screaming at first light, never to be seen again?"

"I canna say that I have." Graham tried hard to keep a serious look on is face. "Thank yer mistress for the warning. I will take heed."

Ada nodded, looked satisfied, and slipped through the doorway.

When her footsteps receded, he wondered what Ada was up to. He stripped and flung himself on the bed and welcomed the cold air on his naked body. He stretched arms and legs wide, rumpling the bed sheets as he sought to relieve muscles too long kept tense from meeting with the girl's father. He had not let his guard down even for a breath after the threat to his ballocks, expecting he would need to fight or take flight at any moment. He scratched them now, wryly thankful they still adorned his body.

Afore they left his solar, Chief Broccin had swilled wine as if fearing never again would a drop pass his lips. That he'd led him to the room the mysterious Ranald used when he visited, told Graemme he thought favorably of him. Else, mayhap the man was so sotted his thinkin' was muddled? Humph. The more probable reason was because it was farthest from the stairwell leading down to the keep's exit.

His future father-by-law might drink enough to topple men equal to his weight, but even so, he ne'er faltered about wedding his daughter to a man who would take her so far away. He was generous in his dowry for Elyne and, in turn, was shrewd in demanding a promise of dower lands in the south for her. Graemme had long earned his way and had coins and jewels enough to find a small manor close to Raptor Castle that would meet her father's qualifications.

Sprawled on the bed, he flexed his muscles and stretched again, feeling tension ease as he did so. Mayhap fashing over his problems that kept his eyes from sleep was a good thing or he wouldn't have noted the door latch easing up. 'Twas the midnight hour by his reckoning. He pretended sleep, but his right hand stole slowly to the bed's side till his fingertips touched his sword propped there. Mayhap the rumors of the castle's haunting were true? The rushlight beside the stairwell was strong enough to highlight a ghostly image framed in the doorway. Were he a superstitious man, his knees would be knocking together. Peering between near-closed lids, he took his time studying the hideous wraith. The form wore a covering from head to toe. Its material was so thin he could see tangled hair falling over a white face heavily streaked with blood.

The eyes staring at him from behind the hair were wide and rimmed with such a large circle of black they appeared to be in hollow cavities. The ghostly crone carried a small iron pot in her left hand, holding it in front of her. By the sounds of clanging against the inside walls of the vessel, she stirred a steaming liquid with a ladle far too big for the purpose.

He pressed his lips tightly together when she uttered a muted cackle, no doubt softened to keep the chief from awakening. He pretended to startle from his sleep and sat upright in bed.

"What ghastly creature is this?"

"I be the murdered crone of Raptor, dead these many years and rotted in me grave," came a high-pitched, quavering whisper.

"What tragedy brings ye to leave yer restin' place?"

"To warn ye that if'n ye dinna ride forth at first light, the curse of Raptor will fall upon ye!" She cackled again, a little louder this time.

"What is this fearsome plight ye speak of?"

"If the sun falls upon ye within the castle walls, ye will sicken. Green slime will spew from yer lips, yer arse will spurt vile shite like water crashing o'er rocks in a swollen stream..."

Her eyes must have adjusted to the darkness, for she hesitated and blinked at his sex displayed between his legs on the white sheet. "Um, and yer tarse will wither like the smallest carrot from two years past!" She thumped the ladle around in the pot, stirring away.

"I canna order the guards to raise the portcullis and lower the drawbridge. I must awaken the Chief." He took a loud, deep breath as if ready to bellow for Chief Broccin.

"Nay! Rest the night. Be first to leave Raptor when darkness turns gray!"

"If ye spare me, I will be in the bailey afore first light."

The crone hesitated, unsure how to deal with an agreeable man. Finally, she nodded.

"I be off to seek me grave, then."

She made a slow turn and walked so smoothly back through the doorway she appeared to float. He almost chuckled aloud when she closed the door slow and easy so as not to make any sound. He fell back on the bed, a grin splitting his face. His bride would have much cleaning up to do afore she could seek her bed and sleep.

Elyne hurried two doors down and slipped into her room. At first, she felt elated that she had blocked another betrothal attempt. But in the space of a heartbeat, disappointment took hold because Graemme so easily gave in. Of all her imaginings, she had not taken him to be a fearful man. Why, she had prepared to chant gibberish and do other ghoulish things to impress him.

After carefully removing the veil and folding it, she poured the kettle's hot water over the cloth waiting in the washstand's basin. While it cooled, she took off the old, torn chemise, wadded it into a ball and shoved it in the corner of her clothing chest. She sighed as she rubbed heather-scented soap over the wet cloth until it was properly sudsy before scrubbing her face. It took several rinses and a lot more soap before she cleansed her skin of the charcoal around her eyes and the cherry goo pasted from her hairline down to her chin.

The Highlander gave in so easily it was near an insult. Ye dimwit! The truth is, he didna think ye worthy of chancing a few aches in his belly. Hah! Much less the loss of his manly parts. Even her brothers as young boys prized those dangling pieces of flesh. When playing in the woods, they would taunt her because they could piss against a tree while she needed to crouch down behind a bush for relief.

And grown men? They preened in front of women when an

obviously hardened tarse nudged their kilts like a ram's horn. Bleh! Mayhap they pilfered a sausage from the cookhouse and strapped it to their belly? She grimaced. With such thoughts, she might never enjoy another plump, juicy sausage.

What was she huffing about? She should be relieved she could go to bed and not worry about saying any silly betrothal vows on the morrow. A grin came to her face as she dumped the stained water out the window opening. She'd best sleep now, for she wanted to rise early and gloat when she watched the weak nithing of a Highlander waiting with his friends to escape the castle walls.

The black of night began to lighten to gray when Elyne woke. She scrambled out of bed and scampered across the cold floor to peer out the window. Graemme and his friends, Colyne and Brian, were ahorse and waited at the barbican as the gatekeeper prepared for the day's coming and goings. When all was prepared, the three near galloped over the drawbridge and across the clearing into the wooded path beyond.

'Twas good to know she was done with another simpleton. If ever she found a man courageous enough not to believe in an old crone's curses, she would gladly welcome him as a worthy husband.

She hopped back in bed and regretted having sent the dog to the stables to spend the night. Why did she feel a need for the comfort of a warm body next to hers?

Too soon, Ada entered, setting peat in the fireplace and lighting it. Elyne pulled the covers over her head, still sleepy from keeping herself awake till so late last eve. She waited until Ada stopped bustling around the room and came over to stand beside the bed.

"Come, lass. I warned the Highlander but he paid me no heed. The crone must have been more convincing!" Ada stopped and winked at her. "The Chief said I was to see ye went down to break yer fast with him and the Highlander when he arises."

"For certs. I am most anxious to start the day." She smiled brightly, hardly holding back her glee anticipating her father's face when Graemme didn't appear.

She hurried donning a pale blue smock with a deeper blue gown.

"Yer hair is in a rat's nest!"

"I worked hard to make it appear unkept for many years." She smiled back at Ada, but the smile faded when she learned how much it hurt undoing her handiwork.

"Did the crone leave yer unwanted guest properly affrighted?"

"Aye. His horse was in full gallop by the time its hooves struck the middle of the drawbridge afore dawn. Like all the rest, the Highlander was a weakling."

She and Ada enjoyed a laugh. By the time she was ready to go below, her stomach was grumbling. She was so hungry she would eat everything in sight!

Even sausage.

She stopped near the foot of the stairwell and leaned forward to peer into the great hall. Colorful banners hung above from every rafter. Done in vivid threads, generations of women had sewn picturesque tapestries on the wall opposite the fireplace to record the family history. They gave the room a warm effect. The far wall was bare except for a standard ten paces on either side of the fireplace. Her father's black silk with a yellow eagle, its talons spread for the kill, hung from a bracket to the left. To the right fluttered a yellow silk with two black eagles, a red bar dividing them. Looking at the two standards, one and all knew the harshness of the Raptor men. Throughout the room, huge iron candle branches chased the shadows into corners.

Servants had set up long trestle tables and benches below the high table. A snowy linen cloth covered the chief's table while pewter plates, drinking horns and pitchers of wine awaited the diners. Where Elyne normally sat, a colorful arrangement of wild flowers stood in a tall earthen vase.

Large bowls of cooked apples soaked with honey and nut

sauce stood at each end of the table, with platters of hard cooked eggs, pigeon pie, sausage and cold roast veal between them.

Such a lovely, cheerful mood. Too bad Father was going to be disappointed without the guest of honor. The Chief stood with his back to the great fireplace, Aunt Joneta was to his one side, Domnall at the other. At least seven castle knights laughed and talked with them, their backs to her. All were dressed in white shirts, their kilts neatly folded and strapped around their waist with heavy leather belts, then draped over their shoulders and held there with crest pins.

As she started to enter the great hall, the little dog streaked into the room, outsmarting a stable boy trying to catch him. Elyne stopped to enjoy the funny dog's bow-legged run as he headed straight for a warrior wearing black tassels knee-high on his boots. At the last moment, the wicked little thing launched into the air and latched onto the nearest black cords in midflight. His forward momentum nearly skidded the relaxed warrior's foot from under him.

"Satan's arse!"

His gaze snapped downward. No doubt thinking to rid himself of the pesky creature, he shook his foot. When the dog did not let go but snarled and tried to shake its prize, he bent and gently forced the dog's mouth open then picked it up. Husky laughter rolled from his chest when he held the scruffy bundle at eye level and studied it. Could the fool not see it was a dog?

She glimpsed his profile and caught her breath. It could not be! With her own eyes she had seen Graemme leave with his two companions afore dawn!

"I take it this misbegotten varmint belongs to Raptor's knotty-pated crone?"

For certs, 'twas him. She recognized the deep voice that made her think of warm, dark honey flowing over hot bread.

"What makes ye think so?" Chief Broccin scowled down at the dog.

"He is as ill-shaped and hapless as the crone. No doubt the two have knocked themselves senseless wandering throughout the castle of a night."

Ohh, she'd show him how senseless she was! She eased herself back up several steps, and once sure they couldn't see her, she signaled a passing servant. Once the girl came, she told her to send Ada to her room. Elyne twirled on the steps and raced back to her bedchamber.

When she descended the stairs a short time later, she could hardly keep a grin of anticipation off her face.

CHAPTER 5

"**N**AY, NOT THE CRONE'S. 'Tis Elyne's," Broccin grumbled and gave the dog a disgusted look. "The day she rides off with ye, I will kick his scrawny arse into the woods and let the wolves chew his bones."

Surprised to learn his bride-to-be favored the small dog, Graemme put it on the floor. Stranger yet was the chief's reluctance to turn the cur out while his daughter was yet here. This ill-shaped bundle with his misshapen back legs made him appear to squat so he could shite.

He looked down at it and shook his head. Hopefully, Elyne would not request they take the dog. Though she may be a bit lonesome at first. Perchance he should allow her maid to accompany them? He would think on it.

The strange dog seemed fascinated with his leg, for now it had locked its front legs around his calf and was...

"Satan's crossed eyes!"

The dog humped Graemme as if he was the hottest bitch in the castle. He jerked his foot off the floor and shook his leg, but the wiry little devil hung tight, grinding away.

"Do not! Ye will hurt him," Elyne called out.

She swayed and dodged people as she ran across the room. When she skidded to a halt beside him, Graemme turned and raised his brows. Elyne scowled back.

"Ye didna leave?"

"A-a-aye, I did," he slowly drawled his reply. He straightened his leg again and held it off the floor. The dog held on. Humping and sliding down Graemme's boot. He ended scrunched up at his ankle. "This... this creature? Ye have a fondness for it?"

"I do."

"I would ken last eve's crone havin' a dog such as this. But my future bride?"

She glared at him but when the chief spoke, she couldn't give him the scornful answer he deserved.

"The crone? She visited ye and yet ye didna flee?" He shook his head and struck Graemme's shoulder with his fist. "Ye will make a worthy son-by-law!"

"I am not afeared of a crazy old crone's threats. 'Tis not possible to cause such dire misfortune simply by saying it will happen."

"Mayhap ye should have listened more closely, Sir Graemme." Elyne bent over to pick up the dog, for he had exhausted himself and released Graemme's leg.

At the same time, Graemme leaned down to adjust his boot.

"Our vows *will* be said afore Sext at midday," he murmured for her ears alone.

"Humph. If ye are still hale and hearty." Elyne turned her back and put the dog down.

"Stop fashing around with the stinking dog so we can eat."

Broccin's growled words drifted behind him as he made his way to the high table.

Graemme was only too glad to sit, having been up way afore dawn. He had dallied at the last moment, feeling a tinge of sympathy for the girl whose father cared so little to whom he married her. He sent Colyne and Brian off to check the village and surrounding countryside for news of his brother.

He flushed when the Lady Joneta leaned around her brother to make mention of the flowers close to Elyne's hand.

"Elyne, Sir Graemme came across a field of wild flowers. Are they not lovely?"

Elyne's eyes widened. She looked at the colorful flowers and then at the hardened warrior sitting beside her. This man had taken the time to pick flowers? She swallowed her surprise.

"They are lovely, indeed. Thank ye."

As Ada and two of cook's helpers hurried through the

doorway carrying steaming bowls of porridge, Elyne felt a stab of regret. Just a stab. Not enough to change her mind. While the servants served the other diners, Ada smiled and set a bowl down in front of Graemme.

"Ah, porridge. 'Tis healthy to start each day with gruel."

"A little milk?"

Elyne handed him the small pitcher setting close to her hand. He nodded his thanks and doused the porridge with it. She watched from the corner of her eye as he started eating.

She put her hand over her mouth to stifle a giggle when her father leaned forward to say something to Domnall. While his back was turned, the dog had stretched tall and took a quick lap of the chief's porridge. It scampered back at the last moment.

"He lives dangerously, as does the crone," Graemme said with a tinge of menace.

Elyne knew it was no idle comment but a warning. The rest of the meal passed quickly, for everyone was too intent on enjoying the fare to spend time talking. All went well until Graemme glanced down and saw the little dog sitting on his hind end, begging.

"Well, now. Yer legs do ye some good after all, Squat."

"Squat?"

"Aye. To call him 'dog' is unfair to the hunting beasts in the castle. Even when walking, he looks to be squatting to sh..., uh, 'tis a fitting name."

Elyne snorted. It was fitting, but she wouldn't admit it.

When Graemme fed Squat a bit of pigeon pie, she did not object.

When he gave him a small slice of sausage, she kept silent.

When he scooped out a small spoonful of leftover porridge, she near jumped out of her chair.

Squat's long tongue lapped over and around the spoon before she could stop him. She bumped into Graemme's arm, hard. She reached down and grabbed the spoon from him before Squat could put his tongue to it again.

"Ye are gawkie, Lady?"

"I am never clumsy. I thought to keep the dog from chewing

the spoon. He is foolish enough to think he can eat wood."

"He looks to eat little of anything that would put meat on his bones." Graemme looked at her from the corner of his eye. "Does his mistress neglect feeding him because she's so busy prowlin' around at night to spy on nekid men?"

"His mistress does not prowl around looking at men."

"Aye. She does."

She snorted and frowned.

"Did ye forget hidin' in the tree while I bathed?"

"I wasna hiding to spy on yer bath!" Her face heated as if she was standing close to a steaming pot of porridge.

"And what of the crone who came into my room?"

"So? I dinna know what the crone saw."

She had an urge to fan her face with her fingers. For truth, he must be taking wicked delight in her discomfort.

"Me. Nekid. On the bed. She stared. I think she feared she would miss something."

"I dinna think so. One nekid man is much alike another."

She had always thought so. Until last eve. There had been little light in his bedchamber, but what there was filtering into the room, she could not miss his splendidly bronzed skin against the white sheets. Never did she think to see any man as finely made as he. Why, she had near forgotten what she had gone there to say. She started to squirm in her seat and planted her feet so close to each other that she couldn't move. It was a trick she'd learned when she didn't want her father to know he'd caught her in a lie.

"I hope ye will rid yerself of sneaking around afore we wed. My brother does not take kindly to women who are loose with their favors."

Graemme shifted on his seat. His stomach was beginning to rumble and gurgle much like someone who had not eaten in days. He cleared his voice, hoping no one else could hear the disgusting sounds his belly was making. 'Twas harebrained. With all the people in the room talking near at the same time, you could hardly hear yourself think, much less hear someone's guts talking.

His mouth filled with bitter water rising in uneasy waves to his throat. He swallowed and needed to swallow again. Lucifer's tainted breath! He was going to spew!

Never had he left a table so quickly. His long strides took him to the door of the keep. From there, he did not stop running until he reached the privacy of an empty stall far back in the stable. He soon put two empty buckets to use.

"I thought you said the old crone's curse was naught but crazy rambling." Brian's red hair and laughing blue eyes peered over the top of the stall.

"'Twas no curse which caused this." Graemme groaned and wretched into the bucket he clutched to his chest.

"Hm. Looks like the curse to me. Ye're sitting on one bucket and hugging another."

"My dafty bride-to-be tampered with my food."

"Did the other diners become ill? What if it is the curse?" Brian' mouth twitched at the corners. "Have you checked your cock?"

Graemme shot him a quelling look. "When did ye return?"

"Brian, why are you hanging over an empty stall?"

That's all Graemme needed. Another witness to his plight. Though to be fair, 'twas only Colyne's footfalls coming toward them.

"Graemme here didna believe in the crone's curse. Seems he should have."

Colyne's brown head joined Brian's. They stood together, gazing at him as if they'd never seen a man with griping pains in his gut.

"Hm. Did your cock… ?"

"Nah, Colyne. Already asked him. He's afeared to look."

Graemme made a threatening gesture with the bucket. He talked fast so as to get it all out in one breath, "Brian, find Lady Joneta. Ask for a potion. She will know what the little devil used." After he heard the man's footsteps pounding away, he sighed with relief.

Never had he spent a more miserable morning. Lady Joneta quickly supplied him with a potion which gradually eased his symptoms. Finally, he was able to control his bodily functions. Before leaving, he gave coins to the stable boys waiting at the huge double doors of the stable. Brian and Colyne helped him return to his bedchamber.

He no sooner closed the door than servants arrived with a bathing tub and buckets of hot water. They said the Lady Joneta had ordered them to watch for his return. Their eyes were wide and admiring, for never had they known anyone to have challenged a curse. Though he felt as drained and weak as a starving kitten, his rising wrath gave him much needed energy for the rest of the day.

"It was not a good thing to take your anger out on Sir Graemme, Elyne." Lady Joneta gave her niece a disapproving look.

"Do ye think I could yell and scream at Father and not find myself abandoned in the convent afore dawn?"

Sickening nausea crept chilly fingers through Elyne's stomach. Could someone feel the effects of another's distress? Mayhap she *had* acted in haste. Too late, now. Sir Graemme would not have to even think on who had made him so dreadfully sick.

"When he came out of his room, his eyes were spitting hot rage every bit as much as Ranald's do when in a fury," lady Joneta said.

Mayhap she had misjudged the size of the dose she'd given to Ada? She hadn't meant to cause the warrior the misery the stable boys reported. Why, with only having licked Graemme's spoon, Squat had soon needed to stop every several paces, leaving foul smelling shite. The servants were not happy. Seeing her father's scowl, she had swept the dog up and carried him out to the pasture.

When someone rapped on the door, it had such a sound of urgency Elyne near jumped out of her shoes.

"Lady Elyne, Sir Graemme requests your presence at the chapel for the betrothal vows. 'Tis near high noon."

From the little she had seen of this Highlander, his blue eyes had always held laughter. Not so now. They looked hard as steel.

"Aye, Sir Brian. I think it fitting I change..."

Brian interrupted her. "Nay, Lady. You are to come at once."

She had to stop herself from stomping her foot when she eased the door shut. She waited to hear his footsteps leave. They did not. So. Sir Graemme didna take any chance she would not appear. No doubt, Sir Brian would enter and drag her all the way up to the chapel if she didna appear speedily.

"He does not even give me time to change clothing!"

"No doubt he expected you to be ready. Come. You need only a silver circlet for your hair and a matching silver girdle about your hips to make your blue gown festive."

Elyne was ready far sooner than she wished. She steeled herself to look calm as she opened the door. Sir Brian lounged against the far wall of the landing, his arms across his chest. He straightened and offered his arm. He raised his brows.

"The chapel?"

"Up the far stairwell." She nodded toward the corner. "'Tis in the east tower close to Father's lodgings."

"You are in a hurry, Sir Brian?" Aunt Joneta's voice was quiet but admonishing.

Sir Brian near skidded to halt his long strides. "I beg your forgiveness, ladies."

Too soon, they were going through the chapel doorway.

"I hear ye had a bout of sickness in the stable?" Chief Broccin looked Graemme over from head to toe then grinned at him.

"Aye. Mayhap I ate too quickly this morn." Graemme shifted from one foot to the other. Even thinking about not having a handy bucket made his stomach clench.

"Ye are white as a lass during her moon's time." Broccin's gaze moved down to settle on Graemme's crotch. "Did yer cock shrink to a nub? It isna about to fall off, is it?"

"Not likely. Why would you think so?"

Piss and shite! Was the man going to demand proof?

"The rest of the curse came full circle, did it not? I heard ye spewed in one bucket till it was green slime while yer arse thundered as it filled another. The stable lads thought better to bury the bucket than to cleanse it."

Graemme knew his face was no longer white but red as poppies in the field.

"'Twas naught but eating too heartily."

Chief Broccin cuffed him on the shoulder as admiration gleamed in his eyes. "Ye are a worthy son-by-law! Not a single bone of fear in yer body. 'Tis likely ye have broken the curse. I will have grandsons aplenty if ye keep a bairn in her belly as oft as Ranald plants his seed in Catalin."

"Ranald has children?"

"Aye. One strapping boy followed by twins, a boy and a girl, the very next year."

When Chief Broccin beamed with pride, he lost his sinister appearance.

"Um. I canna promise twins. I will strive to have Elyne swelling afore we reach Clibrick. 'Tis the one thing that might make her obedient."

"Huh! Good luck on that."

"I would dispense with the common betrothal vows, if ye dinna object."

"Ye dinna have the same custom in the Highlands?"

"We do. Yet I require something more binding from yer daughter."

He took in a slow, deep breath and stopped himself from rubbing his stomach when a pain struck. He wished this whole mess was speedily over afore he needed to run from the room. He rocked forward on his toes when the chief slapped his back and threw a heavy arm across his shoulders.

"Whatever ye need to get the girl bound to ye and wed. If ye dinna, yer prick may not have shriveled off," he paused then turned his head to fix his steely gaze on Graemme, "but yer danglin' stones are still in danger."

"She will wed me. I'll see to it. But the marriage ceremony

will have to wait."

He told Elyne's father, afore he could wed, he had a pressing duty to perform for his family. In one more day, he would have to leave but would return in two months time. He talked quickly, not wanting anyone else to overhear.

The sun's rays glinted on the gems embedded in the cross above the small altar. Flashes of colorful lights danced on the walls, giving the room a festive air. Until Elyne saw the face of the man waiting across the crowded room. 'Twould be more fitting if lightning danced across the sky and thunder rocked the walls of the keep.

Her intended stood beside her Father, talking earnestly to him. Where Graemme's face had been a sun-warmed bronze at dawn, now its paleness accented the dark shadows of his beard beneath. The skin on his cheekbones had pulled taut and his jaw looked as if God had chiseled him from slate. His wide, sensual lips were thin and pressed tight. Was he still in pain?

This morn he had worn a white shirt and tasseled boots with his kilt. Now, his attire looked like a man dressed for war. He had on a black tunic belted around with a sturdy leather belt holding a heavy warrior's sword. His fingers caressing the sword's hilt showed he itched to pull it free from its scabbard.

The closer she came she realized the chest of the tunic was gray. Embroidered in striking threads across the gray, a black wolf leaped from a brown boulder. Recognizing the wolf from her dreams, her knees near buckled. Why would her father not believe her?

She saw Graemme's burnt almond eyes and read the fury flashing there.

The devil of her nights had come to life.

Elyne's hand tightened on Sir Brian's arm.

"Aye, Lady. You did yourself no favor when you angered a Morgan of Clibrick. You have caused our motto of 'With a strong hand' to become 'With a hand of steel.'"

Graemme studied Elyne as she came into the chapel. Watched as her eyes turned from defiant to regretful. Then to something akin to fear when she studied the standard across his tunic and met his eyes. She should have thought of not angering him afore she dosed his food.

Strangely, her father didn't take exception to his curt mood when Graemme insisted they dispense with the normal betrothal vows. He looked around and noted the room had filled with the knights and ladies of the keep. Fortunately, a cool breeze drifted through the window openings, so they would not be unduly warm. After Brian walked Elyne over to her father's side, Graemme beckoned Brian and Colyne to stand behind him.

"Halt yer clack!"

Chief Broccin's voice boomed with such vigor 'twas a wonder the walls did not shake. Two women who had been whispering behind their hands near fell off their bench.

"Ye lack-witted women are here to witness betrothal vows between Sir Graemme of Clibrick Castle and Lady Elyne, not to smirk and slabber o'er seeing his private parts last eve."

Graemme steeled himself from flinching at the reminder. The sooner they finished here the better. He could not be too long away from privacy, for his gut sent up warnings of impending doom. His teeth clenched together to keep from yelling vile threats at his intended bride. He stepped forward to the center of the altar. He studied Elyne like she was some strange creature he wanted to crush.

She was lovely to look at with her curly brown hair restrained with a silver circlet around her brow. It left glossy curls streaked with auburn hanging to her waist. A silver girdle made of circlets hugged her hips, accenting their slimness. To look at her, a man would not guess this woman could be so treacherous she'd near poison a man to keep from wedding him. She would learn a Morgan didna run like some addled lowland Scot with a backbone of sheep's wool!

He stared into eyes the color of wet earth. When he noted her swallow a gulp, he held up his right hand. With one finger, he slowly crooked it, demanding she come forward. When she hesitated, he narrowed his lids at her.

"Go!" Chief Broccin shoved her from the small of her back.

She moved to face Graemme while her father stationed himself facing them, his back to the altar.

"Sir Graemme wants his own betrothal vows and I see no reason to deny him." He looked at Graemme and nodded, then stepped back.

Graemme took Elyne's hands in a hard grip and stared into her eyes.

"My family, the Morgans of Clibrick Castle, have long held honor to be all important. A promise once given is sacred. Our vows bind us one to another for all time. Once spoken, it can never be broken — not by choice; only by death."

"I, Graemme, son to Angus, The Morgan of Lake Naver, betroth Elyne, daughter to Chief Broccin of Raptor Castle, to me forever in righteousness, in faithfulness," he stopped for the length of a breath and his jaw hardened even more, "and with a strong hand. Two months from this very day, we will wed.

"Ye will repeat after me: I, Elyne, daughter of Chief Broccin of Raptor Castle, vow to wed Sir Graemme, son to Angus, The Morgan of Lake Naver, and take him as my husband forever in faithfulness, in obedience and forsaking all others two months from this very day."

Elyne's clear voice mumbled over the words vow and obedience.

"I didna hear ye. Ye will repeat it clearly for everyone to hear." He squeezed her fingers to let her know he meant what he said. She said the vows again, this time her voice was stronger. For truth, it was with anger, but he cared not a whit. He repeated the rest of the words he would have her promise:

"I, Elyne, will not poison, cause to sicken or injure in any way, my betrothed."

She gasped so loudly anyone with half a good ear could hear her.

"I didna poison ye!"

"Heh. I suppose ye will say the crone did? Dinna waste my

time with such foolishness."

"I did not give ye poison. I canna help it if ye have a *delicate* stomach for Cook's fare," she muttered.

"Mayhap I should add lies to the vows? Repeat the words. Now! I have no more time to linger."

Elyne near shouted the rest of the vows, her face red with indignation. He cared not.

When they drew apart, he muttered to Colyne. "See everyone leaves. I would have words with my delightful bride-to-be."

CHAPTER 6

As THE WHISPERING CROWD filed from the room, Graemme watched Colyne lead Elyne to stand alongside the window opening. She glared a look of loathing at Graemme then stared down on the practice field, her shoulders set stiff in defiance. He waited until they were alone then stalked over to her, his fists convulsing with tightly controlled rage.

"Come. Sit." He grasped her elbow and led her to a bench facing the altar. A firm pressure on her shoulder forced her to sit.

"How could I have poisoned ye?" she muttered. "I merely gave ye something to rid yerself of yer ill humors. I give Father the same thing each sennight."

"Hah. You rid me more of my *good* humors than aught else. I had thought to deal lightly with ye, to treat ye kindly. After the way ye made a fool of me afore the whole castle, I have changed my mind."

"I did not make a fool of ye. If naught else, ye are more of a warrior than ever. The men think ye are a gladiator from Roman times. The senseless women drool like Adonis has come to life."

"Aye. An Adonis whose throne was a bucket in a stall; his crown another bucket clutched tight to his chest!"

He burned with resentment at her having made him a laughing stock with the warriors. The stable boys most likely babbled to one and all about the hapless Highlander in the stall.

Elyne looked at him strangely before understanding dawned in her eyes. "Oh."

"I will speak slowly so ye canna misread my intentions. Ye will be here. In this keep. Two months from this day. *We will wed*. Once the ceremony is over, ye will return with me to

Clibrick Castle. Is that clear?" He waited for her nod. She stared stonily at him, her mouth tightened into a stubborn line. He bent down and grasped her chin between his right thumb and forefinger and tilted her head upward.

"Is... that... clear?" The words hissed with menace between near-clenched teeth. His eyes narrowed until he saw naught but her brown eyes glaring at him. To show her he was out of patience, he jerked at her chin.

"Aye! Are there any other orders? Mayhap ye wish to demand what I wear, what I eat, what I think while ye are gone, lord and master?"

"There is! Never again will ye pretend to be a witch. I am surprised no one has sought to burn ye at the stake. I canna have word of yer unholy doings reaching the Highlands. They are not so forgiving."

"Why do ye insist I was the crone?"

"Oh, come now. Do ye think I have not eyes to see?"

"Do I look..."

"Piss, woman! I saw yer near-nekid body atop me in the bailey. Yer wet smock was like a second skin. And when ye stood in my bedchamber doorway, the light was behind ye." He straightened and put his hands on his hips. "No supposed old hag has the body of a nymph." When she opened her mouth to argue further, he added, "And no ancient woman has lush hair guardin' her private parts. Ye stood with yer legs spread, if ye remember?"

Thinking of the picture she had made, his cock pulsed and began to swell. He did not try to control it. He doubted she was an innocent lass, not with the way her eyes had strayed to his cock last eve.

Shame spread heat over Elyne. He accused her of making a fool of him, yet he had humiliated her by making her repeat those horrid vows in front of the ladies and knights of the entire castle.

"If ye are done ordering me around, mayhap ye can go about yer business and get the Hades away from Raptor!"

"'Tis my intention to leave on the morrow's first light." He started to whirl away, then turned back and pointed a finger at her. "See to Squat. The poor beastie canna move without farting and leaving a trail behind him."

As he was leaving through the doorway, he heard her mutter, "Flea-bitten bastard." Had he not needed to seek relief, he would have returned to swat her backside.

He regretted not having the time.

Graemme's favorite warhorse sidled and shook his head, near upsetting the young groom off his feet as they passed the middle stall. The chief's magnificent black warhorse, Goliath, kicked at the walls and trumpeted, no doubt jealous the stable master didn't lead him outside.

"What did you learn in the village this morn?" Gramme asked Brian. He led his horse out the huge double doors onto the cobblestones surrounding the stable. He spied Squat in the grass, and from the looks of his position, he had shite to spare. Poor, miserable little dog. He could smell him from ten paces away.

"Older villagers were less at ease answering questions, but the young lads were only too quick to tell about a lovely girl found beside her dying horse, holding its head in her lap."

"Aye," Colyne added. "Chief Broccin's other son, the one named Moridac, found Muriele and brought her to the keep."

"Ranald has a brother?"

"Dead now. Killed the day afore he was to wed. 'Tis why Chief Broccin forced the monk home." Brian stared at Squat and shook his head.

"Monk? What monk?"

"Ranald. Moridac's identical twin," Colyne chimed in.

"Lucifer's piss! He was a monk?" Graemme's mouth dropped open. No wonder the girl was a fey lass. Her father was ready to cut off his ballocks, and he had called Graemme's future brother-by-law a devil. Her family was even stranger than his own.

"Aye. In Kelso Abbey. Has a terribly scarred face and back.

Father did it," Colyne said. He made a wide detour around a foul looking mess on the ground.

"Near killed him then abandoned him for fifteen years. When the other twin died, Chief Broccin took an army to Kelso and forced the monk to return to the castle to sire grandchildren," Brian said.

"Got a special paper from the Pope and all," Colyne added.

"Humph. No wonder he spits fire with his eyes." Graemme shook his head. Poor bastard. "Did they say more about the woman, other than her horse died and they brought her to the castle? Where is she now?"

"She went with this Ranald and his wife Catalin into Northumbria. She's part Saxon, part Norman. Word has it he went to besiege his wife's castle. Her uncle had taken it over." Brian adjusted his sword and scabbard and swung up into his saddle.

Colyne settled his helmet on his head. "They say the girl with hair the color of summer wheat didna return. Could only be her. There is some talk about her disappearing into thin air."

The stable boy tied a leather bag of supplies behind Graemme's saddle then a second boy handed each man a leather skin filled with enough water for the day.

"There's talk about a man with black hair and eyes hard as granite sniffing around the village. One day he was there, the next he was riding hard toward the English border like a hound with a dripping prick chasing his bitch." Colyne gave his horse a slap on the rump as warning to stand still before he leaped into the saddle.

"Ye dinna look so good, Graemme," Brian said as he eyed him. "Do ye not wish to stay abed whilst we check the other villages?"

"Well, piss and shite. Nor would ye look hale if ye had been shitting yer brains out all day. We will ride out as planned."

Graemme wiped sweat off his forehead and swallowed back bile surging to his throat.

Lady Joneta called to him. "Sir Graemme. Hold, if you please."

She hurried down the path from a small building built against the outer wall. She was walking carefully, balancing a small jug whilst keeping her skirts from sweeping the ground. And Squat's leavings.

"I prepared a potion to soothe your, er, aches. By morning, you should feel your normal self." Her eyes studied him. "'Tis naught but boiled barley water with a bit of savory for you to drink."

"What will this do? 'Tis not the same as ye gave me earlier."

"It will soothe your stomach and, um, quiet your gut. Dinna eat food this day," she reached in her pocket and took a cloth bag tied with string and handed it to him. "If you hunger, boil this barley to make gruel."

He nodded and fastened the items in his saddle pouch. Over the top of his saddle, he spied Squat as he eased himself to lie down in the shade of a tree. "Do ye think mayhap ye could make something for the poor beastie?"

She smiled up at him. "Aye. I await its cooling. He is much better than he was." She tilted her head and studied Graemme's face. "Dinna think our Elyne is always as she was this past day. Things were not as calm as they are now. She's had much to be afeard of."

His eyes widened. What was it like when there was turmoil?

"Thank, ye, Lady." He looked at her and debated. "If ye would have yer niece happily wed, make sure she keeps from me this day."

He bowed and turned to leap onto his saddle. He took a deep breath of air, thankful he would be gone from Raptor Castle for the day.

"The stable boys said Sir Graemme and his men are searching through the villages for a woman with hair the color of wheat. He must be the man Muriele was afeard would find her." Ada finished brushing Elyne's hair, for her mistress had required an early bath after attending to bathing Squat. He would let no one else near him but her.

Elyne nibbled at her lip and made up her mind. "Aye. I will go to Domnall."

"Not yer father?"

"Nay. Father is too pleased with Sir Graemme to think of anything which would put a halt to our wedding." She drew her finger over her lips where she had nibbled them a bit hard. "Domnall will send a messenger to warn Muriele to deny any visitors."

Elyne whirled and ran from the room. She didn't stop until she found Domnall atop the rear barbican talking to the sentries there. He came over as soon as she entered the wall walk.

"What is it, lass? You look like the ghostly crone chased you up the stairway." His eyes twinkled down at her.

"Not ye too, Domnall," Elyne said with a scowl.

"What else sent you in such haste?"

Elyne told him all she had learned from Ada and was grateful to see his face turn as worried as her own.

"Aye. Ranald would be furious if we did not do all we can to keep Muriele safe. I will send a messenger to the convent at once. It may be unneeded. Your brother posted a man to pose as gardener there. He will protect her once he is warned Sir Graemme may appear." He turned and clattered down the stone steps and disappeared through the gateway to the middle bailey.

Elyne breathed a sigh of relief. The messenger had a full day's start ahead of Sir Graemme. But would one day be enough?

Mayhap if Graemme was too tired at first light, he would delay his leaving until well after the noon hour? She took a deep breath and hurried back to Ada. They both watched Domnall's messenger riding out the massive double doors of the stable, and by the time he hit the drawbridge, his horse was in a full gallop.

Elyne kept watch from the northwest tower well into the day. It was past dusk when Sir Graemme and his two men emerged from the woodland path and rode across the cleared area to the drawbridge. As soon as they clattered into the courtyard, the gatekeeper ordered the bridge up, the portcullis down and the gates secured for the night.

She sighed with relief. If Sir Graemme was here, he could not be out hunting down her friend as a wolf does after a fine doe. She hurried back to her bedchamber and prepared for the night. Ada waited with hot water and, after Elyne refreshed her body, Ada rubbed perfumed oils over her skin.

"Did the cooks prepare the special dishes for Sir Graemme?"

"Aye. Sir Graemme will have beef wrapped in a spicy pastry, figs stuffed with cinnamon, sparrow's eggs, clams boiled in ale, turnips steamed with dill and basil and red wine spiced with rosemary, sage and rue." Ada shook her head and grinned.

"Mother's recipes listed each as a stimulant for the male shaft. I fear after the porridge this morn, he will be lacking strength, uh, to be properly, um…"

Ada giggled. She held up her hand with her middle finger drooping halfway down. "Ye mean his prick may not spring to life?" Her finger sprang outright.

"For truth."

"If ye are shy with me, how do ye think to seduce the man? Are ye certain ye should do this, lass?"

"What difference now or two months from now? 'Tis still the same, is it not? We are near as legally joined as if Father Martin was here."

She gulped, for though she knew what happened between a man and a woman, she had expected it to be with someone who excited her. Someone who made her heart beat faster. One who made her flushed and anxious for him to take her.

"Catalin and Letia have said the best part of being wed is bed sport. My friends would not tell me an untruth. They said the worst is answering to another man."

"Aye. 'Tis glad I am to do as I please." Ada grinned at her. "The freedom makes up for being a servant. If I want to swive with a man, I have but to whisper where I spread my pallet and it is filled."

"It isna fair. Men always rule us. My father, my brothers, uncles. A husband is the final straw. Men have freedom from the time their voices change and their first straggly whiskers appear."

"Aye, but they follow their commander's orders."

"This is different. Look how Sir Graemme orders me about." She deepened her voice and strutted around the room. "Vow ye will do this. Vow ye will not do that. Dinna dare think on being somewhere else in two months. Bah! At least this one night, I will have control."

Chapter 7

ONCE GRAEMME REACHED HIS bedchamber, he near tore off his clothing in his eagerness to lower himself into soothing hot water. He had meant to bathe at the well, but after the happenings there last eve, he thought better of it. Who knew if the chief had another kinswoman anxious to spy on male flesh!

One thing for certs, Raptor Castle's servants knew how to treat a guest. He had no sooner entered the room than men arrived with hot water and a bathing tub.

He was tired. No. More than tired. Exhausted. Drained. But he was pleased with what he had learned this day. Leaning his head back on the tub's rim, he bent his legs, letting the hot water flow over his chest and stomach. He rubbed his belly, exploring his sore muscles. The last potion Lady Joneta gave him had worked miracles.

He glanced down, a slight smile spread his lips, for his cock floated and bobbed like it sought to put its head above water. His fingers rubbed lower into the wiry curls surrounding it, then reached to explore his balls. Every inch of his body ached, even there.

"'Tis glad I am ye are still with me," he muttered. "The chief was too eager to nail ye to a tree. Hah! Probably the cursed apple tree beside the well."

He patted the round stones in their sacs then surged up in the water when someone scratched at the door. His hand sought his sword hilt resting on a short stool beside his bath.

"Aye? Enter."

His nose recognized the exciting smell afore the door opened more than a crack.

Two of cook's helpers entered, carrying enough food for two men. Though the tub stood in front of the fireplace and the table was close to the window opening, the full-breasted woman in the lead made a curved path to it. Her black hair bobbed when she swung her head to glance down at his bouncing cock. It was changing noticeably in size. When she giggled, he waggled his brows at her. The young, red-haired lass behind her stared and licked her lips. He near reached out to take her hand and invite her to stay.

Sanity returned.

'Twould be best not to dip his wick in his betrothed's keep. Servants were all too ready to brag of their conquests. Chief Broccin would chase him with his hunting knife if he found he'd been swiving the servants after having supposedly taken his daughter the night afore!

He shook his head at the last minute. The girl's shoulders slumped. 'Twas unfortunate. His cockstand was erect and eager. On their way back to the door, they couldna resist another long look at his body glistening beneath the water.

His sigh echoed in the empty room. The bed would have been most comfortable with the red-headed lass cuddled to his chest and the cushy curves of the taller woman curled against his back.

The aroma of beef floated on the evening breeze making him salivate. His belly grumbled reminding him how empty it was. More than empty, really. 'Twas a wonder his stomach didn't meet his backbone.

He grabbed the bathing cloth and hurriedly soaped it until bubbles floated from it. Water surged in waves and splashed the floor when he stood to scrub his body. After he soaped from his head to his hips, he paid particular note to his sex. He lifted his cock and washed the bottom side and around his ballocks until his skin was pink. When he finished his back and hips, he sat in the water and rinsed.

Never had he felt more cleansed. If he was not so hungry, he would go straight to bed. Wrapping his lower half in a large drying cloth, he padded with wet feet to the table.

Wine. Beef wrapped in something. Clams. Turnips and asparagus. His mouth watered. He popped a sparrow's egg into his mouth while he used his eating knife to attack the beef. The bite of meat was near in his mouth when he hesitated. Should he be wary?

Nay. The girl was troublesome, for truth, but she could not be so fashious she would again tamper with his food. He ate the beef. Not only did he eat the beef, he near ate everything they had brought him. He burped, loud and strong, before savoring the stuffed figs.

He sprawled back in his chair, enjoying the cold air from the window sifting between his legs. The wine was surprisingly good. Better than any at Clibrick. He would have to ask where they secured it.

One thing about eating heartily — it made him sleepy. He stretched, contented. He would make a point of going into Northumbria when he left here in the morning, but since they'd learned what they had today, it was all for show. Still, it would give Magnus a head start. He grinned, thinking of his cagey brother. They would have to ride hard afterward to overtake him afore he reached the Highlands.

He stood and unwound the drying cloth from his hips. He tossed it on the chair's seat, picked up his sword and leaned it against the bed. After pulling aside the sheet, he plopped down on the bed, arms outstretched.

Were angels to lie down on clouds, they would feel as he did as his body settled into the down mattress.

What awakened him? He didn't twitch, didn't move. His chest kept up his quiet, deep breathing. Um, he noted the faint scent of heather and raised his lids 'till only a thin line of vision showed.

Piss! Elyne had come to plague him again. Did she think to cackle and drool, throw cinders around the room or something else to pretend she was a wraith? At least she hadn't striped her face with cherry juice. He waited to see what her new mischief would be.

She hesitated in the doorway, biting her lower lip. So.

Undecided, eh? She'd best be. He'd not go lightly with her again.

He watched as she eased the door shut and walked so quietly her footsteps did not even whisper across the floor. She stood beside the bed hugging her arms then rubbing them before she started inching her smock into her hands and began to lift it. He watched long, slender legs emerge, then the soft material slid up over firm, gleaming thighs. It bunched now in front of the joining of her thighs, and he found himself holding his breath.

Waiting. Tense.

Did she plan to run screaming from the room, claiming he had tried to rape her? Was it her intent? To get him killed afore the nuptials?

Heavy footfalls sounded outside his door. Was this what she awaited? His muscles readied to grab his sword and fight his way from the keep. Interesting. She jumped and scampered to press herself against the far wall. If the door opened, no one standing at the entrance would see her. When the footsteps faded in the distance, he sensed her tension ease and she returned.

No slow disrobing took place this time. She took a deep breath and yanked her smock over her head. As a cloud eased from covering the moon, a thin streak of moonlight crawled with stealth through the window opening beside the head of the bed. It crept across the distance like a lustful hand to stop at the hair covering her maiden's place.

Lush. Beautiful. Curly. More auburn than that on her head. He felt himself stirring and held tight to his control, willing his stubborn cock to stillness. His heart beat faster as his gaze settled on the underside of her firm breasts. He wanted to look higher, but if he did so, she would learn he was awake.

He didn't want her to know. He wanted to see what she would do.

He saw.

Elyne gently eased herself onto the bed, lying rigid as a fence board. He heard her swallow. For truth, more gulp than swallow. Funny, that. He had never noted such a thing before.

The pillow moved when she turned her head to watch him,

and he knew when she made up her mind for she eased closer to him until their skin touched. She stopped like he had scalded her. After several breaths, her hand crept over to stroke across his chest, so light it tickled the hairs there.

He allowed his body to stir. Just the smallest bit, as a man would who is restless and enjoying a dream. Huh! After all, she *was* big on dreams.

He mumbled gibberish under his breath and slowly rolled on his side to face her. He breathed a light sigh and let his arm flop across her. Pox'd Lucifer! She near jumped from the bed. She seemed afraid to breathe but finally quieted. And when she started to put her arm around him, he muttered again and flung himself on his back. He near laughed when she whispered a frustrated response.

"Drats."

Had she slipped him another potion in his food? If it was a sleeping potion, it wasna working. The only thing he felt at the time was controlled lust when she moved to put her left arm across his chest and her soft breasts teased his skin.

"Umph?" He pretended to be reluctantly awakening.

Elyne felt uncertain. What was the matter with Sir Graemme? He should have been mindless with desire by now. Did he not eat the foods she had Cook prepare for him? Cook had laced them with aphrodisiacs taken from her mother's recipes. Elyne had thought such would make a man helpless not to couple with a woman. How was she to keep him here until long after the sun's rise if he wouldna awake and be properly lustful?

She went over all the recipes in her mind, but she could not think of a single thing to make a man groggy. Except too much wine. But, Hades, her father drank more wine than she had sent to Graemme's room. It couldna be the reason. Ah. Perchance he had not the proper, er, stimulation? How did one go about properly preparing a man? She thought over all the rutting she had seen her brother Moridac and his women performing in the darkened corridors.

She would try. There was no help for it.

She eased up on her knees, and remembering how large his body was when atop him in the courtyard below, she reached one arm across his middle to place her hand on the bed for balance. Once there, she stretched her legs wide to straddle his hard, muscular hips.

She near fell forward when the bare cleft between her legs settled down on the hard male heat of a growing erection. She had seen the women sit upright and rock back and forth, making Moridac grunt in agony.

She rocked.

Graemme grunted.

She nodded, satisfied. She must be doing something right.

After her fifth rocking motion, his whole body tensed as stiff as it had when her father's sword had pricked the hollow of his neck. Bleh! She was doing it wrong. She knew she was for sure when his hands flew up to grasp her shoulders and forced her to stillness.

"What in cruddy Hades do ye think ye are doin'?"

She squealed when he flipped them both over until she was beneath him. Now, 'twas his knees which straddled her.

"Tell me!" He shook her shoulders up and down on the bed, making her head bounce on the pillow.

"I wished to seduce ye." Ack! She had not meant to come right out with it. What ailed her? She had to think quickly. "I didna wish to wait two months till ye returned."

He stared at her, not believing a word of it.

"Ye were right. I desired ye from the first moment I saw ye come to the well," she babbled on. "We are as good as wed. No one will think it sinful. Why, most couples seal their betrothal afore they wed. Ye didna have time to purchase a proper betrothal gift, but I thought this would seal our bargain as well."

Where did she come up with such a feckless reason? Her heart raced watching his face tighten, his eyes gleam with hidden fire. For truth 'twas fear sending her blood flying through her body, for the eyes of the black wolf of her dreams gleamed down at her! She felt afire where he started to rock back and forth imitating what she had done to him. Who knew a man's body could hold such heat?

Ah, so this is how to do it. He did not just rock, but bore down with each forward move. And each time he did so, he moved further down on her body until, bit by bit, his throbbing prick caressed her nether lips. He reached down and did something with her springy curls.

"Is this what ye wanted to feel? Hm?"

Hard, hot velvet rubbed against the bare flesh of her nub. Her gasp was reply enough. He chuckled, the sound sinister in the darkness.

"And this?"

His breathing became ragged. Grunting, he leaned forward and brushed his chest against her breasts. The crispy hair there tickled her nipples so much she tried to move from side to side to relieve the itch.

It didn't work. It worsened.

"Do ye enjoy my hair teasin' yer nipples? Hm?"

She grasped his shoulders and squirmed.

Of a sudden, he took in a great breath and held still. As if he had come to his senses.

"Ye should not have come to me."

He pulled upright breaking her hold on his shoulders and stared at her.

"If ye wish to leave, do so now." He started to swing off her.

She grabbed the hard muscles of his thighs and held tight. She could not leave now! If she did, he would not go back to sleep and wait until the sun rose. He would leave! Muriele would not have time to find a proper hiding place at the convent. Elyne could do this for her. Give her time. After all, Muriele had killed a man to keep her safe.

"Nay! I dinna want to leave ye. I burn for ye."

The way Graemme's mouth swooped down to devour hers, she was the plump hare to his hungry wolf. Soft, warm lips greeted him, hesitating when he slid the hard tip of his tongue over them, seeking a slight opening to invade. He nibbled and nipped, nudging at them until they parted in a soft sigh. It was all he needed. Soon his tongue fed from the minty freshness of her mouth. So sweet. So hesitant with each move he made until soon her own tongue explored and played with his.

Hearing her soft purr, he braced himself on his left elbow and moved his right hand to gently brush over the top of her breast. His fingertips trailed the plump flesh around to the side until he cupped its full weight in the palm of his hand. His calloused thumb gently grazed over the hardening nipple then quickly moved on.

"Dinna leave," She arched her breast upward, urging him to return.

He did. He squeezed gently then brought his wet, open lips to brush over the straining flesh. Ah. So delightful. He suckled and drew it out, letting it go with a wet pop, then nuzzled it again and nibbled gently. Her hips squirmed and her thighs moved. Still suckling, he reached between them and moved his cock to nest its length between her nether lips. A groan rumbled from his throat. He feared it caused him to nip harder than he intended. He released her nipple and caressed it.

"Forgive me, little jewel." He lapped and kissed her flesh.

She did not protest. Though she had not the skills of a woman well used to bed sport, from her instant response to his touch, he wondered. Her mouth had been hot and eager. Her breasts had swelled afore he started caressing them. If he read her aright, she was already wet and weeping for him. To assure himself he need not go slowly, he brushed the heel of his hand above her slit. He ran his middle and third fingers along the length of her outer lips. Lightly at first, then harder as her tension built. He cupped her delicate softness and felt the hot wetness dampening the soft curls and spreading its dew over her nether cheeks below.

Elyne arched her hips, not in the smooth, practiced way he was accustomed to with women, but in a jerking motion. His finger entered her, and though she was thoroughly wet, he found she was tight as a woman who had not swived a man in many moons.

He spread her legs wider and settled between them. Moving

higher, supporting himself on his elbows, he brought the base of his cock to slide against her throbbing nub. He thrust slowly on an up-and-down motion, not entering but teasing her flesh.

"Please."

She panted against his neck then bit down. Her legs locked around him, trying to find a way to make him enter.

"Um. Gladly."

He took the head of his cock and nudged it at her opening. Feeling her flesh give around it, he settled himself more firmly on his knees. The calloused flesh of his palm slid over the warm skin of her thigh gripping his hips, then traveled up over her stomach, her waist, her breasts.

With one strong thrust, he slid to the hilt.

"Oh!" She gasped and dug her fingernails into his shoulders.

Graemme hesitated. She had flinched, yet he had felt no hard resistance. Now he was sure, displeasure flooded him. 'Twas too much to expect the girl would be intact when she was bold enough to gaze on naked men at every opportunity.

"I should have known," he muttered.

CHAPTER 8

"**K**NOWN WHAT?"

Elyne gasped and held tight to him.

Graemme raised his head to see her expression in the faint light. Elyne's puzzled eyes questioned him. Angry now, he shook his head. She knew full well what he meant. Coming to him this night prevented him from ever breaking their betrothal. Her being in his bed locked them together as much as any consummation after repeating the wedding vows.

His ballocks quivered and prodded him for attention, while his cock had engorged within her 'till it was likely to burst if he did not gain release. He forced his mind from dwelling on how she had used her body to ensure he would return for her. For certs! She had fooled him by acting reluctant to wed.

He snorted. She would wed the devil and go to the Highlands to escape her father. He rocked and stroked within her. Her muscles tensed and her lips tilted in a slight smile. She arched her head back. Closed her eyes.

"Oh, yes," she sighed.

His thrusts varied, first short quick bursts, then slow withdrawals until just the gleaming head of his cock stayed hidden, followed by a deep thrusts to the hilt. Sweat ran down his face tickling the hollow in his neck.

He watched surprise and wonder building in her expressive face. Her hips began to rotate. She strained to reach up to him when he teased her. Her head fell back. Moaning, she closed her eyes then opened them again to stare up at him. They clouded and her stomach muscles tightened and began to quiver. Reaching between them, he gently stroked her wet, swollen nub. One touch was all she needed. Her eyes flew wide. Startled. She opened her mouth and took in a great gasp.

No doubt, the reckless lass would shout to the world her pleasure. Their teeth clanged together in his haste to thrust his tongue in her mouth and seal her lips with his own.

To keep them locked together, he fought her through her climax, surprised by the intensity of it. He bitterly acknowledged if they had nothing else between them, their bed sport would be enjoyable.

His ballocks throbbed while he bucked and strained and spurted within her with such force he near banged their heads against the stone wall at the head of the bed.

When she stilled beneath him, he heaved off her and fell to her side, exhausted.

Elyne turned her head and stared at the man next to her. She had never thought bed sport could be so intense. 'Twas no wonder Moridac's women had all giggled and bragged about his prowess and how he had pleasured them.

Graemme's eyes strayed to her breast, and she looked down to see they seemed fuller than usual. One thing for certs. Her nipples had never hardened so, not even when she pleasured herself on rare occasions.

Now she knew why they were so rare. They had left her wanting. Feeling unfulfilled. Had she felt the intense pleasure Graemme had given her, she would have made it a nightly ritual!

"What makes ye grin so?" Graemme rose up on his elbow and peered down at her face.

"Foolish thinkin."

"As?"

"Had I known it was so pleasurable, I would have, uh, found ways to secure it."

"Ye didna have the same pleasure with other men?"

He leapt to straddle her on his hands and knees. He glared, letting her know he would not allow her to seek bed sport with another while he was tending to Magnus.

"Other men?"

Elyne stared up at him, studying his angry expression. She had just given him her virtue and now he accused her of wanting to swive other men?

"Aye. The men afore me."

His eyes squinted and gleamed with a feral light. Why, the stupid man thought she had swived other men? While they had made love, she felt a warm feeling of belonging with him. Even hoped they would live well together after they wed. Those feelings flew as if snow had fallen between them.

Her throat closed with the lump forming there. She struggled to keep the tears from spilling from her eyes. She never cried! And she'd be damned to Hades if he would ever see her regret. She heaved at his shoulders with all her strength. When he released her and sat upright, she scooted up in the bed until her feet were free.

"For certs I had pleasure!"

In her attempt to swallow back a sob, the sound came out as a derisive snort.

"They pleased me more than your puny prick did." She held up her hand, forefinger and thumb three finger widths apart. "'Tis naught but the size of a boy half-grown!"

She struck out with her right foot landing squarely on his tarse which had engorged again when she had scrambled from beneath him.

His eyes widened with shocked surprise. He grasped his sex with both hands and bent double while she sprang off the bed and grabbed her shift all in one smooth motion. He rolled around on the bed, moaning and holding on to his cock that had refused to go limp.

Elyne snorted in disgust. Her stupid aphrodisiacs had finally decided to work. Well, a fat lot of good it would do her now. The next time they met, she'd be sure to feed him something guaranteed to shrivel even the most powerful of men!

But then, she didn't *ever* intend to set eyes on him again.

She left the room in a different manner from which she had arrived. She pulled the door shut with as mighty a bang as she could. She slipped inside her own chamber afore she heard the first curious footsteps heading toward Graemme's room.

Let *His Wolfishness* talk her father into thinking a maid had pleasured him. He was too afeard of having his stones hanging from the castle barbican to name her.

'Twas not until she had scrambled into bed and pulled Squat close that she realized the strange sounds she heard were her own sobs. She scrubbed at her face with the sheet. Her woman's place felt raw, and her legs ached from having been spread so wide to accommodate his hips. She felt dirty. All had been fine until he had suggested she was a woman who slept with any tarse that swelled and aimed at her!

She threw her arm over her eyes, but his just-bathed scent of sandalwood near made her scream. Graemme had marked her much like a dog did his bitch. She could not rest until she had washed his smell from her.

Jumping up, she went over to fill the basin. She tore the shift off her body and scrubbed from her head to her knees. When she washed her stinging woman's place, she cried again. The stupid man had thought she was not a virgin because she had not yelled and screamed and bled like a stuck pig.

Well, he would hear yelling and screaming if he ever came near her again.

He could count on it!

Fists pounded on Graemme's door before it swung wide to show Chief Broccin standing there, naked except for the sword gripped in his hand. Graemme wondered how Elyne had already alerted her father when he had heard naught but her footsteps running down the landing.

"Were ye attacked?" Chief Broccin stared at him. "Where did he go?"

Graemme realized he had curled like a sick kitten in the middle of the bed. He forced himself to unwind and appear as normal as possible. He levered his hand on the sheet and slipped on something wet. When he did, it pulled the sheet back about the width of his hand. His startled eyes noted the juices from his release. To cover the stain, he eased the sheet over it as he sat up.

"Nay. No attack. Just the effects still of the stomach sickness from earlier. I didna mean to make so much noise when I returned from fetching cold well water."

He forced himself to straighten and pad over to the doorway, blocking the room from the chief's view.

"I'm sorry I disturbed ye."

"Still, 'tis best to keep alert," Chief Broccin said as he stifled a yawn.

As a guard trotted toward them, he motioned for him to patrol at the end of the passageway then turned his well-honed body and disappeared into the darkness.

Graemme pulled his tumbled hair from his eyes and backed into the room. After he latched the door, he lit the candle and again studied the bed, hoping Elyne's father had not noted the musky smell of sex in the room.

He was truly fortunate he had not.

If he had, Graemme would have been in deep shite.

He did not sleep the rest of the night. He stared at the ceiling and listened for any sound of Elyne leaving her room. If she did, he had no qualms about stopping her from going to her father with some trumped up story of his taking advantage of her.

The slightest sound and his senses were alert. He didna have to try hard. After her foot had near smashed his cock up into his body, he didn't think he would ever have a cockstand again.

He was wrong. After the pain faded, the demented thing insisted on standing erect the entire night. Of course, it didn't help with Elyne's heather scent on the bed linens. And he couldn't keep his mind from reliving the feel of her thrashing beneath him as she climaxed.

What did finally cool his lust was recalling her look of total scorn when she snorted and made the obscene and totally inaccurate judgment about his cock. A half-grown boy? Heat flushed his face and a growl rumbled up from his chest. Why, he had not been as small as she intimated since he was seven years old. Not even in the deepest, coldest winters!

He knew he had always been more than adequate since he

was a youth. All the young lads at Clibrick had pissing contests atop the wall walk overlooking the gardens. One year, they decided it wasn't fair for all to compete together. They busily gathered twigs the same length as their limp cock, then decided the four longest would compete separately.

When he, Magnus, Colyne and Brian proved their pricks were the same length as the twigs they claimed, they were the envy of the other lads. Their seventh year, red-haired Brian had sworn with some envy that Graemme's had grown as much in length as his body had in height.

The contest ended the year they failed to note activity in the shadows below. No sooner had the yellow waterfall burst forth over the walkway than the shadowed ground below them heaved and exploded.

Chief Angus surged to his feet, piss dripping off his hind quarters laid bare from knotting his black tunic around his waist. 'Twas not his shouted curses which sent Graemme and Magnus scrambling away. Nor was it his fists punching the air that made them protect their faces. Nay, it was the naked woman on the ground between their father's feet. They covered their eyes in horror and near backed off the wall walk on seeing her face.

'Twas their mother.

Even the memory made Graemme flush.

"Father, I canna marry him! He's the evil man who pursued Muriele!" Elyne followed her father into the solar, dogging his footsteps.

"Ye can save yer breath, Elyne. Ye repeated the vows well and true."

Chief Broccin yawned and walked over to the large arm chair and settled his arse on its thick tapestry-covered cushion. When he'd complained about his nether regions going to sleep from the wood's hardness, Lady Joneta had made it. He sprawled his legs wide afore him and leaned against the carved back. He waggled his hand at her as if chasing off a pesky bug.

"Ye heard the stable boy," Elyne spluttered. "Graemme is searching for a woman. Her hair is the color of wheat. She's tall and slender."

She paced back and forth in front of the fireplace, ticking off a finger with each point she made. Still, her father refused to budge.

"Mayhap he looks for a thieving servant."

"He's from the Highlands!" There. She had saved her best argument for last.

"Aye. He made no secret of it." Broccin snort sounded impatient.

"He wouldna search this far for a woman who stole a coin."

Broccin crooked a finger at Domnall as Elyne continued to argue.

"And ye know Muriele had nothing of value. When Moridac found her, she had naught but the dead horse beside her."

"Domnall, send a man-at-arms to follow my soon to be son-by-law." His face hardened and his eyes hooded and glinted with menace.

"I already have. I'm waiting for him to return."

Broccin nodded and pointed. "Then remove this yammering girl afore I smash her like a bothersome fly."

Later the next morning, Graemme pulled his mount to a halt and held up his hand for quiet as he eased out of the saddle and stretched out on the ground, his ear pressed to the road. He wasna sure, but he felt it in his bones. Someone followed after they left Raptor Castle.

He pointed to Colyne, then to his own eyes and then motioned to the tallest tree. Colyne nodded. In a few quiet moves, the man was perched atop the highest strong branch without even having made the tree sway. He grinned down at them and held up one finger before he returned to the ground with as much ease as what he had climbed.

"Hm. One man, eh?"

One man meant Chief Broccin's purpose was to learn where he went and not to beat the shite out of him before he carved him up as he would a stag for the fire pit. Elyne had kept her mouth silent. No doubt in fear he would declare he wasn't the first to possess her. His cock still throbbed and tried to swell, reminding him of her insult.

"Aye. He was riding hard until he came to the place where we last took a piss. How in Hades did he know such?" Colyne scratched his head.

A bark of laughter burst from Brian. He grinned as he said, "Mayhap he heard our friend here comparing the length of his cock to our own."

"What caused yer sudden worry, Graemme, hmm?" Brian's blue eyes sparked with mirth.

"Did yer future wife take a peek to see if the curse left yer prick intact to pleasure her?"

Graemme felt heat begin in his neck. He knew Brian fought to keep his expression solemn.

"Shite!"

"Well, Lucifer's wicked funny bone!" Colyne crowed. "That's it!"

"Dinna be a fool." Graemme pressed his horse into a trot.

"Ye were right, Colyne," Brian nodded and grinned. "Not since the day we doused his father has he even thought to have a pissing contest."

"Ye are both blatherin' like lasses. If ye talk less and pay attention to the path, we will make better time."

Graemme urged his mount to a canter and pulled ahead of them. When they quickened their pace, he near put the horse into a gallop to avoid the discussion.

At dusk two days later, they came out of the woods atop a rise. The land sloped downward from there, nearly bare of trees. A lush valley spread before them. At the far end at the foot of the next rise rose the walls of what could only be the Convent of Mary Magdalen. Though several buildings stood within the walls, it was smaller than an abbey would be. From this distance, he made out a narrow tower over the entrance gate. A large, wooden cross stood above it.

"Come. We must pretend we have come upon the convent by surprise. Search along the walls and pretend ye look for a postern gate. Look upward and study the battlements as if seeking a weak spot."

"What is the point, Graemme? We learned yesterday the villager's cousin had talked about seeing a man a sennight ago wearing a strange helmet. It could only be Magnus'" Colyne said.

"To be sure Magnus has a good start before anyone knows he took Muriele, lackwit." Brian cuffed his friend on the shoulder.

"Aye. We aim to mislead anyone following us. It will give Magnus extra days to get ahead before someone tries to waylay him. Besides, we wouldna want Raptor's man to return without something to report." Graemme eyed the convent and made up his mind.

"Colyne, take the left side of the convent and circle around it. Brian, take the right around to the back. I'll take the area surrounding it." Graemme removed his helmet and cupped it in the crook of his arm. "Once I'm done, I'll apply at the gate and ask for shelter during the night."

They made a show of examining the surrounding area and the walls. When they rang the bell at the entrance gate, an old man appeared to question them. Once assured they sought only a place to lay their heads for the night, he returned with a man who appeared to be the gardener. He lifted first one heavy bar and then pulled a second from its iron holders.

Graemme learned the old monk lived out his days helping protect the good sisters and women sheltered there. The second man who looked like the gardener caught Graemme's interest. Mainly because once they entered through the convent gates, he never left them out of his sight. He plied them with conversation. Not just as a man thirsty to talk to another. If Graemme were less cautious, he would not have noted the skill with which the man sought information. He protected someone or something.

While Graemme was near a prisoner with the tall monk, Colyne and Brian talked with the old man. When Colyne caught his eye and gave an imperceptible nod, he knew his friend had learned something of import.

He did not need to question anyone. When he needed to relieve himself, he made his way through the kitchens leading outside. A cook's helper handed one of the sister's a tray. Atop it was a bowl of the hearty chicken soup together with hot bread. She talked low, but he picked up bits of pieces of what she said. "'Tis strange… eating more now… confined herself… commune with God."

He felt a surge of relief. Magnus had come to his senses and left Muriele at peace here in the convent.

When he returned, the gardener made it a point to show him to a pallet near his own, separating Graemme from his men.

The next morn when they rode out, his feeling of ease died a sudden death.

CHAPTER 9

"**Y**E LEARNED WHAT?"

Graemme's relief scattered faster than snowflakes during a winter storm.

"A man who must have been Magnus came to the convent over a sennight ago. He led a second horse with a cloaked woman on its back. The old man likened her hair to summer's grass." Colyne shook his head over the poetic wording by the aging monk.

"And?" Graemme drew his lower lip between his teeth and worried it. Satan's arse! He opened his teeth and snapped them shut again. Without the lip.

"He asked for a night's rest. The woman slept in a cell alone, and he resided in the stable." He looked at Graemme and shrugged. "The same empty stall where we spent the night."

"No guard, eh? Before we arrived at Raptor, they had no cause to be wary." Graemme pulled at a hank of black hair falling over his eye. He had left off his helm to enjoy the fresh air on his head.

"I think not. The woman, either." Colyne slapped his hand on his chest and let loose a loud belch. "The soup," he said, in way of an explanation.

"They left early the next morn, afore they broke their fast," Brian added. "The old monk said the woman must not have been feeling well."

"I asked what made him think she was feeling poorly," Colyne said, "He said the man had to hold her around the shoulders to help her walk. His companion lifted her up into her husband's arms. She appeared too weak to help herself mount."

"Did he see her face?" Magnus hoped the answer was yes.

"Nay, but he saw her hair. He said even though the sun was not as yet up, it looked lighter in early morn than it did in the evening light." Colyne leaned to the side, lifting his left buttock off the saddle.

"How much of the soup did you eat, man?" Brian, who was half a length behind him, waved his hand in front of his face.

"Shite!" Graemme stuck his thigh with his fist.

"Did not! 'Twas only gas," Colyne said, indignant.

Graemme rolled his eyes. "Not that. I'd hoped Magnus realized his vow was not worth the smallest finger on Muriele's hand. But, nay. My brother has to see everything as black and white!"

If he had been on the ground walking, Graemme would have kicked his foot and sent stones flying.

"There's nothing for it, then. We'll have to overtake him afore he forks off to go to Kinbrace. Should he take her there, they will kill her. Slowly. We'll split up to make sure we dinna miss them." He pulled to a halt so they could talk quietly.

"Colyne, cover to the west. Brian, go the eastern route. Make all haste and find out all ye can. If ye see no signs of him, make yer way to the fork in the road leading to Clibrick. 'Tis likely he will head due north. I'll take that route."

They snapped their reins and set their mounts into a gallop. Graemme was glad the paths were now familiar.

A sennight later, Elyne studied horsemen thundering toward the castle. She put her hand up to shade her eyes so she could see who they were. Riding at the lead was her brother's black mount. She grinned, for dressed all in black with his cloak flying in the wind her brother did look to be a huge black raptor.

"Aunt, 'tis Ranald," she shrieked. She near tumbled Lady Joneta over as she hurtled across the front bailey.

"Watch it, Imp." Ranald ordered as he sidled his huge horse away from his sister. "Ye know Satan's Spawn is as bad-tempered as the Chief is when he's deep in his cups."

For a flash in time, seeing the comely left side of Ranald's face, it was as if Moridac laughed down at her. It was oddly comforting knowing how her other brother would have looked if he had been happily married and had children. But then, if Moridac had escaped the hunting accident the morning he was to wed, she would never have known Ranald still lived. He was beauty and darkness all within one man.

Elyne grinned up at him as she backed away from the black horse and waited until he turned and handed the reins to the Stable Master. She near leapt into her brother's arms. Always glad to see him, she was more so than any time in her life. He would be her savior. Ranald would talk some sense into her father and stop this craziness about her wedding a savage Highlander!

Once he and his men greeted everyone and Ranald, Aunt Joneta, her father and Elyne settled in her father's solar to enjoy a private meal, Elyne thought her head would burst from Broccin's shouts.

"The daft lass sprawled atop Angus of Clibrick's son Graemme." He scowled at her. "All but *nekid*. Her bare arse shined in the moonlight bright as the rising sun," he shouted as he slammed his fist on the solar table.

"I did not sprawl on him. Blessed Saints! I fell out of the tree." Elyne was satisfied her shout was every bit as loud.

Hearing her shout, Squat came running into the room leaving muddy paw prints in his path and looked at his mistress then over at the Chief.

"Nay! Ye did not sprawl. Ye were *swiving*, his hands doing the guiding!"

"Lass, how oft did I tell ye spying on men would some day cause ye grief?"

The dog cocked his head and turned his attention to the cause of his mistress' anger. He went behind the Chief's chair and stealthily crept up to Broccin's boots under the table. Balancing on one bandy leg, he lifted the other and let loose with a hot stream of piss. His aim was at the top. It didn't take long before the warmth alerted the chief. As he sprang up, shaking his leg and cursing the dog, Squat skittered away to hide behind Elyne's skirts.

Ranald shook his head and looked stern. At least the scarred side of his face looked stern. His lips twitched at the corner on his comely side, and Elyne could swear she heard the rumble of a subdued chuckle.

"I hadn't meant to spy. I had no place to go but up the tree. I thought to hide myself until he was gone, but the fool grabbed my foot."

"The Chief can do naught else but see ye marry the man. The whole castle, nay, even the distant villagers know of yer mishap."

"Ye jest!" She slammed back in her chair. Surely, a cloud of doom, complete with lightning and thunder, floated above her head.

"I fear not. I was no more than halfway here when I heard the tale."

"Huh! But would ye wish me to marry the man who has gone to steal Muriele out of Mary Magdalen?"

Ranald's head whipped around to look at Broccin.

"Brodie followed them," his sire sad. "They searched the woods then his men spent the night in the stables. The man ye sent as gardener to watch Muriele kept his eyes on them. He had young Graemme sleep in the pallet next to him. They left the next morn."

"Alone?"

"Alone. Brodie didna return until the men were well on their way to Clibrick Castle."

"Well, Elyne, had they been after Muriele, they would not have left. I think 'tis time ye married and had bairns to keep yer adventurous nature busy."

"But I don't want to marry him! For certs, he *is* the man who ruined Muriele's back."

"I'll talk to her. It should set yer mind at ease." He looked at Chief Broccin and saw his rare nod of agreement.

"Aye, do. I would be less fearful if ye find she fares well." Elyne could not expect anything more.

When Ranald and his men arrived back at Raptor's drawbridge several days later, the sun hovered over the horizon. Riding behind one of the men was a woman in a long, black cloak. Wind whipped golden hair with flecks of brown from beneath her hood. It swirled around her face. An unfamiliar face. Elyne's heart sank, for there was no way Muriele had changed that much in little over eighteen months.

Elyne stared. She did not recognize the woman. What she did recognize was the anger on Ranald's face. His eyes sparked with fury, causing wherever he gazed to heat.

Once they had dismounted and were within the keep's great hall, Ranald finally spoke.

"Muriele was gone and this lass was in her place. Elyne, see she has a place to sleep tonight. Once she's settled, come to the Chief's solar. We need to talk.

The woman looked exhausted. Pity welled in Elyne's heart. From her haunted eyes and white face, Elyne saw she was more than a little frightened. Whatever had happened, for truth, Graemme was behind it!

As she led the exhausted woman to her bedchamber, she tried to put her at ease.

"I am Elyne of Raptor, daughter to the Chief. Come, ye may share the room with me this night. Did, uh, my brother say how long ye will reside with us?"

"Thank you, my lady. He did not. I am Ysabel.

"Ye look much like Muriele, the woman taken from the convent." Elyne couldn't help but stare at her. "Where did Sir Graemme find ye and how did ye come to agree to do such a thing?"

"I know nothing of Sir Graemme. The one who found me in a village at Stow was named Sir Magnus."

"Ye dinna look like a village woman. How came ye to be there?"

"I lived at a castle near Clibrick until two years ago. A band of unruly men whose leader looked to be one of God's angels, raided the castle. He killed my husband. When they had their fill of me, they turned me out." Shame and sadness pinched her face. She blinked, trying to keep her tears from falling.

"Why did ye not seek help at Clibrick?"

"I heard the man who killed my husband bragging he had everyone there under his heel. Instead, I spent many months making my way to the Lowlands. I settled at a village in Stow."

"The man who found ye, did he force ye to work for him?"

"I had recently arrived in the village and lived with an old man and woman on a farm. I had no talents other than with the sewing needle. People in the villages canna waste their earnings on clothes. Truthfully, though, this Sir Magnus paid me well for the deception. He even provided farm animals for the old couple. I cared not for the coins he gave me. It was enough to again be treated and dressed as a lady. Even for such a short time."

Elyne's heart melted on seeing tears slip down her cheeks.

"Ysabel is a lovely name. One not often heard."

"Tis an old family name." She stopped and looked around her. "I have heard of the Black Raptor. I feared he would throw me in the dungeons when he arrived."

"Nay. My brother would never be so cruel." Elyne gulped, for indeed, Ranald had once tortured a man then tended his wounds to see he lived to remember what he had lost. To her, such a thing was beyond cruel.

When they reached Elyne's bedchamber, she directed Ada to bring water for Ysabel to bathe. Elyne laid out a cotton smock and a soft, green tunic for her to wear. "Fresh clothing and a good meal will lift yer spirits. I will have a tray sent from the kitchens for ye."

Elyne hopped from one foot to the other, anxious to meet in the solar to find out what had happened. "Cleanse yerself and relax. After ye have eaten, go to bed and rest."

Before Ysabel could answer, Elyne was out the door and closing it. When she found a guard posted there, it surprised her. She didn't stop to question why. She'd find out soon enough from Ranald.

Elyne burst through the doorway of her father's solar and skidded to a stop. The white cloth on the table fluttered. The tapestries and banners around the room flapped softly. There was not a hint of a breeze through the window opening. The castle doors remained closed, too.

Ranald paced back and forth. One look at his tight face gave her the reason why. He was more than upset. He was angered.

Were he any more so, the cloth and all the food atop it would be flying to the floor.

Elyne stopped halfway into the room.

"Father, I told ye I should not wed Graemme. He may not have stolen Muriele away but this dreadful Magnus did. They are Highlanders. Would ye wish me to marry into such a cruel clan?"

"Graemme did naught wrong." Chief Broccin snorted and glared at her.

"But Muriele is now on her way to be tortured or worse!"

Elyne was beginning to get a sinking feeling her troubles with wedding Graemme were not over. "This Magnus who stole her away. Who is he to Graemme?"

"His brother."

"He has a brother?" Elyne's heart gave a sickening lurch.

"Aye. Two years his senior."

Believing she could save Muriele, she had given herself to Graemme. For naught! Naught but insults! Bile surged to her throat. She wanted to heave. Swallowing, she took a deep breath. Realizing Ranald studied her with an appraising eye, she tried to appear only curious.

"Graemme never said anything about him, did he Father? Perhaps his brother stole Muriele to protect her from Graemme?"

"I already told ye, Graemme had naught to do with it," her father's voice rose in irritation.

"Still, I willna marry a man whose brother treated a woman crudely as any unruly serf."

"He didna, lass," Ranald broke into the conversation before it became any more confusing. "Your Graemme and his brother Magnus didna harm Muriele. 'Twas Magnus' foster brother Feradoch who did."

"Bleh!" She glared at Ranald. "Dinna call him *my* Graemme."

"He will be," Chief Broccin warned. "This doesna change

the vows. Finding his brother to protect Muriele is the reason he could not marry right away."

"Both Graemme and his brother are worthy, Elyne," Ranald said. "Their only flaw is they are more honorable than most men."

"How can ye say such when this brother kidnapped Muriele?"

"Magnus is a good man. Too worthy for his own happiness." He paced over to the window and looked out at the bailey below. "He made a vow it is impossible for him to keep."

"Huh! No more impossible than mine, I'll wager." Elyne sucked her teeth. "What was this impossible promise?"

"When he was a youngling, he and his foster brother Feradoch of the Gunn's, made a blood vow to revenge each other if one of them was dealt a terrible wrong." Ranald turned, his arms crossed over his chest. His voice lowered. "The Gunns claimed Muriele entered a handfast with Feradoch"

"Heh! What is terrible about an old tradition?"

"Naught. But she stabbed him in the back the same night. And murdered his leman."

"Did they see her do it?"

"Nay. But they demand she be brought back and hung."

Elyne's fingertips stifled a small cry from her lips. She swallowed and glared at Ranald, as if the bad news was his fault.

"Muriele would never kill anyone! If she stabbed him, he must have done something terrible and deserved it!"

"Never kill? She has already taken a life. Ye saw her slit a man's neck afore." Her father thumped his chest and belched, then downed what was left of his ale.

"Aye. To keep him from capturing her!"

"Then dinna say she would never kill." Broccin scowled at her.

"And this Magnus," Elyne turned her back to her father to speak to Ranald. "Why was it an impossible promise? Seems to me, he found it easy enough to pluck her out of the convent and disappear with her." Her anger built knowing men thought nothing of protecting a woman, only of punishing them.

"It's impossible to fulfill his vow. He loves her." Ranald went over to an arm chair and pulled it back from the table.

Ranald's frustration showed, for though he was a man larger than most, his movements were always fluid. Graceful even. Now, he plunked down in the chair, his legs sprawled in front of him. Everything on the table clattered and finally righted itself.

"Loves her?" Elyne scoffed. "With a love like his, a woman doesna need hate."

"Aye, he loves her."

Ranald pointed to his goblet and Broccin filled it with red wine. Ranald took a hearty swallow and drew the back of his hand across his lips.

"He doesna. No man who loves a woman would chase her down like she was a rabid fox." Elyne was so tense she feared she would explode. "He loves her so much he would take her back to be hanged? Nay. Hate is more like it."

"I questioned Ysabel whilst we were returning here. For truth, this Magnus is in love with Muriele. Ysabel said he could not eat during their trip. He barely slept. When he did, he cried out in his dreams."

"Ha! Ye should know something of that, daughter."

Elyne cast him a scowl as telling as any of her brother's.

"I'm glad the bastard has night terrors."

"Daughter!" The chief struck the table, making the wine pitcher wobble.

Elyne shrugged. "Serves him right for being such a fool." She glared at Ranald. "Why are ye sitting here and not going after them?"

"Because he loves her. And he's an honorable man."

Elyne let out an exasperated shriek. "Dinna say such again! Love and honor with these brothers are akin to hate and shame!"

Squat crept from under the table and dragged his butt on the floor close to Broccin's boots, leaving a foul smell.

"Ysabel doesna believe Magnus can bring himself to return her to the Gunn's. He will fulfill his vow, but he will not allow harm to come to Muriele."

Elyne snorted. Loud. The sound as disgusted and disbelieving as any man's.

"He will drag Muriele to the Highlands, though she is the only woman he has ever loved? How can ye claim he loves her when he knows something dreadful will happen to her there?"

Annoyed because he was not more concerned for their friend, she kicked Ranald's right foot so hard he had to adjust himself in the chair.

"I'll not have a brother-by-law who is so rigid, nor will I live with such a family."

Of all the men she could have given herself to for the first time, it had to be to a deceitful man with a brother who had such twisted morals he'd see his love killed afore he would break a vow.

Well, she didn't intend to tie herself to such a cruel family. Piss on them! And she used to think her own father was harsh!

Graemme would probably think nothing of tossing her off the highest turret if she displeased him.

And she knew she would.

She was too used to doing as she wished. The women in her family were all strong. Not a one would put up with the insult he had handed her after giving him the gift of herself.

Somehow, she'd pay him back for that insult. And he could forget ever having bed sport with her again!

CHAPTER 10

ELYNE STOPPED OUTSIDE HER bedchamber to compose herself before she entered. She couldn't go in and slam the door and kick the bed the way she wanted to do. Ysabel was there and would think she shared a room with a crazy person.

She undressed down to her shift and quietly slid between the covers. The faint moonlight coming through the window opening showed her the lady was not asleep. 'Twas funny she would automatically think of her as a lady. There was no mistaking the breeding in the woman's speech, nor in the manner in which she bore herself.

"Did ye have enough to eat, Ysabel?"

"Aye. Ye were kind to send up such a hearty meal."

"Ye must be very tired. If I know my brother, he would have ridden hard to get here."

"I am bone weary, but too confused to sleep."

"And I am too angry at my father to have naught but nightmares!"

Elyne rolled to her right side and plumped up her pillow then slid her arm beneath it. Watching her, Ysabel turned toward her so they could talk face to face.

"Tell me of Clibrick Castle and the people who live there."

"I have never been to Clibrick, but everyone in the villages between there and my home speaks of them. What do you want to know?"

"Anything you can recall about Chief Angus and his sons."

"I have heard stories of the two young men for many years. The older is Magnus, the younger Graemme. They didna grow up together because of feuds between the Morgans and the Gunns."

"What separated them?"

"The two Chiefs fostered their sons together. They made them swear a blood oath when they were younglings. Strangely, after Feradoch of the Gunns came to foster with the Morgans, the villages far from Clibrick Castle lived in fear. Two weeks of each year, Magnus returned to Clibrick to spend time with the Morgans and Feradoch. The next two weeks, Feradoch would return to Kinbrace with Magnus. The weeks when Magnus was at Clibrick or when Feradoch was away, the village folk relaxed."

"When Magnus was not there, what did they fear?"

"Raids at night where their daughters were taken from their huts then returned in the morn."

Chill bumps formed on Elyne's arms. "Then Graemme and Feradoch preyed on the outlying villages? They raped the women there?"

"Nay. Not Graemme. They only had reports of a man who looked like a blond Viking. And also of his friend. An ugly lout."

She gave such a violent shudder Elyne could feel it in the bedding.

"This Graemme. Does he have lemans living at the castle?"

"Nay. Though he's had women aplenty from the age of fifteen. 'Tis said little by little the village lasses paid heed only to this Feradoch."

"By chance, Graemme was cruel to them?"

"I dinna think so. This foster brother declared to everyone Graemme was soft and weak as a woman."

Elyne snorted. "Soft? He can be mean as a ravening wolf!"

"I wouldna know. Several years ago, we heard he was in love with a blond lass. She was the daughter of a knight at the castle." Ysabel put her hand to her mouth to stifle a yawn.

Knowing Graemme loved another woman made Elyne's anger heat. Some love he had for this knight's daughter when he was only too eager to swive her here at Raptor!

"What is her name?"

"Elspeth, I believe."

Before she could speak again, a queasy feeling made Elyne

swallow bitter water that surged to her mouth.

"Why has he not married her?"

"Graemme?" Ysabel blinked and tried to keep her drooping eyes open.

"Aye."

"I would not know..." She finished the sentence with a soft sigh, half asleep.

"Ye must be terribly tired, Ysabel. Sleep and we will talk more on the morrow."

Elyne tossed and turned and thought she'd never relax. Finally, exhausted, she closed her eyes and drifted off, only to be caught up in one of her foretelling dreams.

She found herself hidden high in a tree watching a giant black wolf in a stream. He stood tall on his hind legs, like a man. Mud covered his body and leaves had tangled in his hairy chest. He covered himself with soap and began to bathe. As he scrubbed his body, the long animal hair washed away with the mud. Beneath was hard, male flesh.

Finally, nothing remained of the wolf except his face.

Her heartbeat pounded in her ears. She tried to hold her breath, afeared he would hear her breathing. The wolf man's face turned from side to side. Moonlight hit the slanted eyes showing they were so deep a brown as to appear black. Satisfied he was alone; he began to wash his face.

As he splashed water on it, the branch she perched on broke away. She tumbled to the ground. Jumping to her feet, she ran as fast as a fox. His terrible snarls were thunderous, crashing behind her. The earth vibrated when he ran. His panting drowned out any other sounds as he gained on her.

His breath stirred the hair on her neck and his massive arms grabbed and pulled her against a hairy body. The hair did not feel coarse and thick as the wolf's had looked, but soft and tickled the flesh on her back.

With her tight against him, he grunted and nuzzled her ear. With horror, 'twas not a man's face caressing her cheek, nor a man's lips tasting her flesh.

A long, hot and wet tongue started at the throbbing pulse of her neck and trailed up her jaw, savored her cheek and stopped at the edge of her lips.

She shrieked!

Elyne was still splitting the quiet night with screams when Ranald and her father found her in the apple orchard. Her eyes were wide with fright. When Ranald kneeled to take her by the shoulders, she fought him as fiercely as a demented barn cat. He grabbed her wrists as she tried to gouge his eyes and held tight to them, talking to her all the while in a quiet, soothing voice.

"Lass, 'tis Ranald. No one is going to hurt you."

He looked at Broccin, for Elyne did not seem to hear him. Aunt Joneta ran up, knelt on the ground behind Elyne and pinned her arms to the side.

"Wake up, lovey. 'Tis naught but one of your dreams." She repeated it over and over, and finally Elyne began to quiet. She blinked, holding her eyelids tight and then opening them.

"Dafty! 'Tis a wonder any man would consider her!" Broccin shouted and pulled his hair at his temples. "How many times have we found her roaming the castle grounds, the fields, even the pig sty sitting in the midst of their slops?"

Elyne put her arms around Ranald and sobbed, muttering the wolf would tear out her throat. Joneta and Ranald kept up a soothing, wordless murmuring in her ears until she stopped shaking.

"If Sir Graemme hears of this, he'll think she's crazy as a loon and will likely murder him whilst in one of her wild dreams." Broccin stomped around in a circle, kicking the earth with each step. "If he refuses to have her to wife, she'll spend the rest of her life in the nearest convent. Let them deal with her."

Ranald lips thinned and his fingers twitched. He had an overwhelming need to do something physical. Fury churned in his mind at the cruel statement. He'd not let his father lock her away in a convent the way he had discarded him at Kelso Abbey to either live or die. Broccin hadn't cared which.

He knew why his father had hated him. Had even come to terms with it. A common superstition in the Highlands was the belief the second born of identical twins had an evil soul. But surely, Broccin had some love for his only daughter?

"You'll do no such thing, brother!" Lady Joneta said firmly. "She has the dreams for a special reason. We should all pay more heed to them." She frowned and smoothed back Elyne's hair. "I think this will not be the end of them, lovey. Ye have not seen the wolf's true face. It may not be Sir Graemme, but someone else. Your gift may be trying to warn you about a man you dinna yet know."

Rising with Elyne sobbing in his arms, her face buried in his neck, Ranald ignored Broccin and headed toward the keep. He held tight to his fury, not wanting to lose control. If he did, he couldn't stop the winds from blowing or objects flying around when his gaze touched them. As it was, a forceful gust banged the heavy doors of the keep open as he approached them.

Squat shot out of the open doorway like someone had booted him in his bowlegged hindquarters. He took a quick look at each of the humans and must have decided Broccin was the one who had caused his mistress to cry. Without hesitation, as Broccin passed him, a hot stream of piss soaked the Chief's left foot. Squat skittered away afore a forceful kick could meet his malformed body.

Elyne felt the rigid control in Ranald's body and stopped sobbing. She hiccupped and patted his scarred cheek, trying to soothe Ranald as he had quieted her.

"Dinna let him spike yer temper, Ranald. I know ye would never allow him to lock me away."

Taking a deep breath, he hugged her tighter.

"Ye must not tell Ysabel anything of yer dreams." Ranald shook his head. "Ye know how frightened most become of anyone not alike themselves." He chuckled. "Look how quickly they believed me a Black Raptor and thought I could change into a huge bird of prey."

Ranald's body relaxed as he calmed. He picked his way amongst the sleeping men on the great hall's floor and entered the solar.

"I'll fix ye an elixir to sleep afore ye return to yer room," he said. He turned to Broccin and tried to smile, but 'twas more of a grimace. "Go to bed, Father. I will handle this from now on."

"Ye'd best. Can't have everyone in Scotland believing both of my children are beset by mad spirits!"

"Oh, go to bed, Brother, afore I take a broom to you," Joneta said with a scowl.

Grumbling about senseless women, Broccin stalked out of the solar and walked the short distance to the door of his bedchamber. When the door closed behind him, they could hear a woman's voice urging him to climb under the covers and give her a good swiving.

Ranald sat Elyne in a chair and quickly went to a chest beside the wall to withdraw a leather bag filled with herbs and potions for all kinds of remedies. He never went anywhere without it. Quickly, he stirred herbs ground into a powder in a small amount of wine and handed it to Elyne. She swallowed it without asking anything about its contents.

Elyne had complete faith in her brother's healing abilities he'd learned in his years as a monk in Kelso. She spread her arms and stretched, unable to stifle a yawn while she did so.

"I think it safe for ye to return to yer bed with Ysabel. Should she ask anything of tonight's events, tell her ye couldna sleep and went for a walk beneath the fruit trees. An owl swooped so low his talons slid through your hair and frightened ye."

"I'll be asleep afore I even finish telling her." Elyne stretched up on her toes and kissed her brother's scarred cheek.

Aunt Joneta took her by the arm to steady her to her room. When they opened the door, they found Ysabel sitting up in the middle of the bed, the covers drawn up to her eyes. Joneta calmly walked over to the bed, pulled back the covers and tucked Elyne in.

"Go to sleep, ladies. 'Tis hours afore the sun rises." She looked at her niece and smiled. "Next time you canna sleep, come to me to accompany you in the orchards. We will both be afeared of the night creatures." She chuckled and motioned for Ysabel to lie down then tucked the covers around her.

With no other words, she left the room, pulling the door silently closed.

CHAPTER 11

SIX DAYS AFTER LEAVING the Convent, Graemme was near ten leagues from Clibrick when he saw a flash of light on the hill ahead of him. 'Twas enough to know the lowering sun had glinted off a shiny helm. His horse snorted, weary from their fast pace, but Graemme urged it to a burst of speed. Before the evening hour, he knew he had caught up to them.

He left the mount hidden in the bushes until he was sure it was Magnus and not some lawless party going over their loot. He used his broadsword to hold back the bushes, confident he could handle anything awaiting him.

When he came to the last line of the trees before the camp, he studied the scene before him. A comely woman, long and naked, lay on a kilt on the ground. Cuts, scars and bruises covered her back. Magnus must have sensed his approach, for when he jumped upright, his bow was already arced as bulging arm muscles pulled the nocked arrow back. He stood between the trees and the unconscious woman.

Graemme's brother' face looked drawn as tight as the hide cover on a war drum. His lips, white-rimmed with strain, clamped together in determination. Haunted near-black eyes within equally dark circles reminded Graemme of the charcoal Elyne had worn as the crone. But his husky voice sounded as strong and forceful as ever.

"How in Hades did ye approach without us hearing?"

Magnus sounded irritated but Graemme ignored him for his body seethed with anger.

"What have ye done to the lass?!"

When his mount burst out of hiding on hearing familiar

voices, Graemme ran his hand down the steed's neck and praised him. As he tied his reins to a bush, he gazed intently at the girl on the ground then turned to fix his brother with a cold stare.

"None of this was done by my hand." Magnus voice was harsh with worry, answering his brother's unasked questions.

"She's bonnier than any lass ye have ever bedded." Graemme rubbed his cheek as if the stubble of hair there annoyed him then nodded. "From the looks of ye while ye tended her, she must be Muriele of Blackbriar."

He noted her hair was short, not flowing down her back as Ranald had described her.

"Did ye cut her hair as punishment for the months ye spent searching for her?" He tensed, not wanting to believe his brother would do such a dim-witted thing. 'Twould be as much punishment to him as to Muriele, for he had more than once described the beauty and warmth of her tresses.

"Nay. Her hair was as we found her in the convent. These latest injuries ye are staring at are by her own doing. The lass tried to hide atop a tall pine and ended up crashing to the earth." He realized he was making excuses to his younger brother and stopped. "How did ye find us and why are ye here and not at Clibrick or Kinbrace?"

"To keep yer sorry arse from making the worst mistake in yer life."

Magnus folded his arms across his chest and scowled at the disrespectful way his brother spoke to him.

"And this horrible mistake is?"

"Believing anything coming out of the lying mouths of the Gunns."

Graemme stopped and pulled out a packet of cut leaves and asked Sweyn to brew them. He was bone cold and wet from chasing two steps behind them for days. They moved to the other side of the fire to talk where they wouldn't disturb Muriele. Once they had the hot brew in their hands, Magnus became impatient.

"Start talking."

"I went to Kinbrace and pretended great alarm that anyone

had dared attack Feradoch." He took a great gulp out of the pewter cup and sighed. "All was not as I expected there."

"What had ye expected? All grieve in different ways. Olaf lost a son, his only heir." He shrugged at Graemme. "'Twas natural if he stayed drunk and his temper was short. He often picks fights with his men."

"Olaf acted as worried as any father thinking his son near death."

"Near death? He yet lived?"

"Feradoch pretended to be dying around the servants, myself and his father." He wriggled his shoulders, relaxing his tense muscles. "After all were abed, I was as quiet as a church mouse as I made my way to an alcove near the dying man's door. I wanted to watch all who entered."

"He didn't believe overmuch in priests or such," Magnus added, thinking his brother was surprised Feradoch didn't have a priest standing watch at his bedside.

Graemme snorted. "No priest could provide the *comfort* he required. He needed only women." He sucked his teeth in disgust. "Two at a time. I put my ear to the door. I didn't mistake the sounds of him swiving his newest whores. Both of them."

"He was able to swive after losing so much blood?"

"Aye. And boast of all he would do to Muriele once he had his hands on her." He held out his cup for Sweyn to refill it. "She was canny to insist on a handfast instead of a wedding. After Feradoch intercepted a king's messenger outside Clibrick and relieved him of a missive, he plotted to marry her."

"A missive? What missive?"

"It was about ye."

"Tell me afore I throttle ye!"

"King David's missive stated the conqueror of Blackbriar was to marry the heir and hold the castle in the king's name. Feradoch cleverly planned to force Muriele to marry him. Once he consummated the marriage, the king couldn't do anything about it. After he seized a firm hand on Blackbriar holdings, he planed to make her sorry for the rest of her very *short* life."

Graemme let out a gusty sigh. "All in all, I think I have

been a very good spy."

"Huh! Did you find anything of Grunda or Esa's body?"

"I couldna at first. Then I remembered Muriele had lived deep in the woods. I finally found the old hut. When Grunda first saw me, she nearly ran me through with a rusty sword!"

Magnus grunted. "She must have heard ye comin' for leagues. 'Twas a wonder she didna lay a curse on ye."

"Nay. She stared into my eyes. She walked circles around me then grunted and said. 'Ye are the younger son of Clibrick. The one with compassion and brains to think.'" He laughed at Magnus' insulted expression.

"Did she know aught of Esa's killing? Where her body lies?" Sweyn asked, his face twitching from trying to keep himself under control.

"I'm coming to Esa's story. The seer claimed Feradoch beat Muriele because she wasn't perfect. He couldn't consummate the handfast. He sent guards to bring Esa to the room to help him have a cockstand. She resisted. As he was trying to strangle her, Muriele stabbed then hit him on the head. She kenned she was too late."

"Kenned?" Sweyn straightened, for he had ever tried to hide his love of the dark, beautiful Esa.

"Aye, she lives. Grunda gave her an elixir to make her appear dead. When Olaf had her thrown into the forest, the old seer rescued her from the woods. She lives there with her. I had sent Colyne and Brian on different paths, but met them at the fork. I left them to guard over the women."

Muriele must have awakened and heard Esa was alive, for she struggled up and bundled the robe about her. She stumbled close to the men sitting by the fire. Ignoring Magnus and Sweyn, she talked only to Graemme.

"Ye say Grunda and Esa are safe in the forest?"

"Aye." Graemme bowed to her. "'Tis an honor to meet ye, Lady Muriele. I have heard of yer good deeds from the common people at Raptor Castle. Even how ye saved two ladies' lives afore ye reached the Convent of Mary Magdalen."

She shrunk from Magnus when he extended his hand to

steady her.

"I have something from a seamstress in a village halfway here. Something the woman thought ye would welcome," Gramme said as he made his way back to his horse. He looked over his shoulder and grinned at her. When he returned, he had a soft package he handed to her.

Her beautiful eyes looked questioningly at him, but she couldn't take it as she had to clutch Magnus' cloak around her naked body.

"'Tis clothing. I told her of yer plight. She kenned a woman might need extra clothing if she was taken on a hurried trip." His eyes studied her face and he shook his head. "If ye rest until dawn, it will be soon enough to dress. We will be off to Clibrick. Ye will be safe there with my father and Magnus to guard ye."

Graemme knew Magnus would never turn her over to Chief Olaf after he knew the whole story. There had to be some honorable way out of his vow.

But Magnus stayed silent. Unmoving.

Graemme scowled and helped Muriele back to her pallet. Sweyn fixed her a hot potion to drink. Her eyes soon closed and she was fast asleep, holding the gift of clothing close to her chest. He and Magnus slept on either side of her throughout the night, keeping her warm and also assuring she didn't try to steal away whilst they were asleep.

"Well, brother, we are west of the forest between Blackbriar and Kinbrace. I still have a loch to ford and it looks to be calm weather for the next days," Graemme said as he saddled his mount the next sunrise.

"Aye. Ye should find the hut easily now ye know where it is. Be stealthy and dinna linger. If Feradoch or Olaf learns ye are anywhere near, they will suspect something." Magnus buffeted him on the shoulder, something he hadn't done since they were lads together.

"Uh, Graemme?" Sweyn spoke softly so as not to awake Muriele.

"Aye?" He turned his head slightly to the side, wondering

what Sweyn wanted.

"Be gentle with Esa. She has had naught but strife at Kinbrace. Her mind canna take more of it." Sadness filled his face. He lowered his eyes to look at the ground. "If ye should be captured with the women, 'twould be a kindness if ye slit her throat and quickly ended her suffering." His body shuddered. "Feradoch would torture her for days if he laid hands on her."

Grief flooded Sweyn's eyes. Graemme knew this rough knight loved her.

Magnus scoffed to make light of his worry. "Olaf and Feradoch had best beware of Grunda. She will cast a spell turning their balls to huge cherries and have ravens plucking at them as they fled through the whole of Scotland!"

"Grunda seemed a harmless sort to me." Graemme looked puzzled.

"Her ancient appearance hides a mind which can strike fear with but a look! If she warns ye, pay heed to her."

"For certs I will." He swung up into the saddle. Reaching beneath his kilt, he settled his sex betwixt his legs and grinned. "Cherries, huh? 'Twould be most uncomfortable sitting atop something that popped every time ye hit a bump in the road."

"Off with ye, eejit! And dinna forget yer caution!"

Gramme chuckled as he walked his horse as quietly as possible through the woods until he was far enough away the sounds wouldn't wake Muriele. The beautiful woman had looked exhausted even in her sleep. His brother had best be good to her else, he would have to answer to him. Now he'd reached his full growth, he was equally as strong and capable as Magnus.

The two days it took him to ford the loch and ride through the forest gave him time to think. He would gather the women and the two guards he'd left with them, and then make all haste to Clibrick. The faster the trip, the sooner Magnus would learn the whole story. Once he did, Graemme knew his brother would break this unholy blood tie with Feradoch. Once it was finished, then Magnus would be married. He didn't doubt Magnus loved Muriele. When he looked at her, Graemme had seen the worry and tenderness lurking there.

He wished he felt the same for Elyne. But each time he thought of her, his anger rose and he wanted to throttle her for her tricks. She'd made a fool of him in the eyes of every man at Raptor Castle. Had she done so with any other man, after they spoke their wedding vows, her husband would take her to the woods where he'd slap her pretty nether cheeks until she couldna sit to eat. She wouldna dare to rile his anger again.

He felt sorely tempted to do it.

And, aye, he had to admit he felt lust apleanty. Just the memory at the well of her plump breasts beneath the wet shift made riding difficult. His stones hardened and his tarse swelled near to bursting. Would that she was here to soothe them!

The idea made him groan. It was not likely a wife would take her husband's tarse into her hot mouth to soothe. For such a thing, he'd have to dally with one of the laundresses' daughters. 'Twas their favorite pastime afore they swived a man.

His daydreaming made him near miss hearing a horse pulling a cart on the forest path ahead of him. He pulled off the road and blended in with the trees. He wanted no one to see him and report a lone man riding. Every lawless lout would be on the lookout for him. For a man without a master, even worn out boots would be worth stealing.

He reached forward and rubbed his hand along his horse's jaw, distracting and soothing him. Between the leaves, he made out a cart with produce from a garden. A husky but not-quite-right-in-the-head lad shuffled behind it. He carried a club, ready to swing at anyone or anything the old man driving the cart would order him to.

He had no quarrel with them. But if the man's helper spied him in the woods, the boy would probably charge into the underbrush swinging his club thinking he was thwarting a robber. Graemme didn't want to hurt the poor lad, but he didn't want a delay, either.

Soon the man and boy were gone, and he continued on the north-eastern road. The loch was easy enough to cross. The men he'd left to protect the women met him in the woods.

They'd seen him coming, for they were adept at climbing trees and spent most of their days as lookouts from one.

"Well, 'tis about time ye got here. If we dinna make haste to Clibrick, yer rock-headed brother is liable to try to force Muriele. She is not a lass who takes kindly to demands made by any man."

Graemme noted Esa clutching something in the pocket of her outer dress. He would bet it was a sharp knife, for she moved to keep between him and Grunda, as if protecting her. To test his theory, he moved closer to the old crone. Esa eased between them, her eyes never leaving his face.

"I mean ye no harm. Sweyn would cut off my, er, head if aught happens to either of ye." He flashed a smile, hoping to reassure her. She seemed to relax her shoulders a slight bit.

"I knew ye would come today, so all is in readiness to leave." Grunda said.

Glancing around, Graemme saw small cloth bundles carefully tied and waiting neatly beside the door.

"I cooked oat cakes enough to last us two days, then ye'll need to hunt for hare. I banked the fire when I heard ye within a league of the hut."

Grunda looked at the two guards with squinted eyes. "Did ye saddle yer mounts and fill yer water gourds?"

"Aye!"

The two men nodded and near bowed, anxious to show respect to the old woman. No doubt, they'd heard of her dire threats to the louts' prized possessions when the Gunns first captured Muriele and took her to Kinbrace Castle.

Graemme shrugged, seeing no reason to linger since everything was in readiness. The faster they left Gunn territory, the better for their necks. Besides, 'twas near dusk. A bright moon would guide them back the path through the forest. They could travel most of the night, cross the loch and be on solid ground way afore the sun rose.

He tossed Esa up behind the youngest warrior and Grunda up behind the burly one. It would distribute their weight and be easier on the mounts to carry two people.

They left as quietly as possible, riding at a slow pace until they were well away into the night. As dawn began to dim the sky, they picked up speed. For the next sennight, they rode hard. When the mounts needed resting, they put kilts on the ground for the two women to relax as well. On the fourth day, he thought it best to make loops to put over the women's hands and attach them to the saddle. Doing so would allow the man to keep his hands on the reins when the women fell asleep. He feared in their exhaustion they would slip from the back of the horse and do themselves an injury.

Once in Morgan territory, they slowed their pace and rested at night. As they had ridden during the day, the men had used their bows and arrows to bring down game for their meals. They ate well when they rested at the noon break, then finished off the days food afore they went to sleep at night.

When they stopped to rest each evening, Graemme thought he'd never had such agreeable company. Grunda amused them with tales of Muriele when she was young. His brother was going to marry a woman worthy of him. 'Twould be a good match.

One night, the old woman had him stand and again paced around and around him, studying him from the tip of his head to his bare toes.

"Ye know, dinna ye, this Elyne of Raptor ye're to marry will not accept yer rule without a fight?"

"How do ye know of the lass?"

"I see things. She also does."

"I know ye are a soothsayer and see hints of what is to happen, but I think ye are wrong about Elyne."

"Nay. I am never wrong."

"It seems to me she but mimics the poses and gestures of women of sight such as yerself."

"'Tis different ways for different seers. She has dreams which she knows are telling her what is ahead."

"She also tries to make herself appear an old crone. She paints ashes around her eyes, streaks cherry juice on her face and blackens her teeth." He stopped and frowned. "She also tangles her hair and streaks it with ashes. She has fooled her other suitors and Chief Broccin, but she didna fool me."

"She is yet young. Her understanding of her dreams has not fully grown." Grunda nodded, her eyes showing she thought ahead. "When ye return to Raptor, I will travel with ye and guide her."

Graemme spluttered and shook his head.

"I dinna want my wife to believe her fanciful dreams." He gritted his teeth then burst out, "She believes I'm a wolf come to eat her for my noon meal or some such nonsense!"

"If ye were a youngling in a keep who saw yer father near beat yer brother to death and then abandon him for over fifteen years, ye'd have developed gifts to help keep ye alive. And this Ranald of Raptor Castle has special powers."

Graemme snorted. She ignored it.

"Aye. His first year at Kelso, his raging fevers affected his brain."

"Chief Broccin warned I am to have the devil as my brother-by-law."

"Nay, not the devil. But if a fool causes his temper to unleash, he may lose control over his gifts."

Disbelieving her, Graemme raised his brow and smiled.

"Watch him. When he and his father are together and argue. Ye will see wind blowing objects when there is no wind. If his father doesna stop, ye'll see Ranald's eyes heat and anything they touch will alight. If he loses control, doors will slam, platters will fly."

"Why are ye telling me this?"

"Because, Ranald will protect Elyne. He'll not let Chief Broccin force her into marriage. Or to be thrown in a convent and locked away."

"She must marry me. No other man will have her after we were seen together bare arsed on the ground."

"Do what ye have to do." She grinned at him. "But if this Ranald doesna want Elyne pushed into wedding ye, be sure ye are not atop the keep at the time. 'Twould be a nasty spill."

It was too much for Graemme to take in at one time. He

didn't believe in seers. Yet here was one who had proved it. He didn't believe in a man who could control objects with his brain and eyes. Yet she was telling him to watch Ranald for the truth when he returned to Raptor.

Most of all, he didn't want to believe the beautiful lass Elyne was truly a seer of another kind.

He should believe Grunda. But everything he heard was not possible. Though not as rigid as Magnus, he was practical and logical. 'Twas hard to accept happenings that had no rightful explanation.

Hmm! What could be more unusual than a woman like Elyne? She'd made him laugh at her make-believe crone in the middle of the night — and made him furious enough to kill when she'd dosed him the next day.

Cold trickles of sweat ran down his backbone. He truly hoped his imaginative to-be-wife was sleeping peacefully.

Dreamlessly!

chapter 12

At Raptor Castle, Elyne had done all she could to talk her father out of this betrothal. As they were eating their supper in the great room, he turned a baleful look on her and said she had two alternatives.

"One! Ye shall marry this Graemme of Clibrick in a fortnight and learn to be an obedient wife. He is kindness itself to ye, allowing ye to take the mangy cur. The dog is good for naught but to keep the squires busy covering his shite in the bailey."

As if by habit, he picked a scrap of food and threw at his feet. Squat wolfed it down.

Lady Joneta winked at Elyne. "The poor little beast's stomach is unsettled and you dinna help feeding him from the table. He needs only barley water to soothe his stomach and naught but gruels," she said.

After Squat broke wind loud enough to have come from one of the knights, Broccin waved his hand in front of his face.

"I've added a bit of savory to prevent building up his wind," Elyne said while she too fluttered a small piece of cloth with rose water under her nose.

"It isna working!

"These things take time, Brother." Joneta patted his hand and stifled a grin. "Eat the pigeon pie afore it gets any colder. I do wish the kitchens were closer to the great hall."

"Stop trying to distract me from reminding Elyne she is soon to be wed. Ranald and his family will be here afore ye know it. I think he intends to meet young Graemme afore the wedding, though if he doesna like him, 'tis Graemme's bad luck."

"Father, please believe me. Graemme means me harm."

"The only harm ye are in is falling off the battlements with yer crazy sleep walking."

"I have not moved from my bed for the past sennight!"

"Aye. Now Ysabel sleeps with the other unmarried lasses, a firm rope tied around yer ankle keeps ye there."

"Pish!"

Elyne had to admit she had been dreamless these past fortnights, but she wasn't going to give her father the satisfaction of telling him so. She bit her fingernails until there was nothing left to catch between her teeth. The thought of traveling to the land of the bestial Highlanders turned her stomach.

She had heard they ate like pigs, preferring their food half-cooked, the meat still dripping blood. She near gagged at the thought. The only saving grace was Muriele would be her sister-by-law, though she wouldn't live at the same castle. When things got too bad, she could always run off and join her at Blackbriar.

The thought heartened her a bit. Then she kicked herself under the table for even considering going through with the wedding.

Not many nights later, her sleep was again fraught with nightmares.

'Twas but four days afore her wedding day. She dreaded seeing Graemme's coming with foreboding. She twitched in her bed. Her legs thrashed and tried to reach the floor. Sitting up, she found the knot in the rope.

In few quick swipes, she was free to run as fleet as a doe to the top of the castle. She could hear the horses in the distance. She stood from the tallest point watching the forest path. A man and his horse burst from the trees. His face was a blur, but she knew it was Graemme. He seemed triumphant, for he reared his horse. The magnificent beast's hooves clawed the air, and the man let out a warbling war cry from deep within his chest. An army of savages followed him, riding horses shooting fire from their nostrils. Each warrior seemed taller than the other, some with hair over their faces, others with pointed ears and long, sharp snouts. They were a clan of half-human, half-animal giants!

Elyne stood on solid ground and grasped the stones on either side to steady herself. Looking down, she found him directly below her. His shadowy face showed his fury, for though guards had lowered the drawbridge, they had refused to open the great teeth of the barbican entrance.

"Ye will marry me this day," he snarled, "else I will destroy every stone betwixt us!"

"Huh! I am not such a fool. If I married ye, ye would soon feed me to yer hungry army. Why they drool at the mouth when they look upon me!"

A dog's frantic barking caught her attention away from him. She looked around the ground, thinking he had brought a devil hound with him to help in his hunt for her.

"Order the men to raise the teeth of the portcullis, woman, or I will destroy ye afore ye can move!"

When she did not, his eyes became narrowed slits. Blue lights glowed from them. Fury turned his face as red as the hottest fire. The wind ruffled pale, gold hanks of hair below the edge of his helmet.

The hanks of gold hair distracted her until the dog began to howl. Could it be the specter of a dog and not a live one? The man's next words drew her attention back to him.

"I am warning ye. Do not thwart me in this. I have vowed ye would be my wife. As the Devil is my master, ye will wed me this day!"

As he slowly lifted his sword, fear paralyzed her. She couldn't move. He pointed the sharply honed tip at her. She watched, fascinated as it began to glow. Sparks sizzled off it and lit the night sky.

His face seemed to lift in a smile. Not a smile of kindness, but one of malicious triumph.

A lightning strike started slowly to grow from the sword.

'Twas beautiful to see. The startling hues of blue and silver and blinding white fascinated her as they neared.

"Order the iron gate up, else I will strike ye down!"

She didn't move. Finally, the lightning bolt's tip was so close to her eyes it blinded her.

Elyne screamed as she fell to the beasts below.

She awakened in a panic. She was not the only panicked one, for guards were leaning over the battlements. One man grasped her around the waist, near falling off himself.

Her feet flailed naught but air!

The shouting of the guards and the frantic barking of what she now knew was Squat drew her from her frightening dream. Blinking, she looked down and saw emptiness. Her waist felt near squeezed into half where her rescuer had a steel-like grip on her. When her arms cleared the stone battlements, others grabbed them too, not wanting to take a chance she would stumble forward and fall.

"Hold on to the dafty girl!"

Her father's face loomed above all the guards as he charged through them to get to her. Fear filled his eyes. His lips were bloodless. Why, he did care for her but didn't want anyone to think him weak because his daughter meant something to him. After all the years of fighting with him over every little thing she wanted to do, it was a strange thing to realize.

When he reached her, she felt like he carried her wrapped in a huge bear rug, for he held her in his arms close to his heart. He didn't speak but headed down the spiral stairway. Reaching the solar, he allowed his sister entrance but no one else.

Once he released her to stand on her feet, he started shouting.

"Has Lucifer addled yer brains with maggots? I have a mind to send a patrol to Sir Graemme and tell him he'd best make haste to get here else he'll be without a wife come the wedding!"

Broccin unconsciously shook his leg, for Squat had not liked his yelling at Elyne.

"Father! He's going to kill me with his sword the first time I make him angry!"

"Ye talk like an eejit! Never has he given ye a reason to not trust him."

"Perchance because we hardly know him?!" Elyne shouted as loud as he and felt her face redden with the effort.

"I know him enough! He did the right thing. I didna even have to burn his toes to get his vow to marry ye."

"Burn his toes? Ye threatened to hack his stones from his body! Any man faced with losing his treasures would utter an unwanted vow."

"The short time he was here, he talked of fulfilling a promise to his brother. It proves he is a man of honor."

Broccin realized Squat had pissed on him again and aimed a kick at him. The dog scurried away, his hind end nearly sweeping the floor of any debris.

"What? Because he made his brother a vow?"

"Nay, fool! Because he didna have him killed so he would be first in line for his father's estate."

Elyne's mouth dropped open. Did men really think only of their own possessions and not of their loves ones? Nay. The men in her family… except her father, perhaps… loved each other. Ranald and Moridac had been as close as any identical twins could possibly be. Moridac grieved for years after he believed Ranald had died at Kelso Abbey. She realized her father had started talking again.

"Sir Graemme doesna look like a man who would kill his wife without reason." He stopped to take a breath. "Though the way ye are actin', 'tis more certain ye have lost *yer* mind. Should he hear of this, he'll fear ye will skewer him afore he comes to the bridal bed!"

"I have told ye a score or more times, I canna marry him!"

"And I have told ye time aplenty ye have no choice!"

"Enough!"

Aunt Joneta's shout would have scared birds from the rafters, had there been any there.

"Such frightful dreams are caused by naught but a maiden's fears. Come, morn will be here soon enough. By the shadows beneath your eyes, you need to sleep peacefully. I will sleep with you this night." She put her arm around Elyne's shoulders and hugged her. "You'll see. Your dreams will stop."

Neither spoke again until they reached Elyne's chambers and they were abed.

"Mayhap it is not even Sir Graemme you dream about. It could be some other man in his family or thereabouts?"

Elyne frowned. Nagging thoughts took hold. Why did he have golden hair when it was black? A trick of the light, mayhap? His head had been hard to see through the blur. Had his eyes been blue, or were they brown? She didn't remember. And didn't really care. Sir Graemme meant to kill her. She would be long gone from Raptor afore he came.

Chapter 13

Relief washed over Graemme when Clibrick Castle loomed in the distance. The sun was high and the waters of Loch Naver were calm. The large field of grass and wild flowers showed no enemy encampment, nor was there any hint of sun flashing off a helmet in Ben Clibrick behind it.

He had arrived in time.

Guards and welcoming people from the castle swarmed over them when they rode through to the keep. Sweyn was there to help with the women, and Graemme smothered a smile at the way he treated Esa. Why, anyone would think she was a young eyas out of a falcon's nest he was so gentle with his touch!

Muriele's light brown eyes lit with happiness when she saw her two friends. She hurried Esa and Grunda into her chambers When Muriele studied their faces, she saw the same hurt and fear reflected in Esa's eyes as was in her own. Men had badly mistreated both in their lives. Her back had near healed and she'd determined she'd have no qualms of killing any man who took a hand to her again.

"Grunda, they say I must marry Magnus tomorrow!"

"And what say you?"

Muriele looked at her like she had asked if she was planning on taking a broom ride to the moon the next day!

"Nay! Of course. They may force me to stand before the priest but I'll not repeat the vows." Her chin hardened and her eyes narrowed, waiting for Grunda to argue with her.

Grunda's face didn't show any reaction, but she shrugged and said, "The Gunns have gathered all their clan and are already riding west. From what I see, they will be here within two days time."

The words were no sooner out of her mouth than Fergus knocked on the door. Chief Angus summoned Grunda to the men's solar. She slid from the room without a whisper of sound.

She returned some time later, her face firm and determined. "Ye are to marry tomorrow. Sunday. There will still be a battle with the Gunns over it, but Magnus will be the master of Blackbriar and ye will be its mistress."

"Magnus can stand afore the priest waiting on my vows until his hair turns gray, but I will not repeat the vows."

"Aye. Ye will."

Sure enough, Sunday saw a wedding at Clibrick Castle. Grunda saw to the bride, giving her mulled wine and keeping her calm. Though done hastily, it was a beautiful wedding. Graemme presented the rings belonging to Muriele's parents, the rings only the rightful owners of Blackbriar could wear by the King's decree. When Muriele had left Kinbrace so abruptly, Grunda had kept them safe in a box beneath the dirt floor of the hut.

When time to repeat the vows, Muriele clamped her teeth together. They would not stay closed. She replied as if someone else were in her brain and formed the words that came from her mouth.

During the night, Graemme grinned to himself, hearing his brother and his bride's frequent outbursts of pleasure. Both looked a little bemused the next morning.

They had one more night of bliss before peace erupted into chaos.

Graemme spent the night watching atop the castle wall walks. The hairs on his arms told him the Gunns were close. The people of the outlying villages were already within the castle walls, and Magnus had armed the warriors with weapons aplenty. They all waited, anxious for the battle to begin.

He heard the Gunn's long before anyone could glimpse them.

Horses pounding. Men yelling war cries passed down by their ancestors. Torches glowing high over the water where they should not be.

Hell broke lose outside the castle.

Chief Olaf came not over the hills, nor through the mountain passes. Around the foothills reaching out into Loch Naver, horses thundered through the surf, kicking up huge splashes of water. As they carried torches to light the still dark sky, their riders looked like phantom warriors from Viking raids a century ago.

The built their camp on the sand and the grass field while Chief Olaf walked far out onto a series of flat, large rocks jutting into the loch. The glow from the torches played over his beard and long, shaggy hair making them look redder than usual. He wore animal pelts covering his shoulders and a wool kilt bunched securely at his waist. Water lapped against the rocks, splashing near as high as his knees. Looking like a statue of an ancient leader, he stared across the dark water.

He did not speak, nor did he pay any heed to the castle at his back.

Graemme almost pitied him. He looked a man torn between two sons.

One of his blood whom he had fostered at seven; the other he had raised until he was a man.

Olaf's shoulders slumped. At the middle of his dilemma was the huge fortress of Blackbriar and its riches.

Which *son* would be its final owner?

Later the same day, Graemme had his answer.

The two chiefs wanted the matter settled without bloodshed, for each had raised the other's son. Chiefs Angus and Olaf, the sons Magnus and Feradoch and Father David agreed to meet outside the castle on open ground. There would be no weapons on either side.

When Feradoch claimed his rights to Muriele for she had killed Esa and attempted to kill him, Magnus pointed to the top of the barbican. Sweyn moved aside and Esa stood there, her tall, dark beauty outlined by the blue sky behind her. She spoke loud and clear and told what had happened that fateful night.

Feradoch near frothed at the mouth, saying she lied. Then

as if she had never spoken, he went on to claim Muriele by his rights of handfast. Father David confirmed Muriele had sworn afore Chief Angus, Sir Magnus and the castle commanders as witness, that Feradoch had not consummated the handfast. And Muriele had been absent for more than a year and a day, so the handfast was no longer valid.

Feradoch was incensed, knowing they would thwart his plans at every pass. His hand flashed down and retrieved a hidden dagger from his clothing. He leapt at Magnus. Magnus ordered everyone not to interfere.

Behind them, Muriele had found a way out of the castle. Fleet as a doe, her feet barely touched the ground as she raced to protect Magnus. Chief Angus grabbed her as she tried to streak by him. He held her tight until both men tumbled to the ground.

Neither moved. Feradoch sprawled atop Magnus. Blood seeped between them to the ground.

When the two fathers separated the men, both were lifeless. Feradoch showed no wounds, but they could not hear a heartbeat or see any motion from his chest. Blood spread so fast over Magnus they despaired over being able to help him in time.

Muriele sprawled in the dirt, holding Magnus' shoulders and head on her lap, keening. Rage overtook her. He couldn't leave her after they had finally realized their great love! She screamed and beat him on the chest. Tears streamed off her face as she ordered him to come back to her. Then, remorseful for doing such a cruel thing to his body, she hugged him to her breasts.

'Twas then he decided to again reside upon the earth.

Muriele felt a gasp of air upon her breasts then heard his smothered words.

"I canna breathe."

After a fortnight, Magnus had healed enough to take his meals again in the great hall. They were having the final course of their evening meal when Graemme brought up the subject of leaving.

"I vowed to return to Raptor Castle when my business of

pulling your arse out of the fire was settled," he said.

Magnus gave him a threatening look.

"What business? Ye weren't there but two days from what ye said before." The more Magnus studied his brother's face, the brighter Graemme's face flamed.

"Aye. Two days and a vow. Enough to settle a lifetime for me."

"How is that possible?"

"It seems Chief Broccin's daughter sleepwalks while having foretelling dreams."

"Ah, Ranald's sister Elyne! Her dreams really do portend the future, Graemme. I myself have witnessed one come to pass," Muriele said.

"But what does all this have to do with ye, Graemme?"

Magnus studied his brother's eyes and saw the anticipation and the dread there. What caused it?

"Searching for ye, I arrived late at Raptor. It was dark and everyone was abed. I thought to clean the dust from my body at the well."

"'Tis reasonable. No one likes to have a dirty traveler breaking his fast at dawn. But why must ye return?" Sweyn said.

"When I was bathing, I was, um, nekid."

"How else were you to wash?" Sweyn raised his brows.

"Aye. But a comely young lady was in a tree overhead. Spying on me. I grabbed her ankle and she fell. I ended on my back. She lay sprawled atop me."

Muriele burst into laughter. "Her brother Ranald has forever warned her saying she would spy on one man too many and would pay the consequence!"

"She has done this often?"

"Well, the windows to the solar face over the well. She near fell from it one day when Ranald and his cousin Raik proved what fine bodies they had. Not to mention men often stripped to bathe there. They make no secret of strutting around, liking to be admired."

"She wasna ever hurt? What does this have to do with a vow?" Magnus' black eyes began to twinkle.

"Broccin's beloved daughter Elyne was near as nekid as I."

"Aha! Why didn't you both hurry and dress?"

"Because by the time I caught my breath, Chief Broccin's bare feet were on either side of my head...."

Laughter rippled throughout the room as the story passed from one ear to another.

Graemme gave a good-natured shrug.

"Why didna ye tell me ye were betrothed?"

"In the midst of yer debating whether to marry Muriele and tell the Gunns they could take their tarnished vows straight to Hell?" He shook his head. "Nay. I could not distract yer dim-witted mind while pondering yer decision."

"Nothing is to stop ye now." Magnus sprawled out in his chair and studied his brother. He nodded and said, "Grunda."

"What about Grunda?"

"She must go with ye." Magnus straightened up and leaned his arms on the table in front of him. "If anyone can help ye with her visions, she can."

"Grunda has already demanded I take her. The girl is lively, but I had to make her vow not to poison me again."

"Again!"

"'Tis best forgotten," Grunda's eerie voice said behind him.

"Then mayhap ye'd like to be my taster?" Graemme hooked his brow at her and grinned.

"She'll not do it again." Grunda had a far away look in her eyes, as if watching something no one else could see. "We had best make haste afore she throws any delays in the way."

"When is the wedding to take place? My brother canna wed without me."

"In three sennights. I should arrive a sennight before the ceremony." He gave Magnus an accusatory glare. "If I'm late for my own wedding, I fully plan to blame ye."

"I'm going with ye. Sweyn will escort the women at a slower pace."

Elyne slept well for the next several nights and everyone began to relax. Broccin decided he had finally talked sense into the girl. Aunt Joneta thought it safe to sleep in her own bed, but propped her door open to listen in case Elyne needed her.

One rainy day, Elyne told her aunt she wanted to sleep in a little longer and stayed abed. While Lady Joneta told the servants to leave Elyne alone until she caught up on her rest, Elyne busily searched through her clothing chest for garments of brown and greens. Colors nigh impossible to spot in the forest.

The trickiest part was keeping Squat from pulling the bundle out from under the bed as soon as Elyne shoved it there. Finally, she picked him up, closed the door firmly behind them and went down to the stables.

While she whispered and talked to her favorite mount whose hair matched the deep brown of Elyne's eyes, she casually made sure all she would need for the horse was stored neatly under a stack of hay within the stall.

From the time she could walk, she had screamed if anyone tried to make her ride in a cart. She'd insisted on riding a pony like her brothers and cousin when they were younglings. She had snorted, most unladylike, when potential suitors arched their brows at her riding astride with her slit skirts. She secretly took pleasure in shaming them by her greater ability. She regretted she'd not had time to prove to Sir Graemme she could outride many men.

Early in the afternoon, Chief Broccin thought she had come to her senses when she didn't scream and object to the seamstresses fitting her bridal outfit for the last touches. 'Twas a beautiful garment, one she'd have enjoyed wearing to a wedding or a banquet — as long as it wasna her own celebration.

The seamstresses used a sheer silver material for the outer tunic, while beneath was a deeper, shimmering gray. They lined the bodice and upper arms to the elbows with the same matching gray material. The sheer silver covered from the elbows down, with flowing sleeves floating wide and free. An embroidered, beautiful deep-green trim surrounded the bodice edges. A belt and matching veil with a shiny, silver circlet topped it off.

'Twas an elegant gown. One made with loving hands to

welcome a joyous marriage.

She felt a pang of regret when she took it off and the women carefully folded it. Its splendor looked lost lying atop the other new garments they had made for her to wear at her new home.

Elyne took special pains when she dressed for the evening meal. She was especially courteous to Aunt Joneta and her father, and pampered Squat by giving him the juiciest pieces of meat on her trencher.

She felt like she was seeing the great hall for the last time. Her chest hurt when she looked up at the family banners hanging from a rafter. The Chief's black banner with a yellow eagle at its center, its talons spread for the kill took the center spot. Her brothers had shared a banner. 'Twas made to picture a sunny yellow field with two black eagles flying, a red bar dividing them. Moridac had ordered the red bar sewn between them when he believed Ranald had died of his injuries. On the other side of Broccin's was her cousin Raik's, Aunt Joneta's son. A yellow gryphon on a field of red, its beak stretched wide as if screeching. All fitted a castle called Raptor.

Banners hanging from other rafters belonged to either relatives related by marriage or the knights themselves who came from high-ranking families in the Highlands. On the morrow, they planned to make room for Graemme's wolf banner to fly between her cousin's and her father's. The idea of looking up and always seeing the stalking wolf above her head made her cringe.

No fear of that. She would be long gone by sunlight. They'd never think to look at Mary Magdalen for her. Not after she'd made such a scene when her father had threatened to have her placed in a convent after she'd balked at wedding Sir Graemme.

She blinked to keep tears from forming. Why, she never cried! Not even when she'd had her bottom strapped for trying to make her way to Kelso. She'd wanted to see for herself her dear Ranald no longer lived. A lot of good it had done her to try, for she had never made it past the last village before Domnall had caught her up on his warhorse and returned her to her father's wrath.

She had to fight herself to go to bed after darkness fell. Her stomach was queasy thinking on what she planned to do. Why, she might never see her home again! She swallowed a lump in her throat and quickly kissed her father's cheek when he ordered her to bed. With Squat following close behind, she went to her bedchamber. In case Aunt Joneta decided to sleep with her, she put a small potion in the watered wine beside the table.

Nibbling on her fingers, she hugged Squat in her lap and fed him a tiny portion of wine-soaked bread. Soon, his snores assured her he was sleeping heavily. She climbed into bed and knew she had time for a good nap before the castle guards would be lulled into their normal routine. Raptor guards were more efficient than any neighboring castles, for when Ranald had returned, he made sure they were the best trained in the Highlands. She'd have no easy time leaving by the postern gate. She'd studied their pattern and knew it was possible in the short space of a few breaths when their backs would be to each other before they turned at the corner turrets.

Elyne had picked a good night, for clouds filled the sky. She put Squat on the bed, his head on her pillow and felt his reassuring breath on her cheek when she kissed between his eyes. She would miss and worry about the little strange dog. Surely, Aunt Joneta would see he came to no harm.

In the darkest hours of the night, she slid out of bed, shivering as her bare feet met the cold floor. Where were her shoes she had carefully placed so she could slide into them? Ah. She knew. Soft snores lead her to kneel and swipe her hand across the floor beneath the bed.

"Got ye, little thief," she whispered.

Squat was sleeping comfortably atop her bundle of clothes with his head resting on one shoe. She tugged the culprit and her belongings from their hiding place. Holding the still snoring offender close to her chest, she put his head back on her pillow and brought the still-warm covers close around his body. He opened one eye, scowled at her, and then licked his lips and went back to sleep.

Finally clothed and with her shoes on, she tossed her cloak around her shoulders and stole from the room. Walking close to the wall where her footsteps were the quietest, it took her longer than usual to descend to the great hall and make her way through the pallets filled with snoring, farting and grunting men.

It was much easier than she thought. And also much harder. Easy to gather her belongings and her horse, and make her way slowly in the shadows until free of the castle grounds out into the forest beyond. But, oh, so much harder to glance over her shoulder and see the fortress looming against the sky!

Her home. The only one she'd ever known. Though Broccin was a harsh father, she fought the lump rising in her chest. Her leaving should be on her wedding day, a happy occasion. Instead, she hated Graemme for forcing her to flee.

She wasn't suited for convent living. In a few days, she'd be sure to cause some terrible commotion. If the kitchen help and cooks weren't doing their job, or the laundress didn't know the proper way to get stains out of clothing, she'd likely lose her temper and insist on changing their procedures.

Not to mention her need for physical labor. The thought of being on her knees and praying all day near made her turn back. And men? Regardless of what her father thought, she didn't spy on them for thrills. She envied their flawless bodies. Their muscles and bones which enabled them to do all the things she couldn't. No matter how hard she pulled the strings of a bow, she couldn't fly an arrow as far as Ranald or their cousin. Aye, she could hold her own with most men, but she wanted more than equal strength.

She refused to think of what this *more* was. At the thought of Graemme's impressive cockstand, she gritted her teeth. His lovemaking had been all she'd dreamed a man could do.

Until he ruined it by making her feel like a whore.

She shrugged off the thought. She must have done something right to have given him such pleasure. If she hadn't, he'd have known she was a virgin without a maidenhead to prove it.

Every step of the way, she imagined she heard horses pursuing her. She slept only when she could not see or when her horse needed rest. She had no trouble finding the convent, for she'd been with Muriele and Ranald's wife, Catalin, when they'd sought sanctuary there. 'Twas when Catalin had clung to Elyne's waist as Elyne urged the horse across the valley riding like the devil pursued them.

He had been.

If Muriele had not urged the two women on and slowed her own mount, the lout would not have had a chance to grab her friend's long hair. She'd backhanded her knife and slit his throat, but his foot caught in the stirrup. The horse had galloped on. Her tresses, tangled and caught in the dead man's glove, held her prisoner. Muriele had managed to hack through her hair in time to free herself.

Once Muriele healed from her ordeal, Elyne and Ranald's wife had cropped her hair so it would be even when it grew back.

The convent looked familiar in the early morning light. Halfway across the clearing, she saw the gate swing open. Two people stood there, shading their eyes from the sun, anxiously scanning the area behind her.

Her heart did an extra beat as she turned to look, afeared her father or Graemme was charging down the mountainside after her.

Once she rode through the gateway, she breathed a sigh of relief.

"Is there no one traveling with you, Elyne of Raptor? Chief Broccin or your brother Ranald?" The Mother Cecelia asked quietly as Elyne slowly dismounted.

She was bone weary and stiff from riding more in these past days than at any time in her life.

"Nay. I come alone.

"No one pursues you with an army as they did afore?"

The woman's eyes looked doubtful she would travel for three days without an escort. Any time Elyne had showed up at the convent, chaos followed.

Her gaze roamed over Elyne, taking in her soiled clothing and matted hair. Elyne put one foot behind her and tried to swipe off the dust with the back of her skirt. She wished she'd taken time to bathe in a stream this morn. With the surprised looks from everyone as they looked her over, she knew she must have dirt smudged from hairline to chin. Looking down at her hands, she decided she'd best put them behind her back.

"Come, we will talk as we go to the dormitory." She motioned with her hand for Elyne to walk beside her. She also cleared her throat, reminding Elyne she had not answered.

"Pursue? Not as yet. They will not expect to search for me here."

"They?"

"A barbaric Highlander who forced a betrothal on me."

"And? There is more to it than this, I believe."

"My father, perchance. Though he may be pleased I came here, since he threatened me with the Convent if I didna marry Graemme of Clibrick Castle."

"Ah. 'Tis wedding this Graemme that causes you to run away. Is there anyone else who may threaten the peace of the Convent?"

"My brother Ranald. But he would not cause anyone unease."

"I cannot help but ask if this has to do with your *unusual* dreams?" When Elyne didn't answer right away, she continued. "Once you have bathed and are properly attired, Brother Hugo from Kelso Abbey will give you guidance. He arrived yesterday and is very learned. He came to Kelso as a wounded Crusader who wanted nothing more to do with killing. He had meant to leave tomorrow, but I'm sure he will be pleased to counsel you."

Elyne gulped, knowing she would get little sleep this night. "I dinna think the good Brother should delay his travels on my account." She crossed her fingers and sent up a quick prayer for forgiveness before she lied to this good woman. "I haven't had troubling dreams in a long time. Since I left here with Catalin and Ranald, they seem to have disappeared."

"Then how are we to help you? A daughter must marry where her father wills."

"Ye offered sanctuary to Muriele when you knew someone pursued her!"

"Aye. But the man seeking her meant her harm."

"Then I seek sanctuary for the same reason. Graemme of Clibrick plans to murder me."

CHAPTER 14

GRAEMME AND MAGNUS RODE ahead of the small army behind them. The iron bars of the portcullis were still down, which was unusual for this time of day. When the captain of the guards recognized Graemme, he ordered them raised.

"Mayhap they didna recognize ye in yer fine clothes?" Magnus offered.

"They sure as Hades know our standards, though." Graemme frowned, knowing something wasn't right. The guards refused to meet his eye and Chief Broccin appeared on the keep's steps looking a little red about the face.

Graemme's gaze searched the stairs behind the chief. Where was Elyne? Courtesy demanded that she meet him with her father. Instead, Lady Joneta stood there. His shoulders began to relax when the door opened and another woman appeared. She moved to stand behind Lady Joneta looking like she needed her protection.

"What in Lucifer's hairy arse is she doing here?" Magnus exclaimed.

"Who is she?"

"The woman I hired to impersonate Muriele at the convent."

"No wonder she looks like a rabbit about to be thrown in a pot with carrots and turnips!"

Chief Broccin descended the steps to meet them, a broad smile on his face.

It didn't fool Graemme. Deep in his bones, he knew Elyne had pulled one of her tricks on him, and he was in no mood to allow it.

"Welcome, Sir Graemme. I recognize yer two friends from

afore. Sir Brian and Sir Colyne. This man who looks much like you? Your brother Magnus?"

Chief Broccin was trying to delay by making small talk. Graemme's eyes narrowed in a withering stare.

"Aye. He is. Sir Cormac is his commander." He motioned is horse forward a pace. His nostrils narrowed and his lips thinned. "Where is the Lady Elyne?"

"We did not expect you until another two days."

So, he did not want to speak of Elyne. Graemme dismounted slowly, hearing Magnus' boots also strike the cobblestones. Magnus went to lift Grunda from behind Sir Colyne and brought her over to stand beside him.

"We traveled lightly, leaving the rest of the women to follow. Well escorted, of course." Graemme stepped close to Broccin. Though the older man was his equal height, Graemme had an advantage — he was not trying to avoid an issue. "This is Grunda, a healer and seer. She was of great help to Lady Muriele and her family."

"All went well with the Lady?" Broccin turned to Magnus and smiled.

"Aye. We have wed, thanks to Grunda. My wife will arrive with the rest of our family in time for the wedding." Magnus cleared his voice and looked at Ysabel. "How came ye to be here?"

"Sir Ranald became suspicious and arrived at the convent. He was kind enough to bring me here."

"Aye. Once she told us of your family, we knew ye would see no harm came to Muriele. Only a fool would keep to a false oath, and we learned ye were no fool," Broccin said.

Graemme didn't know if his brother would be insulted or not, but he nodded solemnly.

"I dinna think Ysabel need fear Muriele's blade. She will be too angry at me for making her travel with the rest of the women."

"This brings a special woman to my attention." Graemme turned frosty eyes on Chief Broccin. His words near grated through his teeth. "My bride?

"Not here." Grunda said quietly.

He looked at Broccin, not Grunda.

"Where is she?"

The horses shied at the explosive volume of the words. Chief Broccin stood up to him. After all, no one else could compare to Ranald's ferocity when in a bout of temper.

"She disappeared two nights ago. She could not have gone far or for long, for she left Squat behind and all of her clothing."

"Have you searched the castle grounds?"

"Do ye think me an eejit?" Chief Broccin seemed to grow a hands width taller with indignation. "We have even checked the dungeon and every hut from here to seven leagues away. I have sent word to Ranald at Hunter Castle, in case she sought refuge there."

"But Hunter Castle is in Northumbria."

"Aye. In Crookham. Belonged to his wife's family. They were Norman/Saxon mix."

Squat eased himself around the keep's door and slowly made his way down the steps, his one ear stood at attention, listening to every word. The other flopped like it was too tired to bother. On the last step, the poor beast fell forward and was slow to pick himself up. When he approached Broccin, the man sidestepped. Sure enough, 'twas a wise move. Squat wobbled like a drunken chicken when he tried to lift his leg to pee. He shook his knobby gray head, planted all four legs firmly and leaned forward to piss like a bitch.

When he was done, Graemme squatted and picked him up, holding him beneath his front legs so he could look in the dog's face. He studied him a while and frowned, then held him to his chest.

"How long has he been like this?"

"I found him under Elyne's bed. A wine glass had been on the bedside table, but somehow he knocked it over. I'm afeared he drank all the spilled wine."

"And he's still drunk?"

"I'm afraid it had more than wine in it. I think there was also a light dose of a sleeping draught."

"What are ye doing for him?" Grunda came close and held the little dog's face to stare at it.

"I'm afeared to give him any elixir, since he is so small. Instead, Lady Ysabel and I have kept him walking. We make sure he drinks a lot of water and eats something every hour. We hope it will flush it from his body." Lady Joneta looked at Graemme cradling the dog like a baby and smiled.

"Um, Sir Graemme?" Grunda caught his attention.

"Aye."

"Perchance ye had best not hold him now. I will prepare something to ease his suffering. The pitiful beastie will be right in no time."

When Squat passed wind with the vigor of a warrior, before the noxious smell reached their nose, Graemme bent fast as lightning and put him on the grass. Just in time.

He straightened, and all the sympathy for the dog vanished from his face, leaving his features cold and forbidding.

"I came as promised but the girl has insulted me by ignoring her betrothal vows. I dinna plan to take this lightly. It isna a maiden's fear of marriage."

Graemme tried to keep his voice calm and soft, but even to him the words were harsh, angry. When he found Elyne, she would learn he was not a man she could trifle with as her other suitors had been. If she were here now, he'd take her by the scuff of the neck to a private room and whale the Hades out of her lovely buttocks!

His cock stirred. His hands remembered the feel of the wet flesh of her nether cheeks — perfectly formed, smooth and firm. He wanted to either kiss or nip her flesh there, but in his anger, the nip would probably leave teeth marks!

Magnus slapped his shoulder and brought him out of his abstracted musings.

"Come, brother, we will sit with Chief Broccin and piece this together. Between us all, we should come up with some idea of where she has hidden herself and why."

"Right, right," Chief Broccin seized on an end to the awkward meeting. He had feared the Highlanders would draw their broadswords and fight first afore thinking. "Come." He motioned not only the two brothers but their men with them.

They followed Broccin into the keep and up to his solar. Graemme was in no mood for small talk and only grunted if anyone plied him with inane questions.

Once the men entered the solar, Graemme took Grunda's hand and led her inside. Chief Broccin near slammed the door in the faces of Lady Joneta and Ysabel. He hastily filled his goblet with wine and shoved the pitcher and tray of goblets to the men seated around the table.

"Did she make any other attempt to leave Raptor in the past month?"

"Nay. She seemed anxious. She was unwilling to participate in the wedding plans."

"No more than anxious?" Magnus asked in a calm voice. It prompted Broccin to respond.

"Her usual nonsense about not being able to marry Sir Graemme because he intended to kill her."

"Kill her?!" Graemme slammed his goblet on the table and splashed wine on the top of his hand. He unconsciously licked it away. "How did she get such a flea-brained idea?"

"No real reason. Evidently, something frightens her about your standard."

"My standard?" Graemme's eyes widened. He looked down at his tunic where the seamstress had embroidered the black wolf leaping from a large rock. "Does she think I keep a pack of wolves?"

"Nay."

"Then why would she be afeared of a simple standard?"

Broccin squirmed on his chair, reluctant to answer. Graemme knew he wouldna get the truth from him. Without asking permission, he rose, threw the door wide and bellowed for Lady Joneta. He didn't have long to wait. She was in the first alcove to the left of the door.

"I wondered how long it would take you to realize my brother would wind his way around your questions."

"Please, Lady, enlighten me about my lady bride."

After he pulled an arm chair from before the fireplace and seated her at the head of the table, he noted Broccin bunching his brows, giving little shakes of his head and whatever means he could think of to signal her to silence.

The lady snorted. "Brother, don't be a fool. 'Tis best the boy knows afore the wedding than after when he finds her atop the turret roof."

"She's never been to such heights!"

"Nay, just every other strange place you could name."

"What are you talking about? Does she take to climbing? I know she likes to sit in trees, but high on the keep?" Graemme's eyes widened. "The demented girl could fall to her death with her adventures!"

"Not adventures. The results of her dreams." Lady Joneta went on to tell him of all Elyne's dreams and the strange places they found her when she awoke.

Graemme felt like he should put his fist below his chin to keep it from dropping after each telling of a dream.

"When did she first start having these 'foretelling' dreams?" Graemme wondered if she had been born with a curse or a gift. Or was the beautiful girl lacking in wits?

Before Chief Broccin could answer, Lady Joneta supplied the answer. "'Twas right after Ranald was sent to Kelso Abbey." She gave her brother a withering stare. "I think the horror of watching her brother hauled away in a cart like bloody refuse was too much for her young mind."

"Ye blame me for her crazy dreams?"

"If you must know the truth, Aye!" Lady Joneta slapped her hand on the table, surprising Broccin to silence.

"'Twas the shock of seeing ye thrash her favorite brother near to death then discard him." Grunda said. Her eyes looked like she was watching the actual beating, for she grimaced. "Ye told them he died, did ye not?" Her gaze bored into Broccin's eyes.

Broccin gave a jerky nod. Instead of rebuking Grunda, he looked frightened of the old woman.

"What happened just before I first arrived?" Graemme

expected he knew the answer already.

Broccin shook himself and answered.

"The first night you came to Raptor? She knew you would come. She awoke on the ground and climbed the tree when she heard your footsteps. Ever since, she has been having night visions of a wolf bathing until all but the hair on his face was gone. The wolf threatened her in different ways. Chased and grabbed her then tried to kill her."

Graemme wondered if the surprise showed on his face, or if he had hid the shock. When Magnus squeezed his shoulder, he guessed not.

"And the night before she disappeared?" Grunda asked.

Lady Joneta told them.

"'Twas Squat who warned us. His barking brought us to the wall atop the corner tower. She stood between two merlons. Just as the guards reached her, she screamed you were pointing a sword of lightning at her and meant to strike her down. She shielded her eyes and lost her balance. One of the guards grabbed her around the waist, but she near pulled him over with her. They would have both fallen to their death had the other guards not grabbed his legs. They had a difficult time lifting them both back through the opening."

Graemme ground his teeth together. How had the girl formed such a hatred for him? The night she came to his bed, she had been eager enough. She was wet and ready for him in a short time. How could anyone so afeared of a man be so eager to swive him?

"She will not go to places where there is family or friends. She hides where ye will not think to search for her." Grunda looked at Broccin and Joneta. "Ye have threatened her with something. What was it?"

"A convent!" Graemme broke in for them. "When she argued with ye about marrying me, ye threatened to remove my stones." He stopped to glare at Magnus, who tried to cover a laugh with a cough. "Afore ye were through cleaning my blood from yer blade, ye said ye'd have Domnall get coins to pay the sisters at Mary Magdalen to keep her there for the rest of her life. She was terrified. She knew ye meant it. Ye reminded her of the last time a child of yers sought to thwart ye."

"'Tis true, brother. I thought she would spew her dinner. She quieted when I reminded her Ranald would never permit it."

When they all gave him disgusted looks, Broccin looked shamed, probably for the first time in his life.

Grunda rose and walked around the room, her eyes vacant. Broccin jumped when she touched his shoulder then released it. She went to the open window and threw back her head. Anyone would think she was sniffing the breeze or enjoying the night air, but she waited quietly. She opened her eyes and stared to the south.

"We need not search further for her. She arrived at Mary Magdalen this night. I have no doubt she'll have a sound, dreamless sleep for she will feel safe." Grunda nodded her head.

"Why do ye think this, old woman?" Broccin's brows met as he asked. "'Tis the last place Elyne would go."

"And the last place ye would look. They recognized her. She asked for sanctuary saying Graemme of Clibrick means to murder her."

If Elyne had been with them, Graemme was so angry at the words he would be tempted to shake her until her brains became so scrambled they would turn to mush. Ha! If they weren't already.

"She will be safe there whilst ye decide what to do when ye go for her," Grunda added. "Stand so I may tell if ye have changed this day."

They could all go to Hades and back before Graemme married a woman who was so piss-brained she could think he'd do such a thing. He was ready to tell them so when he looked at Magnus. Magnus shook his head and murmured for him to humor the seer.

Graemme stood, rigid and straight. Anger streaked through his body like thunderbolts.

Grunda stared into his eyes. "Angry enough to kill. 'Tis not her, though, but the fool who mistreated his children."

Broccin spluttered, but Lady Joneta slapped his arm and

told him to hush!

Graemme could swear he heard Grunda ask if he wanted to swive Elyne, but no sound came from her mouth. She chuckled and looked down. His cock had stirred to life. By Satan's bug-riddled navel, was she a witch who could control his cock?

Slowly, she walked around him, stopping at different spots as she had done to so many people. Did she read them by the set of their shoulders, the rigidity of their muscles? Mayhap she could see a person's aura? She took so long he began to fidget.

Finally, she surprised him. She faced him and put both hands on either side of his head. She held still a bit then ran her fingers through his hair. She smiled, dropped her hands and motioned for him to sit.

"Well, now. This lad will make a fine husband for the girl. If he uses his heart and handles her right, she will lose her fear that he will beat and discard her. She will think only of having his bairns suckling at her breast."

Graemme felt his tension ease at the picture her words created.

"I leave when the sun rises," he said.

"Nay. Ye are still angered because she broke her vow to be here. Bide for a day. Take only enough warriors for protection so ye may travel fast. Few men together will not look threatening." Grunda gazed at Broccin and studied him. "There is a small hunting lodge in the woods nearby surrounded by Scotch pine, juniper and birch trees. I saw there a man who has black hair and deep eyes. 'Twas Ranald's brother afore he died. He took women there to spend slow days of making love, eating and drinking. 'Twill be the perfect spot for Graemme to take Elyne."

"The wedding is less than a sennight." Broccin sounded impatient, though he looked like he didna dare turn his back to this ancient soothsayer.

"Pshh! It can wait for a few days. Cook enough food for yer guests to gorge on." Grunda dismissed his words like a mother would an annoying youngling.

"They come for a festive occasion. They'll not sit around and gorge themselves all day," Broccin snorted.

"Men find their days fly by with contests of feats of strength. They will be more than happy to drink and fight for an extra day or two. Plan some hunts. It makes them feel powerful to kill something. When Graemme returns with her, his bride will be tame and peaceful."

"A good plan. We leave in two days." Graemme stopped and stared at Grunda. "Ye are sure she can be found at this Magdalen Convent?"

"Aye. 'Tis the only place she could travel to in a short time with no baggage. And she trusts them to protect her. I will tend to the wee dog tonight. He will be his old self when ye make the journey. Seeing him will soothe her."

Graemme nodded and picked up his forgotten wine goblet and drank it down. As his stomach felt its warmth, he began to feel more confident.

"Wouldn't she be more soothed if we take you and Lady Joneta with us?"

"Are ye such a weakling ye must have women do yer work for ye?" Her voice was like thunder.

"Dinna call me a weakling, old woman, else ye will see how far ye can fly out yonder window. Without a broom!"

Graemme's voice roared. If he were on a battle field, his enemies would think twice about attacking him. He put his hands on his hips, his eyes shooting sparks of anger.

When Grunda cackled with laughter, he felt like a fool.

"Dinna be chicken-brained, lad. Were I a witch, I would pull ye with me and drop ye in the same pig sty where Elyne awakened one morn."

Broccin's eyes widened. "How came ye to know of that?"

"Same as I know where she is. I see things no other can." She shook her head at him. "Nay, I am not a witch as ye are thinking. Just a seer with many years of living."

Magnus grinned at her. "When Muriele first came to Kinbrace, Grunda laid a curse on all who would do harm to Muriele. 'Twas so dire, men went around checking their tarse at every chance, afeared it would shrivel to a thin nub and fall off."

"Huh! Elyne must have taken lessons from her!" Graemme

scowled at the old woman. He shook himself and forced his face to hide his anger. "We will take only ten men so we will not frighten the good sisters."

"Ranald has a man from Kelso Abbey who tends the gardens at the convent. Now Muriele is no longer there, he still comes weekly. Likely, with Elyne there, he will challenge your right to enter." Broccin rubbed his belly and burped. Wine fumes wafted through the air.

"A monk willna keep me from bringing Elyne out."

"So you think. This is no usual monk, no more than Ranald was. A crusader who tired of killing. This Brother Octavius can snap a man's neck with his hands and not break a sweat," Broccin supplied.

"Then we shall make sure he never has the opportunity to have his hands on us."

"'Twould be better if I give ye a missive stating she is yer betrothed and Ranald agrees to the wedding. They willna argue with his choice of husband for Elyne."

Graemme nodded.

Lady Joneta stood and got their attention. "We will show you to your quarters. The men who came with you before and your warriors will sleep in the men's tower. Graemme and Magnus will take Ranald's bedchamber. Grunda can share a room with me. Take time to refresh yourselves. Dinner will be at dusk." She looked toward the window opening and sighed. "'Tis near upon us."

"Ye will need yer rest, for ye may have a small fight wresting Elyne from the convent," Grunda said.

"A *small* fight?" Graemme looked at her and quirked his brow.

"Aye. She will not leave through the gate. Ye and Sir Magnus must stand close to the castle walls and be vigilant." She twisted her head to the side and looked him up and down.

"Old woman, ye have studied every inch of me. For what do ye search?"

"Are ye good at catching things hurtling toward ye?"

"Aye. We played at tossing a blacksmith's hammer when

we were lads."

"This will be heavier than ye are used to. Brace yerself when the time comes."

Grunda cackled with laughter as she left the room.

CHAPTER 15

THREE DAYS LATER, IT was near dawn when Gramme and the men rode across the clearing between the convent and the surrounding forests. The entrance gate of the convent faced east. With the sun rising behind the men, it flashed on someone standing on the gateway battlements.

"Magnus? Is that a guard atop the left gatehouse tower?"

Creases formed between Graemme's brows as he squinted at the Convent of Mary Magdalen from atop his great horse.

"Hm. If it is, he doesna have his hair clipped and tonsured. Nor does he wear a robe with a cowl over his head like most."

The sun rose a slight bit higher and seemed to focus its strength on the person's head. Did he really see auburn fire flashing off hair? He kicked his horse into a gallop. On seeing the fear in Graemme's face, Magnus spurred his own mount. The rest followed as quickly.

"By Lucifer's crossed eyes! She must be as beetle-brained as a molding acorn," he shouted to his brother. "If my eyes dinna deceive me, Elyne is standing on the edge of the tower!"

"Slow to a walk when we draw near. We dinna want to startle her," Magnus cautioned him.

"Ye are right. Half way there, he slowed his horse to a walk and prayed his bride didn't panic when she saw them. She seemed puzzled as she studied their approach. She might not be able to see them clearly with the sun in her eyes, but they sure as Hades could see her! She wore naught but a thin shift, her form outlined by the first golden streaks of dawn.

They approached the gate slowly as Graemme spoke to Magnus, his voice so furious the words near hissed between his teeth.

"Am I so horrid to look upon that my bride would try to kill herself rather than bear the burden of the marriage bed with me?'

"Horrid? Not when ye have every woman at Clibrick and Kinbrace after yer cock!"

"We must move beneath her, as close to the wall as possible in case she falls."

"Aye. 'Tis a good plan."

"Keep close beside me in case I dinna get a good grasp on her. The old seer was right. Elyne will be much harder to catch than a blacksmith's hammer!" He looked over his shoulder and called out, "Colyne, go to the gate and demand entrance."

"I'll go too," Brian said. "Two fists are better than one if the man is aged and hard of hearing."

Brian, with Squat snuggled in a sling around his neck, looked up then followed Colyne. His face looked strained. Seeing the worry in his friend's expression frightened Graemme even more. The man was always full of laughter and never seemed to care a whit about danger.

Squat recognized his mistress, for he started barking and trying to get out of his makeshift carrier. He scratched Brian's arms and whined until Brian took him from the sling and leaned over in his saddle to place him safely on the ground. The dog raced to the wall and barked up at his mistress, most likely demanding she come pet him.

Graemme didn't dare take his eyes from Elyne's face. She finally seemed to take in her surroundings with more interest when she heard Squat barking. When Colyne and Brian banged their fists on the gatehouse door and shouted for the gate-keeper, her eyes opened wide. Graemme inched his horse even closer and pulled to a stop directly beneath her. He dropped the reins across his horse's neck, which signaled him to stand still. Magnus moved his mount a small distance to the left of Graemme's. If she fell and Graemme missed her, he would be in position to catch her.

She had never been more beautiful. The sun lighting her

brown hair caused the fiery auburn to shine much like torch-light. Her tall, slender body looked ripe for the taking. Graemme and Magnus moved in their saddles, leaving only the tips of their boots in the stirrups so they could stand with arms outreached.

Graemme's broadsword was in the way and bounced against his left leg. He reached up and drew it from its holder. When he did, the sun seemed to turn it to a beacon. Flashes of light streaked off it.

Elyne's intriguing brown eyes opened wide as she gaped down at the men. Recognition finally shone there, as well as horror. She forced her gaze from him long enough to look over the men below as if searching for a familiar face. Probably Ranald. He'd bet his horse on it! When she didn't see her brother, her eyes filled with panic.

"Elyne, get back from the edge," he shouted as the other men yelled at the slow gatekeeper. When she didn't obey him, he shouted at her again. "Get back and listen to yer husband," he yelled. He felt his face tighten in a scowl, a look which told his men if they didn't instantly obey, they would be in deep shite!

Never did he expect a scowl from him would cause a woman to scream and totter, setting off a fearsome event!

Elyne heard the sounds of mailed fists pounding on solid wood and angry men shouting. And strangely, a dog frantically barked and yipped. It wasn't the type of sounds she would expect to hear in this quiet, prayerful community. Wind was blowing her hair. Had she left her cell window open to the night air before she went to sleep? It was cold. She reached for the thin blanket but touched stone instead. Strange. Her cot was far from the wall.

She blinked her eyes and realized she was tottering on the edge of a crenelated wall, much as she had at Raptor not many days afore. The stone she touched was still cold from the night air. She heard someone shouting at her, but the sun was in her eyes.

Taking her hand, she shielded her eyes. And gasped. Below was a small army of knights. Why were they here? They usually sought a place to sleep as night fell. The stiff wind picked up and teased a standard until it lifted to fly upright.

God help her. The man-wolf had tracked her down!

But now there were two of them. His brother. Much alike, though a little older and even sterner. Her man-wolf yelled again for her to move back. Back where? She wobbled. Afeared to chance turning her head to see where she was, she hesitated. Before she could decide what to do, he drew his heavy sword. Light flashed and streaked from it. It seemed to seek her out, for it reached her eyes.

Heaven help her. Her dream at Raptor had come to life!

Horror filled her as she lost her balance. Her hands flew out to grab onto stone, but they clawed empty air.

Screaming, she toppled off the tower. She was falling to her death. When she struck something hard as stone, she expected to die. Male voices shouted but she couldn't make out the words. The loudest was near her ear as sturdy, muscled arms grabbed hold of her shoulders. Her head cracked hard against something and her legs tangled with a horse's head. The animal stamped and sidled.

"Shite!"

Graemme's voice.

The two tilted back and forth and rolled to the left side of the saddle. It was as if a giant hand meant to shake them senseless and nearly threw them off the horse. Another set of arms grasped her hips and legs. They had not finished falling. 'Twas a short distance from saddle to grass. They landed with a thud, amidst more cursing. Two hard bodies cushioned her from the ground, one with arms around her upper body, another cradling her hips and legs. Her forehead hit something softer than before.

Their legs tangled with the horses' legs, but both men barked orders for the mounts to stand still. Battle-hardened, they obeyed.

Elyne opened her eyes. She squeezed them shut again and wished she could rub them. Had she traveled back in time? Except when she'd landed atop Graemme before, her head didn't feel like it had struck an anvil. And before, she'd stared into startled brown eyes. Now all she saw was a large bump on Graemme's forehead and blood flowing quite impressively from his nose.

"What in Hades were ye trying to do, woman! Fly like a hawk?" The man's voice nearly snarled at her, he was so angry. "This habit of knocking my brother on his back has to stop."

She felt the man release her hips and legs. She was able to raise her head to stare down at Graemme, who appeared to be senseless. His arms still tightly gripped her to him, and blood flowed down the sides of his cheeks.

"I think he broke his beautiful nose!" Elyne tried to pull her shift closer to staunch the bleeding.

"*He* broke his nose? More likely 'twas yer hard head. But Graemme will be pleased ye think his nose beautiful." His voice no longer sounded angry but a bit amused.

She near jumped up, if she'd been able, when the voice's hands pulled her clothing down over her buttocks and legs. Squat tried to wrench the material from him and near tore her shift.

"Stop it, Squat!"

Was it her who spoke or him? Nay. 'Twas him. Squat had shut his mouth and looked up at the man and not her.

"Tsk! Ye need not show the men how fortunate, or mayhap unfortunate, my brother has been in catching a bride."

Laughter was in his voice, but beneath the tone was a hint of worry.

"Come, let me help ye up afore the good sisters think something is happening between ye right here for all to witness. Fortunately, ye knocked us off our mounts onto a grassy area."

Hearing him mention the sisters, she turned her head and saw women in their habits running toward them, some carrying shovels or brooms, others buckets of anything they had gotten their hands on when they heard the commotion. Leading them was a visiting monk carrying a broadsword and looking like he could demolish any intruders with one hefty swing. Behind him was Brother Michael, whom she'd found most enjoyable the night before for he'd regaled her with stories of Ranald as a monk.

Graemme's arms still clutched her to him. When Magnus on one side and Colyne on the other, tried to open them so they could lift Elyne off him, Squat snarled and barked. He headed straight for Magnus' arse.

"You had best fend off the wee dog, else you won't sit for several days," Brian warned him.

"And ye had best catch him afore he does if ye dinna want yer arse kicked from here to the Highlands! Ye were responsible for him."

Why were Magnus and Colyne arguing about Squat? Graemme felt something hot running down the sides of his cheeks and opened his eyes. He'd though Squat had used him for his own purposes, but Brian already had him in his arms.

He hurt all over. Had Lucifer been there to poke him with pitchforks and pile stones on him? His ears rang and his eyes started to clear. Someone was tugging his arms. Another was crawling all over him. Pray God it was a lass! Surely, if some simpering man took advantage of his senseless state, it would be a mortal sin!

"Graemme, ye can let Elyne go now. She's safely on the ground, thanks to yer soft body!"

Magnus voice! He looked. His gaze clashed with Elyne's beautiful dark brown eyes. Everything started to make sense to him now. He sighed and let his arms relax. He felt a cold breeze when Colyne and Magnus carefully lifted her off him.

"Someone cover her. She has a habit of running around near nekid for all to see!"

"I do not! Ye keep showing up where ye're not wanted and battering me!"

"Here now, ye have a lifetime to fight." Magnus turned to the closest nun. "Please, Sister, tend Elyne to see she isna hurt and is properly dressed." He looked at the two men. The giant was Elyne's brother's friend. He didna know who the other monk was. "Does either of ye know of healing? Catching the lady seems to have caused my brother some injuries."

"I am Brother Michael from Kelso. I have some training from our former Brother Ranald. This is Brother Hugo," He said as he came forward and knelt beside Graemme. "He came to Kelso as a wounded Crusader sick to the soul from slaughter. Brother Ranald cured his wounds and mind. Hugo decided to become one of us."

As the monk talked, his hands gently probed over Graemme, feeling for broken bones or other serious injuries.

"His nose is not as straight as before. And her elbow cracked against his head when he first caught her." He chuckled and glanced at Magnus. "The three of you looked like people with cords attached while someone jerked you every which way."

Brother Michael paid particular heed to Graemme's fore-head. "We'll need some cold cloths there and an elixir to ward off pains in the head." He pulled a white linen cloth from a pocket of his robe and held it to Graemme's nose. "We'll need to do a little work on his nose. I dinna think 'tis broken, but she dealt him a blow hard enough to cause bleeding and mayhap some swelling. It should heal with naught but a slight mark."

Asking Graemme questions as his hands traveled over Graemme's neck, arms and felt over his ribs and stomach. Finally, Ranald's giant friend Brother Hugo helped Magnus to stand Graemme on his feet.

"Check my horse, Colyne. I came down on him pretty hard when I stood to catch her," Magnus said.

"Already have. Only a small scratch on his left cheek where her foot struck him. I'll put something on it when we unsaddle."

"Unsaddle? No need. We leave as soon as Elyne's properly clothed." Graemme ordered.

He swayed back and forth when Brother Hugo let go of his arm.

"Still think you will ride this day? You wouldn't get a league away afore you fell off your saddle… or bled to death." Brother Michael chuckled. "And I think you have much explaining to do to Mother Cecelia."

The monk was right. While the sisters tended Elyne for her bruises and cuts, Graemme and Magnus followed the monks to the Infirmary. Brother Michael cautiously pulled the cloth from Graemme's nostrils.

"Let us see if your nose is broken or just had a hard knock." He watched as a slow trickle ran down toward Graemme's lips. "Nay. Her head isn't as hard as you thought."

He dipped a clean cloth in cold water and handed it to Graemme.

"Here. Hold this on it while I check you over. It should stop the bleeding."

He had Graemme bend and straighten his arms and legs, felt every bone in his spine and checked every muscle.

Graemme answered Brother Michael's questions of, "Does this hurt?" with a muffled voice. Finally, he threw the cold cloth onto the table.

Thankfully, nothing had broken when Graemme slammed onto the ground. The most serious injury was a gash on the outside of his left thigh where he'd scraped against a sharp rock when landing. Graemme gritted his teeth while Brother Michael cleaned dirt out of the wound, flooded it with an astringent made from moneywort. After placing a pad over the injury, he bandaged it closed with precision, just tight enough his flesh would heal together but not too tight to cause trouble. When he finished, he massaged ointment into sore muscles and checked Graemme's bruises.

"Brother Michael must have magic in his fingers. I feel as rested as if I'd slept a bit," he told Magnus as they went to meet with the head of the convent alone. Well, not alone, for Brothers Michael and Hugo were there leaning against a wall. Elyne's brother Ranald had appointed Hugo Guardian of Mary Magdalen while Muriele was there.

He took his duties seriously, for he didn't let Graemme out of his sight. 'Twas strange. For such a big man, his touch was gentle as he helped Graemme.

The spacious, sunny room was bare but for necessities. A small table with two chairs waited beneath the window. A pewter pitcher, its sides sweating from cold water, looked inviting.

Small pewter cups circled it and a basin sat just a hand's-width away. Statues of the Virgin Mary, Jesus and various saints stood in niches in the room. A single candle in a glass holder flamed in front of each.

A desk covered with missives took up half of one wall with Mother Cecelia's wooden armchair in place. A charcoal sketch of Jesus on the cross hung behind it. Two straight backed chairs awaited before the desk.

Graemme looked at Magnus and again glanced around the room. "I have seen the Abbot's office at Melrose Abbey. It seems an Abbot lives with more comfort than a fragile woman."

"I met Mother Cecelia when I came for Muriele. She is capable, not fragile, by any means," Magnus whispered to Graemme as footsteps approached the door.

"Please. Take a seat," Mother Cecelia said as she entered.

The men politely waited until she sat before they did. The two monks leaned against the wall and watched the room in a protective way.

"Fragile?" Mother Cecelia's voice sounded surprised when she sat down. "Nay, we are strong women here. Ranald of Raptor can tell you of us. We kept his wife safe from him for a sennight or more while his army camped outside the walls."

"Surely a former monk wouldna have used force to enter!" Magnus looked shocked.

"Nay, he would not. We released her into the care of monks from Kelso Abbey who came to settle the dispute. Ranald disguised himself as a penitent bound to silence. A good thing, too. Anyone who has heard him chanting the psalms at Matins would recognize his voice."

"Were you not furious for his deception?" Graemme couldn't imagine this new brother-by-law doing such a devious thing.

"Nay. I knew from the first."

"Then why did ye allow him to leave with her?"

"Brother Ranald is the most honorable monk or man I have had the pleasure of knowing," Mother Cecelia said. "He protected Lady Muriele by paying much more than necessary for her keep. He had the Abbot of Kelso send Brother Hugo to us as her guardian." She raised her left brow at Graemme. "By the way, Brother Ranald was no more devious than your brother. 'Tis the reason Brother Hugo keeps Sir Magnus in his sight. He was much shamed when Sir Magnus was able to spirit her away."

Magnus looked at the big man and nodded. "I regret the distress I caused ye."

Brother Hugo inclined his head and crossed his arms inside his wide brown sleeves.

"Word travels quickly to us here in Northumbria. I have heard of two brothers, Magnus and Graemme. One is righteous to the bone and will not bend. The other as honorable but lets common sense guide him." She stopped and stared at them.

Magnus and Graemme felt the urge to squirm on their seats, knowing they must both appear as fools to her.

"I knew you were Magnus, "she said, looking at Graemme's brother. "You look to have the gall to hire a young woman, enter a convent and kidnap the lass who sought sanctuary with us. By all rights, I should have Brother Michael and our faithful Guardian toss you back out the convent gates."

"What good would it do ye? We would still return. And anger makes us more powerful," Magnus said with a cheerful smile.

"Agreed. So it is with me."

"We came to retrieve my betrothed, Elyne," Graemme interrupted. "She has addled dreams which led her to fear me. All I intend to do is the honorable thing."

"Her dreams are not addled, by any means. She envisioned the battle outside our gates when Sir Ranald fought off an evil baron who intended to murder Lady Catalin," Mother Cecelia said.

"Not foolish? When she thought I was a wolf turned man and was going to tear out her throat?" Graemme raised his brows and awaited her answer.

"Well, now, she may have been wrong. But you must admit your standard was what caused her to picture you as a wolf."

"Aye. And ye must admit if I intended to murder her, I would have let her fall." He leaned forward to brace his arms on his knees, but winced when the movement disturbed his wound. He sat straight again. " 'Tis more likely the daft girl and her father will be the end of me."

"Nay. She will soften once ye are married," Magnus said. "Muriele hated me for something I failed to say when I left Kinbrace. Once she knew I loved her, she was free to love me in return."

"Aye, but ye are in love. In my case, there will be a wedding or I lose, uh, part of my personal treasures."

"You must pay if you do not marry Elyne? I do not understand." Mother Cecelia said, a slight frown creasing her brow.

Graemme's face turned hot as the blood dripping from his nose. Magnus snorted trying not to laugh aloud. Fortunately, Graemme remembered the missive Chief Broccin had written. He pretended he hadn't heard her question and rose to his feet. Fumbling with the wide belt holding his kilt around his waist, he withdrew the message from a fold in the leather. He hoped to distract her by producing Chief Broccin's letter saying Ranald had given his approval for the wedding.

"I should have given ye this sooner." He handed her the small, folded parchment with a raptor on the seal. "I canna help but be curious about all I've heard of this brother of Elyne's. Her father said the day we wed, I would have the devil as my brother-by-law. I dinna see how he would say such a thing while ye talk about his son as an honorable man."

While Mother Cecelia read the note, Brother Michael answered for her.

"Other than God, his son Ranald is the only man Chief Broccin will heed. He is shamed because he cannot frighten his son as he has every other man. Over the last couple years, they have learned to deal with each other. 'Tis a kindness that Ranald has forgiven his father for many things. But the father knows he can never cross his son. He would not survive the outcome."

Mother Cecelia cleared her voice to get their attention. When they looked at her, she pressed the paper out flat and stared down at it. Her face appeared flushed and she made a small sound in her throat as if choking on a laugh.

"I think you and Elyne should spend some time alone together afore the wedding vows."

Graemme sat up straight, surprised when this saintly woman suggested such a thing. Had she read his mind and known he intended to take her to a hunting lodge in the woods? Or did she mean for them to sit across the great room from Chief Broccin and talk to each other?

From the twinkle in her eye, he didn't think it was the latter.

"A good start would be a walk in the orchard surrounding the small chapel on the grounds," she said, understanding his shocked look. "It was Lady Muriele's favorite pastime. It will take you at least two days before you are fit to ride. And once Elyne reads this, she will be reassured. She trusts her brother with all her heart.

"Chief Broccin was short and to the point. He stated they should open the gates to Sir Gramme. He and Elyne were properly betrothed, and her would-be husband had fulfilled his end of the bargain by appearing at Raptor Castle at the appointed time. His son Ranald approved of the wedding and he and his wife will be in attendance."

She stood and handed him Chief Broccin's note. "I think her father expected you to give this to the guard at the gate.

All would have been fine, if the Chief had only stopped writing then. But he stated if Graemme changed his mind and left without his bride in tow, he would forfeit his ballocks when he returned.

No wonder Mother Cecelia had a hard time keeping her laughter from rising when she handed the missive to Graemme!

CHAPTER 16

GRAEMME NEAR SHOUTED AN obscenity as he shot out of his chair. He clamped his teeth together then sat back down as abruptly as he'd stood. His nose started to bleed again. He fumbled around for something to stop it. He couldn't use his kilt because it would expose those very ballocks Broccin wrote about.

Blood blurred Broccin's signature, which was fitting.

Brother Michael sprang to his aid and tipped Graemme's head backward. Magically, Mother Cecelia placed a small cloth in the monk's hand, which he used to cover Graemme's nose. She must have dunked it in the basin with water from the pitcher. Its coldness was a welcome shock and seemed to help staunch the bleeding.

Magnus took Broccin's letter from Graemme's hand. He had the nerve to laugh.

"Well, now, young man," Mother Cecelia said. "You need not worry further about forfeiting any of your *treasures* for Elyne. I am sure she will come around once she understands how serious her father is about this marriage." Graemme snorted then choked for his efforts. He barely heard someone scratch on the door.

"Come." The older woman called out. Elyne entered and jolted to a stop when she saw the blood on Graemme's face. Calmly, she looked him over then decided it was not from a dispute with the monks but simply from getting his nose in the way of her chin.

"If ye had caught me properly, ye could have saved yourself

an injury."

"Caught ye properly?" Graemme's muffled voice growled. "If ye were a proper lass, ye wouldna have been upon the gatehouse in the fist place!" His narrowed gaze shot sparks of rage.

"If ye want a *proper lass*, dinna fear I will be insulted if ye look elsewhere for one."

All he had shown her was anger and dislike. Why didn't he disappear and hie himself off to the Highlands where he belonged? He could take his evil temper out on the wolves that probably raised him! What had he said his family motto was? *With a Strong Hand?* Seemed to her it should have been *With Slashing Teeth and Claws.*

He turned and looked at her through squinted eyes. If a cold, menacing stare could kill someone, she would drop to the floor and breathe her last. Good thing she wasn't a weakling or she'd have backed up, gained the door and ran.

On hearing Graemme's voice, Squat bounded into the room and made directly for him. He stood on his barrel-shaped hind legs and clawed at Graemme's arm, demanding attention. Unconsciously, Graemme reached over to ruffle the hair behind Squat's right ear. It stood at attention even in his sleep. Squat leaned his head back pressing into Graemme's hand, his eyes half-closed in enjoyment. The fool dog had taken a liking for the enemy. The little traitor!

Elyne whistled to him, but he ignored her. Graemme didn't, though.

"Yer father has grown tired of yer strange and unmaidenly behavior. He selected me to tame ye and bring ye to the chapel in time for the wedding. He is determined to ruin my life. Why, I dinna know."

He reached up and took the cold cloth from his face, giving her a baleful look. "We will walk on the garden paths and learn to know each other."

He glanced over in time to see the amused look on Mother Cecelia face.

The woman had a warped sense of humor!

"I already know enough about ye to know marrying ye

would be the worst mistake of my life!"

Graemme snorted. "How do ye think I feel? I'm in dire need of hiring a taster to assure ye dinna poison me again."

Elyne put her hands on her hips and scowled at him. "'Tis unfortunate ye forced me to vow not to." She mumbled under her breath, "A shame, truly!"

Brother Michael changed the water in the basin and rinsed the cloth. When he handed it back to Graemme, he wiped his face as best he could.

"Ye bleed like a stuck piglet! Ye had best wipe yer neck and chest too." Elyne turned her nose in the air and sniffed, like he was doing something dim-witted and she wasn't going to fall for it. "If ye think a little blood is going to make me soften to yer high-handed ways, think again!"

"Where might I go to properly cleanse myself?" He ignored her and turned to the monks.

"We have a well in the orchard," Brother Octavius replied.

"A well?" He glowered at Elyne then turned to Brother Octavius. "Will ye stand guard so my future bride doesna spy on me again? She'll likely follow. She is known for her fondness of watching men bathe at wells."

Elyne's face flamed so hot she wanted to grab the cold cloth, blood and all, to cool it down. The nasty man was blaming her for his own predicament. If he'd been polite and apologized to her while she was still in the tree, this never would have happened. But no! He had to put on a show fit for only a whore to watch then pulled her down on top of him. And he blamed her?

"Bleh! I hope ye use as much soap and water as I did washing the stench of yer body from mine! May I be excused, Mother Cecelia?"

On getting a nod of the head in reply, she turned on her heels and strode to the door, keeping her back straight and haughty. At the door, she skidded to a stop, remembering Squat. His tongue was half in, half out the side of his mouth, and his straggly, bent tail beat the floor. 'Twas obvious he wanted the loathsome man's attention.

"Come, Squat!"

When he looked at her and then back at Graemme, she slapped her leg and whistled, loud enough to make Mother Cecelia wince.

He came.

The frisky little dog followed her to the kitchens, where the sisters there made over him and found a bone left over from the soup last eve. She sat and talked to them while Squat happily chewed on it until his few teeth grew tired. She thanked the women and led him out of the back door leading to the gardens and the cleared area where a small chapel stood.

Brother Octavius had made paths winding around in no certain way other than to give the walker beautiful plants and flowers to observe. She stopped to listen to the wind blowing through the trees and birds talking and singing. Closing her eyes, she took it all in, at peace for the first time since she'd been at the convent.

Finally, she opened her eyes and found Squat inspecting the flowers. Some must be flavorful, for he'd nip one off then swallow it. But then, he was as likely to eat dead, shriveled worms so she doubted he had much taste in food. She sighed, wondering if the flowers would upset his stomach. She didn't look forward to cleaning up the aftereffects.

"Ye should be ashamed of yerself, little mister, falling for a scratch on the head," she grumbled as she started walking again. "He might pet ye now and mayhap kick yer arse this next morn. I'm telling ye, Squat, everyone knows ye canna trust a wily Highlander."

She followed another path, mumbling to the one listener not likely to disagree with her. "Why, Magnus must have put a spell on Muriele for her to fall in love with him. I willna believe it until I see them together."

She kept mumbling and grousing to herself hoping Graemme took overlong in cleaning himself. It was such a lovely day. With him around, he would spoil it. A few footsteps later, she jumped. Someone followed behind her.

"Should I add talking to yerself as one of yer virtues or is it another of the crazed things ye do?"

Bleh! When in Hades did Graemme get there? She turned and raised her brows at him.

He snorted like a horse with a fly bedeviling his nostrils.

"Ye don't even have to mumble for me to know yer thoughts. I've been in back of ye since ye left the kitchens. Did ye not notice Squat looking behind ye and sweeping his crooked tail on the stones?"

"Ye should have made a noise!"

"Why? Are ye hard of hearing, too?"

"Listening in on someone's thoughts is nay an admirable trait in a man."

She really didn't care if he'd heard her or not. Mayhap her opinions of his brother and him would cause him to think twice about wedding her.

"And watching a nekid man is nay an admirable trait in a maiden."

She stopped walking and turned to stand near toe to toe with him. With hands on her hips, she scowled up at him. The man was so thickheaded! Why would he keep insisting he'd marry her when they both knew they hated the sight of each other?

"Aye. Mayhap ye should tell my father the betrothal is nay to yer liking? If ye tell him I am not the right wife for ye, he will listen. Ye can even tell him I'm knotty-pated, if ye like. Even he would understand a man not wanting to marry a daft woman."

"Yer right. And the next breath he took would be to order Domnall to sharpen his sword!" He shook his head and looked at her in amazement. "Can ye be so bug-brained ye believe yer father wouldn't do what he's threatened?"

"He would not. He just said it knowing ye were a coward and wouldna dare to thwart him."

By Lucifer's saggy man-breasts! She truly believed it. After what the man had done to his son, she should know Broccin wouldn't think twice at gelding him!

"Nay. Ye are wrong. He'd do so and laugh whilst he did. Believe me, if I even had the slightest thought he didna mean it, I would have gladly stayed in the Highlands, honor or not."

He shook his head and glared down at her. 'Twas not a good idea. Blood again began to trickle from his left nostril. He grabbed the bottom of his kilt and, without thinking, held it to his nose.

If her eyes had not strayed immediately downward, he wouldn't have thought anything of it. But her face turned pink. It didn't stop her from staring, though, when his cock became interested in her scrutiny.

"Take yer eyes away, woman, else the good Mother will find ye indulging in yer favorite sport!"

Her gaze snapped up to his. When he dropped his kilt, a look of disappointment came over her face. Did her father even suspect she went around giving men a cockstand whenever she wanted?

He grabbed her arm. She tried to pull away.

"Walk. The good Mother suggested we get to know each other better afore we leave."

"Humph!"

She turned her nose in the air and called to Squat, who had decided to dig in the middle of a flower bed. What did Graemme want to talk about? She had one thing she wanted to find out. His women in the Highlands.

"Do ye keep a leman at Clibrick Castle?"

She worried her lower lip with her teeth. Oh, pish! She shouldn't have asked. He might think she cared. Perchance he'd even think she wanted his attention or some such rot. Now why did he stop so abruptly his boots kicked up a dust storm?

"What did ye say?"

Why, he looked dumbfounded. Did he think women didn't know what men did all the time? She really didn't care if he had one or not.

"Ye are the one hard of hearing! Do ye have someone ye beckon to when ye feel like tupping?"

"Are ye witless? I canna believe ye would ask a man such a thing. It has naught to do with ye whether I have a leman or not."

"Naught to do with me? And ye think I'm witless? It has

everything to do with me. If ye have a leman, then I will feel free to have one myself."

Now why was his mouth dropping like he'd seen a horse with ears long as a hare's?

"Ye would take a *leman*? Women dinna take lemans!"

"Little ye know about it. I know several knights wives who are tupping other than their husbands."

She shook her head wondering why he hadn't noticed it in his own keep. He stopped shaking his head. Finally. If he'd done it any harder, his nose would spray blood all over her clothes. What was making him snort like a horse?

"Women dinna take lemans. They take *lovers*."

"Isn't a leman a man's lover?"

"Aye, but if a woman is interested in another man for bed sport, he isna called a leman. He is considered her lover."

"Means the same, doesn't it?"

"Aye. Take my word for it. And nay, ye will not have a lover."

"Then ye'd best get rid of yer leman!"

Elyne started tapping her right foot in irritation. She might not want a husband, but if her father forced her to marry and give up her freedom, then the man was going to have to give up something equally as important to him!

Graemme ran his fingers through his hair acting like she was making him crazy or something. No, wait. Maybe it was the wrong thing to demand from him. If he had a leman, she could just refuse to share his bed when they wed. She would have to suggest that he occupy himself with his leman. He shouldn't mind that. After all, he certainly didn't want her and had made no effort to deny it. All he wanted was to save those impressive ballocks of his.

She thought he was going to shake the leaves out of her hair when his fingers dug into her shoulders. Why did he stare so hard at her? Was he thinking whether she was worth losing his leman over?

"Do not ever think on demanding anything from me, Elyne. Ye will be deeply sorry for it. I think I know what ye are doing. Ye think to make me so angry that I will be a gowk and defy yer father." He shook his head and scowled down at her. "Ye can forget that idea."

When she started to reply, he squeezed her shoulders again. Hard.

"I am neither afraid of yer father nor his threats. I am wedding ye because I vowed I would. Ye are soiled goods and no other man in Scotland will offer for ye. Everyone saw ye atop me. Even yer brother says we should marry. But had he disapproved, we would still wed. A vow from my family is never broken. It is our honor ye ask me to defile and I willna do it. Marry me ye will, and dinna doubt it!"

He gave her another little shake. Did he think she hadn't been listening? Why did he have to have such piercing dark eyes? And smell so good. He had bathed before he met her on the path. A lock of his black hair fell over his left eye when he shook her. She reached up and lifted it out of the way. He had lovely brows, too. As dark as his hair. She was tall for a woman, but she didn't quite reach his chin. She cleared her throat and couldn't think of any more objections at the moment.

Drats! His scent did funny things to her stomach. And her nose. She kept taking deep breaths. She stared at his neck and remembered when they made bed sport the hollow of his neck smelled of warm sandalwood and pine. When she felt her muscles tense to lean closer, she stopped herself and pulled back.

"Well, dinna expect me to like it," she muttered.

"Judging from the last time we were nekid together, I think ye will like it verra much." His voice was husky as he stared at her lips.

By instinct, she started to wet them but stopped herself in time. She didn't want him to think she craved his kisses — or anything else, for that matter.

He lowered his head to kiss her. She lowered hers to deny him.

He softly kissed her forehead pretending it was all he intended in the first place.

"I thought we were supposed to be talking. *Only* talking!"

He dropped his hands and took her elbow to guide her.

"Do ye think I'm some brainless, scrawny lass who canna stay on a path?"

"By yer habit of falling all the time, ye need help of some kind."

He lurched as he walked and he complained about her? Before she could respond to his dig, he spoke again. "Tell me how ye came to have such an ugsome dog as Squat? And does he always do this?"

She looked down to see Squat was on his hind legs, his teeth locked onto the hem of Graemme's kilt in back. He was worrying it as he would a rat or hare. If he kept it up, Graemme's kilt would be on the ground. He'd likely blame her for his being bare arsed again.

"Squat. Leave it!"

Squat stopped shaking the cloth but didn't let it go. He questioned her, looking up at her with his beady little eyes, why she didn't want him to play. "Leave it. Now."

The dog opened his mouth wide and emptied it of a wad of soggy cloth.

Graemme leaned down and ruffled the hair on the dog's sides. Squat plopped down on the grass and turned his belly upward, begging for him to rub his chest. Graemme complied, telling him he was a beastly looking little devil but was one of a kind.

"Ranald brought him to me after saving him from a baron who was torturing people and animals. He'd mistreated Squat so much Ranald feared he would never stop cowering when he saw a man. He felt the poor little thing would trust a woman. It took me months to gentle him. 'Tis funny, but I think Father likes him. Even though Squat pisses on his boots sometimes."

"Yer brother must have a kind spot for mistreated beasts."

"Nay, he has a kind spot for everyone. Everyone who is good, I mean. He wouldna hesitate to put his blade through someone evil."

"Yer father made him sound most sinister. He said he was the devil on earth."

"Bleh! Father exaggerates because Ranald willna back down

to him. Not unlike someone else I know."

"Woman, will ye let it be? I told ye it wasna the threat but the vow I canna break!"

He really *was* very easy to look at. Especially when his feelings were ruffled. It made his eyes flash black streaks and when he clenched his teeth together, his jaw hardened like Welsh slate. She'd get back to learning about him.

"Do ye have a dog at Clibrick?"

"Nay"

"Nay? Why? Ye seem to like dogs."

"Every time I had a dog, it disappeared."

"Disappeared? Did they wander off and get lost? It doesna sound likely."

"I found out why, finally. Magnus fostered with Chief Olaf at Kinbrace Castle. Their son, Feradoch, fostered with us at Clibrick. He was with us most of the year. It was always when he was there that the dogs disappeared. After a while, I decided 'twas best for the animals not to befriend one."

"He must be a hateful person to do such a thing." A shadow passed over Graemme's eyes like he remembered the sadness.

"Feradoch is gone now, never to return."

"He's dead?"

"Aye. Quite dead. He tried to kill Magnus over Lady Muriele's fortune. Instead, they near killed each other. When the fight ended and we lifted him off Magnus, Feradoch didna have a killing wound on him but he didna breathe. Magnus near died, too. Muriele was so angry she struck him on the chest. That lass has the strength of a man when angered. He finally drew a breath. She nursed him back to health. She's coming to see us wed with her friend Esa."

"Muriele lived with us for a while. Until she came here. I know of her strength when she's protecting someone. Yer brother was hateful for tracking her down like some wild animal. He is another reason why we dinna fit together."

"And ye think yer brother Ranald is without faults? We have even heard of the Black Raptor in the Highlands."

"They are exaggerations, nothing more."

"In the woods, when ye see smoke, ye will find fire."

When Graemme saw the anger in Elyne's eyes, he knew she wouldn't take any criticism of her brother lightly. This man was beginning to fascinate him. He seemed to have two very distinct sides to him. A cross between Lucifer and a saint. He wouldn't speak more of him with Elyne. After all, they were trying to make peace with each other.

She looked lovely with the wind blowing her curly hair around her shoulders. The creamy skin above her breasts peeked above the neckline of her green kirtle. His blood stirred, remembering how sweet her skin was to his tongue when he licked around her breasts. 'Twas a saving grace they fitted together so perfectly in bed.

If only she had been a virgin. He wondered who the man was before him. He felt his temper heat. Was he still around? If he ever found them together, she would forfeit her lover's life! He felt his hands clenching.

Without conscious thought, he jerked her to him and started kissing her. When she whimpered, he realized he was grinding her lips against her teeth. He softened his own and kissed her as softly as he would a bairn. He felt the heat of her stomach cradling his hard shaft and wished they were not on such sacred ground. Likely, the monk Hugo would tear his head from his body if he found them swiving.

For that matter, if Ranald learned of it, he'd probably unleash his infamous fury. He eased his lips from hers, but couldn't resist kissing her closed lids. She may protest she hated him but when his lips touched her, she became soft and pliable. 'Twould be a blessing to have a wife who liked to swive — as long as she remained faithful. Likely, Elyne would keep him sated for a time. Until he tired of having only one woman, he'd leave the lasses at Clibrick alone.

Both startled when footsteps approached. When Magnus came around the bend in the path, Elyne flushed and looked away. The corners of his mouth twitched. Squat got between them and Magnus and eyed Magnus like he was a new bone for dinner. Graemme was about to warn him when Squat ran, barking at him. The dog latched onto Magnus' boot ties and tried to stop his feet from moving. Magnus halted and let Squat think he'd done a good job protecting the couple. He patiently waited until the dog tired himself out.

"Mother Cecelia sent me to tell Elyne 'twas time for the ladies to attend Vespers afore supper." He put on a solemn face and nodded, glancing down at Graemme's clothing. "I think it was a timely interruption, dinna ye?"

Graemme near groaned when Elyne, too, spied his tented clothing. It couldn't be a surprise to her, not when his eager member had pressed between the two of them as sturdy as the pine tree on the far side of the path.

"I am glad of the interruption, Sir Magnus. Yer brother seems to think he can maul me any time he wishes."

"Didna look like ye disliked it, lass." Magnus shook his head and grinned.

She flushed so hotly the men laughed aloud. For once, she didn't have a rejoinder.

Graemme extended his arm. She hesitated a moment before she put her fingertips on it. She was glad when Magnus stepped to her other side. All the way back to the buildings, he made pleasant observations about the lovely garden pathway.

Since they first met, body to body, Graemme was the most comfortable with Elyne these last fifty paces.

Whenever Magnus spoke, Elyne took the opportunity to study him. The resemblance was so strong anyone would recognize them as brothers. Magnus was slightly taller with near black eyes where Graemme's were the shade of burnt almonds. Graemme shaved his face each day with a sharp blade, for the shadow of his beard darkened his face as the day grew. Magnus wore a clipped beard framing his chin and up and over his lips. Their lips were full, but Graemme's were wider, more sensual.

She was so engrossed she almost missed his questioning look down at her after he spoke. What had he said? He was smiling, so he must have made some remark he expected her to agree with.

"For certs," she replied and smiled back.

Magnus' laughed outright. She skidded to a halt. What had she just agreed to? The men stopped when she did.

"'Tis obvious ye were gathering wool between yer ears to have agreed so readily," Magnus voice softened.

Graemme's full lips quivered at the corners.

"I am most grateful ye will be ready at daybreak two morns from now so as to return to Raptor." He looked down at her and quirked his right brow. "For the wedding," he reminded her.

"Truthfully, Magnus, ye were correct. Had I been paying attention, I would have replied 'Nay' loud enough for Father to hear at Raptor."

Graemme could forget trying to intimidate her. She'd learned never to back down to an overbearing male or he'd think he had complete control over her. If she'd not let Father's yells of outrage subdue her, she wasn't going to let Graemme think she'd jump whenever he commanded. He may as well sleep late the morning they were to leave. She wasn't going back to Raptor.

Ranald should be at Hunter Castle in Crookham with his wife and children. It was due east, an easy ride from the Convent. Regardless of what Ranald had told Father, she would convince them both that she and Graemme hated each other and would likely fight till the day one of them killed the other.

Yew! But there was the case of Graemme's impressive ballocks.

Heat built between her legs remembering how hot and massive they'd felt bumping with every thrust against her nether cheeks.

For truth, Ranald would demand Father left them attached. Wouldn't he?

CHAPTER 17

GRAEMME'S MOUTH TIGHTENED IN a stubborn line, wiping the smile from his face. He knew she hadn't been listening, but for just one tiny bit of time, he'd felt relief. Why did he even think she would comply? She was going to make this as hard as possible for them both. He looked at Magnus and nodded. Though he'd been with his brother for only two weeks out of each year as they grew to be men, they thought much alike. With a simple nod of the head or question in their eyes, they did not need words.

They left Elyne with Mother Cecelia at the women's quarters. As they walked from there into the chapel for Vespers, he and Magnus stood to one side as everyone filed past them. Once the mass began, they quietly slipped back out the door.

Things were just as tense throughout the following day. When they escorted Elyne to the women's dormitory for her last night there, both men were uneasy. As they had done the night afore, Graemme dozed hidden in the shadows inside the stable where he could watch the front door while Magnus did the same at the back. Well past midnight, Graemme jumped up and hid behind a post. The figure of a monk came quietly through the doorway and eased it shut. Nothing gave him a hint the person was not as he seemed, but to be sure, Graemme watched quietly. He waited as the monk walked down the row of stalls. About average height for a man. A good stride, if somewhat stealthy.

His eyes widened and he hesitated when he noted a portly bulge in the monk's robe. Mentally, he pictured each man who had gone into the chapel and later to the men's supper. He didn't recall any of them being rotund. When he stopped at the stall halfway down where Elyne's horse waited, he furtively followed in the shadows.

The monk looked behind him. Graemme stood quietly. The man entered the stall, looked around again, and hiked up his robes. He fumbled around awkwardly, trying to lift only the front of it. Was the man meaning to take a piss in the horses stall? Why not outside against a tree?

Graemme realized why and was relieved. No man possessed long, shapely legs and creamy thighs. The figure juggled the heaving bulge around his stomach into position.

He almost laughed aloud when he heard Elyne mutter, "If a bairn is as much trouble as ye, squirming and thrashing about, I'll nay be havin' any little ones!"

The bundle jiggled again and out of the pile of clothing popped an uneven head. Squat's little beady eyes looked straight at him. His tail must have been beating against Elyne's sides, for he wiggled in rhythm with his tail. When the dog whined, the horse snuffled and moved restlessly.

"Shh. Ye two are makin' enough noise to wake someone," she whispered. She leaned over and carefully placed him on his feet. When he whipped his tail faster and started to move toward Graemme, she hissed at him.

"Stay!"

Graemme waited until she had her back turned to him. As she adjusted her clothing, he shook his head at Squat and put his hand up, palm toward the little dog, biding him to stay. Graemme silently moved in back of her to lean against the stall's entrance.

"Ye are goin' somewhere, Brother?"

She didn't turn. "I return to Kelso afore first light," she said in a husky voice.

"Ye are aware this horse belongs to a young lady?"

She hesitated. "Ye are right. I am one stall too far." She pulled the cowl low over her lowered face.

Gramme followed her as she turned and went to the stall to their left. When the horse snorted, she halted.

"Now ye mean to take my horse?"

Her hands fisted and she kicked straw on top of the hard-packed dirt floor and sent it flying. He could tell she was trying to remember the color of his and Magnus' horses.

"Nay. My horse is deep brown. Not black."

"And ye were goin' to take this wee, handsome dog with ye?"

Squat's tail thumped against his thin sides. Graemme smiled down at it. For truth, if the dog liked you, he had such an agreeable disposition a person forgot how ugsome he truly was. She cleared her throat, probably preparing to keep it lowered.

"Aye. The lady thinks Kelso's healer can help him. He has malformed legs, ye ken." She started to edge past him but had to stop when Squat leaned forward and pissed like he was a bitch.

"With that, too," she muttered and nodded toward the dog.

He straightened and reached out a hand and cupped what could only be a soft breast beneath the robe.

"Ye are the shapeliest monk in all of Christendom," he whispered as he pulled the cowl back. She didn't have a chance to protest, for his lips swooped to seal hers.

He startled for he didn't free her long curly hair. Mayhap the cowl covered it. He felt all over her back, but the hair was missing. He snapped his head up to look. By Lucifer's tainted breath! If she'd cut her glorious hair off, he'd be tempted to beat her.

In the darkness of the stable, he twirled her around and felt the back of her head. Relief spread through him. Braiding her hair in tight rows must have taken her a goodly time. He twirled her back and found her lips again.

Elyne was near dizzy, but not enough she lost her strength. She shoved against his hard chest, but he didn't budge. She tightened her right leg muscles to lift her knee and give him a more potent message. Instead, he shifted his body to lean back against the stall and wrapped one leg across the back of her knees. Did he read her mind? Foolish thought. He'd felt her muscles tighten and thwarted her.

Had he known all along it was her? Of course, he had. After

all the hours of preparing and planning, he had known right away. How was she going to replace the monk's clean clothing? It was one thing to 'borrow' them and have them returned later than it was to have to admit in person to Mother Cecelia that she had taken them.

Her body warmed and all thoughts flew her mind as he deepened the kiss. His hands roved but seemed to catch in the excess clothing she was wearing. He stopped in frustration, took her by the hand and led her to an empty stall.

She was prepared to defeat his efforts, but he moved too quickly and she too slowly. Mayhap she really didn't want to pull away? Memories of their night at Raptor brought more heat to her body than his hands did. In an empty stall, he whipped the robes up and over her head. They stuck and wouldn't come off.

"Bend over a bit. The sleeve is stuck on a pin in yer braids."

To her shame, quite willingly she did as he commanded. The robe quickly fell to the floor.

Feeling it around her ankles, she cooled to the idea again. He sensed it. Gathering her in his arms, he covered her face with kisses.

Kisses on her forehead. Kisses on her cheeks and nose. Kisses to keep her eyes closed.

When was he going to thrust his tongue in her mouth? She wanted him to most of all. She'd never admit it, but she felt small and helpless when he did that. Not helpless like she was when faced with her fathers demands that she marry some old, smelly, toothless man with a belly as large as an increasing woman, but helpless because she liked far to much what Graemme made her feel.

He kissed her quickly and slid his tongue down to the top of her breasts. He must have been afeared of tearing her kirtle, for he laved the material over her breasts, wetting it until he could draw her nipple into his mouth. He nibbled with his teeth then pulled on her nipple until she groaned. When she did, he reached down and grabbed the hem of her kirtle and smock and yanked upward. He was taking too long. She helped him by wriggling down as he pulled up. Suddenly she felt the cold air on her legs, her bare buttocks and her breast.

The dress caught around her head. She reached up to free it, but he took both wrists and held them together over her head while he lowered her to the floor.

"Nay. Let me."

His voice was more of a growled order than a request for her to remain still.

She couldn't see him. Felt vulnerable as he attacked her breast, first one then the other. He suckled so hard hot wetness flooded her woman's place. She could feel it seeping down between her nether lips and was embarrassed he would notice.

He did. He cupped his hand between her legs, his palm over the opening to her body, and rubbed back and fourth. His breathing became harsh and fast.

"My God, ye are beautiful. So beautiful I want to swive ye till ye faint. Feel how much ye are welcoming me."

He slid his wet hand over her stomach. She thrashed, wanting to cover herself. He was looking at her bare flesh, yet she couldn't see him. There was something erotic about it.

When he left her breast and attacked her quivering stomach, she was lost. Why did his kisses on her lower belly cause her to quiver and squirm? Wanting more? She couldn't control her movements and started to moan. He must have liked the sound, for he chuckled and spread her legs, holding them wide with his own. Then he became very still.

Was he looking at her private place? Shame filled her. Desire too. Then she felt one lone finger tracing the opening to her body. Around and around, he teased her flesh but didn't allow her relief. When he lightly tweaked her throbbing nub, she threw her legs wide. Inviting him to enter. He did, but only with his fingers. She wanted him to fill her!

Still holding her hands above her head, he kissed down to the curls guarding her sex. He wouldn't go any further, would he? She was too wet, too exposed. She wanted to cringe at the same time she wanted to demand he plunge himself in to the hilt. Oh my Saints! His hot tongue flicked her nub while his finger entered her. Planting her feet firmly, she lifted her hips, pushing herself at his face. How shameful! She started to pull-back, but he touched her nub again and inserted a second finger.

She panted and all thoughts of running away fled her mind. Well, Hades! She couldn't move if she wanted to. Not until he satisfied her. She hadn't known swiving could make you so powerless.

Powerless? Why, it was what he was after! To make her vulnerable and pliable so she would go back to Raptor and marry him without a single protest. Well, she'd be damned if she would. She fought the cloth. Tried to thrash free of it. He chuckled and grabbed one leg at the time and wrapped it around his waist. She ignored it while she was trying to free her arms. Then she realized his cock was poised to her entrance. She caught her breath, waiting.

Just a touch. Why was he waiting? She thrashed about again. He shoved his cock a slight bit inside her and held still again. Her stomach heaved. Her frustration raged.

"Tell me ye are sorry for running away and Ill give ye what ye want."

"Ye pig-witted lout! I'm not sorry. I'll keep running away."

"Tell me!" He pushed in a little more then near pulled out. He reached down and circled her nub. Her juices flooded the head of his cock.

"Ye flea bitten, rat-brained..." She ground her teeth together then shouted, "I'm sorry!"

"Sorry? For what my delightful, obedient lass?"

She near bit her tongue, trying to keep from groaning out the rest of the apology. When he wriggled his hips, she tried to push up to take all of him, but he rose up as much as she tried to lift. Finally, she thought she'd scream with frustration.

"Sorry I ran!"

She near screamed the words for he pushed in all the way. She felt triumphant when he began a steady rhythm. When she stiffened and started her climax, she locked her ankles tight around his buttocks. As she came and she felt he was ready for his own release, she spoke up.

"I'm sorry...," she gasped with pleasure, "ye caught me."

She groaned and swiveled her hips the way he had done his. "Ye won't next time."

She was at the peak of her climax when all of a sudden, his cock was gone and cold air swept over her naked body. Her ecstasy came to a dead stop as soon as he removed his cock. He released her hands. She grasped to pull him back. She swatted the clothing down and sat up, as furious as she'd ever been in her life.

Graemme had risen to his knees; his hand pumped his cock. Just as he had by the well! She got all the hotter looking at what he was doing. The head turned deep red, his balls swelled till she didn't think she could have cupped one in her hand they were so large.

He groaned again.

She stared, fascinated as he leaned backward, his face staring sightlessly at the roof as he spurted his seed. Why did he pull away when he could have come within her?

He had found his relief without her. 'Twas not fair! How did a woman find her own relief without a man? Her efforts had been futile.

Her frustration raged with her anger. She prepared to kick him backward onto the floor. He caught her foot and glowered at her.

"Ye didna do as I told ye."

He looked her over from head to foot. She must look a frightful mess, her hair near undone from her head thrashing back and fourth. She bit her lips to keep from screaming. 'Twould not do for anyone to find them here in such a condition. She turned her back and pulled her smock and kirtle into their proper places. She reached up and undid her hair. Better to have it hanging wild than to have her braids looking like she'd caught them in a bramble bush!

Graemme calmly stood, smoothed his kilt over his belly and hips, ran his fingers through his hair and calmed it. Cruddy Lucifer! He looked normal, while she must look like a fright.

Where was Squat? Why hadn't he defended her by biting Graemme's nether cheeks while they were doing their worst?

"Squat?" she called.

A voice answered, not a bark.

"He's here with me, waiting on ye two to finish yer argument."

Magnus' voice! Oh, Saints help her! How long had he been out there?

She found out when Graemme called to him.

"Ye are good at walking silently, brother. But not good enough."

"Good enough? Ye couldna have heard me over her moans of pleasure."

"I heard yer boots brush against the wooden bucket in front of the third stall."

Graemme adjusted his belt and slid his sword and scabbard into the loop at his side.

"And ye didna call out?"

Magnus came around the wall to stand and grin at them. "Nay. 'Twas just about the time ye flipped her skirts over her head. I thought it best ye continued her lesson of obedience to her husband."

Elyne's face flamed so hot she thought she could by chance have the power to light a candle like Ranald. She stared hard at Magnus' nose, but it didn't even turn pink. Well, pish!

Ranald had told her he thought his powers came from the blows on his head and the terrible fever which raged for a sennight in Kelso. Six months later when landless knights raided the abbey, Ranald grabbed a sword and went berserk. The thugs turned tail and rode from the area like Lucifer was after them. It took the Abbot to calm Ranald and bring his reasoning back.

Well. Maybe that's why it didn't work. She wasn't in an uncontrollable rage!

"What is it?" Magnus asked. "Do I have somethin' unsightly on the tip of my nose?"

Graemme laughed. "Nay. From the look of her concentration, I think she believes she can set yer nose aflame."

"I dinna think Muriele would like it changed. She often says 'tis noble and full of strength." Magnus grinned at her.

"I told ye Elyne created a legend that Raptor was haunted by an old crone. The funny thing is, the men believed her. She tried to send me flying with my arse on fire."

"Ye were enjoying being nekid on yer bed. I only warned ye what could happen."

When the words were out of her mouth, she realized what she'd told Magnus.

"Aye, I was fine for the night. But the next day when yer haunting proved futile, ye tried to poison me. My arse was on fire and I spewed for hours."

"Well, now, my soon to be sister-by-law. Do ye intend to poison my brother every time ye have an argument over who is in charge of yer life?"

"Huh!" She ignored him. With a rosy face and nose in the air, she folded the monk's robes into a neat pile, the same way as she had found them.

"Nay. She canna try it again. As part of the betrothal vows heard by all at Raptor, she promised never to do so again."

"Dinna push yer good fortune," she muttered so low he almost didn't hear her.

"Eh?" Graemme came so close his lips near touched her ear. "Breaking a betrothal vow is near a mortal sin. I would be tempted to beat ye for it."

"Ye try and ye'll find a blade at yer precious parts when ye sleep!"

Graemme stared down at her, his eyes searching her face for the truth of her words. Her father never laid a cruel hand on her in her life, even though he had threatened many a time to do so. In no way would she allow a man to mistreat her. She narrowed her eyes and glared back up at him.

He must have sensed she meant it, for he shook his head slowly at her, his mouth grim, and turned his back.

"Where did ye get the robes? We must replace them afore the sisters notice," Magnus broke their concentration on each other.

"The laundry room. They always keep fresh robes for traveling monks. They exchange the soiled ones for these so they may complete their journey in comfort," she replied.

"It will be our first stop," Graemme decided. When he spied Squat snuffling among the bits of oats and hay on the floor, he smiled at him and added, "This sorry sample of a dog needs food." The words might have been harsh, but Squat wagged his crimped tail all the faster, a look of adoration on his face.

"It is near time for the sun to come up. If ye dinna stop yammering, the sisters will soon gather for mass. If they spy us, ye will be to blame." Elyne gathered the clothes to her chest and haughtily brushed past them and headed out the door.

She replaced the robes atop the other two already on the shelf in the laundry room. Towels and sheets were already in woven baskets waiting for the day's washing. A sizeable stream ran beyond the grove. Since it was still within the outer walls of the convent, the laundresses were safe using it.

While Muriele, Ranald's wife Catalin and she were here over a year ago, she'd explored it. She wanted to be sure no one could enter by going beneath the water flowing under the stone wall. She learned the Tyronesian monks from Kelso had built the wall and added iron grating in the open space, assuring the sisters no one could invade the convent by the stream.

Graemme nodded to Magnus. They walked beside her as they left the laundry room. He didn't intend to let her out of his sight until they reached the hunting lodge. And especially after arriving there. He could near hear the explosion from her when she found out their first destination was not Raptor Castle!

They attended mass but couldn't kneel beside her, for the nuns and women were at the front of the chapel and the men at the back. But if she thought to sneak out of the cluster of women, she was sadly mistaken. He had already warned Colyne and Brian to place the other eight men to watch the chapel exits and gates leading out of the convent. Though they looked to pray as devoutly as the women, they watched her through downcast lashes. Graemme gritted his teeth at the furtive way Elyne glanced around her and toward each exit. No doubt, she judged what her chances were she could steal out beneath their noses when they were supposedly deep in prayer. Several times, she started to rise, but when she did, a knight quietly moved closer to the door. When she scowled back at Graemme, he kept her in place with an ominous stare. Her shoulders were rigid with defiance, but she stayed on her knees until mass ended.

Graemme studied her mulish expression. He caught and held her gaze with his, making his face as sinister as possible. The woman didn't know when to stop fighting. Though he understood why. With a father like Chief Broccin, she'd had to be as belligerent as any man to survive. If she hadn't been, she'd probably have been married off to the oldest man he could find with enough land and coins to tempt Broccin. And the man would undoubtedly be toothless, pot-bellied and bald with a castle filled with illegitimate children. Broccin wouldn't want to wait long to take over his daughter's holdings. No doubt, he'd have her married again within a year.

When he looked at her beautiful face and saw the vulner-ability lurking in her eyes, he felt a twinge of conscience about forcing her into the wedding.

It didn't last long.

He reminded himself of his two infamous buckets.

CHAPTER 18

ELYNE KEPT HER HEAD bowed, which wasn't difficult since they were supposed to be in silent prayers most of the time. But she couldn't keep herself from looking for a way to escape. Whenever she glanced up, she felt the threat in Graemme's gaze and squirmed. Magnus' observance was less intrusive. At least his looks didn't bore holes in the back of her head.

She almost sighed with relief when the mass was over. It was thoughtless of her though, for now she would be leaving the convent after they broke their fast. The two men stuck to her like nettles on bushes as they left the chapel. She'd best act like she was too dim-witted to protest further. It wasn't a long trip to Raptor, but somewhere along the way, they might relax their vigil. When they did, then she'd take her chances.

Her father and Ranald only saw a man who honorably kept his word. If they could have seen her dreams of him, they'd know he was dangerous and likely meant to kill her. She didn't know why she felt so strongly when he seemed concerned for compromising her. It had to be the frightful dreams, for when he wasn't fashed with her he was playful and treated her gently.

When he grasped her elbow, a soft breeze wafted his scent to her. She breathed it in as much as her lungs could take. How could he still smell so fresh of sandalwood? He must have taken time to wash at the lavatorium during the night. Visions of his naked body as he bathed invaded her thoughts. Heat spread to her belly thinking of his lips and hands caressing all over her, making her feel desire so hot she forgot the threat he posed. Her breasts tingled. She pretended she lifted her right hand to brush back her hair, while she really needed to brush her arm across her nipples to soothe their strange itching.

Well, piss! Graemme squeezed her arm and gave her a wicked smile. The dratted man knew what she was doing. From the twitch of Magnus' lips, he did too. Knowing he likely thought of his brother's nasty love making, she wanted to fan her cheeks.

Graemme had left her hot and wanting back in the stall. All he'd needed to do was touch her one more time and she'd have spent herself as explosively as he had. The hateful man hadn't hesitated to satisfy himself, though.

How did one squirm and walk at the same time? The memory of him pumping his tarse like he had not needed a woman to satisfy him made her want to kick him square in the arse. Nay. More likely in those precious parts he so loved!

Why did he pull her to a stop? Oh. They were at the doorway to the women's quarters.

"Go collect anything ye left in yer room. Dinna think to sneak away. Magnus will be at the back door and my men guard all the exits."

"Nay. I plan to vanish into thin air." She snorted when Magnus disappeared around the corner. If she could, she'd stamp her feet on the ground and scream in aggravation. "Come, Squat." She beckoned her hand at Squat. He started to follow her until Graemme spoke.

"Stay, dog."

She jammed her hands on her hips and glared at him. Now he controlled her dear little dog, for Squat slammed his butt on the ground and looked up at him. The hairy little thing was smiling as much as a dog could without it becoming a snarl.

She stomped all the way to her tiny room, even though she had left nothing there. Shutting the door behind her, she went immediately to the small wooden stool and brought it over to the small window. The dense orchard started no more than ten paces from the window. The men would be guarding the doors, so if she was swift enough, she could climb out the window. In her muted brown and green clothing, she could lose herself amongst the trees before they even saw her!

Once she stood on the stool, she opened the wooden

shutters and gathered her skirts tightly around her. Carefully, she balanced on her right leg while she swung her left leg out and over the windowsill. She stifled her shriek when a warm hand closed over her ankle and slid sensuously up to her knee.

"'Tis much easier to walk to the door, but since ye like falling into my arms, at least this time ye'll not shove me to my back, love."

"Nay. Thank ye."

She didn't like his reminder of how she'd landed in this predicament in the first place. She tried to shake off his hand, but he held firm.

"Nay? Because I have all my clothes on?" He cocked his head and considered. "Do ye wish me to disrobe?"

"Ye are a fool! Go ahead and I'll scream as loudly as I did the first time. Then I'd like to see ye talk yer way out of Brother Octavius really breaking yer nose and throwing ye off the gatehouse!"

"Then I would suggest ye scramble down here. I believe Mother Cecelia's coming around the corner."

Without thinking further, she hurriedly drew her right leg out and heaved off the windowsill into his arms.

"It wasna necessary to catch me," she said, shoving at his chest. "'Twas a short distance."

"Oh, but ye feel so soft and pliable, I like it. Ye should practice jumpin' when I beckon."

His hand moved up to the back of her waist and pressed her stomach against his body. She shoved back when she felt his hard as an anvil shaft near bruising her.

"Ye'll see how pliable I am when Mother Cecelia asks what ye are doing. And ye may as well forget my jumping at yer commands."

"Why not ask her?"

"Mother Cecelia is behind me?"

She looked toward the front of the building, but all she saw was Squat wagging his tail and throwing spittle with his flopping tongue. Mayhap the sweet woman was at the other end. Her head tilted back away from his chest so she could look to her left. Only Magnus stood there. Grinning at her.

"Ye lied!"

She shoved him with both hands and tried to lift her right knee and aim it at his private parts.

"I wouldna do it if I were ye."

Her foot slammed back on the ground. His tone had changed from teasing to sinister warning. He nodded and pulled back from her, holding lightly to her elbow.

"Ye are learnin' to be less fashious. 'Tis a good thing."

"I am *troublesome*? How do ye think I feel about ye, ye chicken-brained oaf!"

"Ah, ye are right."

His eyes narrowed with icy calculation as his gaze roved from her head to her toes.

The hair on her arms and nape rose. She wanted to step backward out of his reach but she'd not back down. If he knew he could make her fear him with naught but looks, she'd be lost. When he spoke again, his voice was so low if she wasn't listening she wouldn't hear him.

"Any man who would marry ye without yer father holding a knife to his skin would have to be an eejit."

His words sent sharp pains through her chest. Was she so terribly plain and unwomanly? Was her looks why her father could only entice the weak or elderly men to offer for her hand? He had to threaten a virile, comely man with gelding him afore he would consent to marry her? Her chest became so heavy it was hard to breathe.

He whistled loud and shrill. Squat came at a run while Magnus sauntered up to them.

"Time to leave?" His gaze took in Graemme's emotionless face and stopped to study hers.

"Aye." Graemme's voice sounded loud in the peaceful surroundings.

"But we have not broken our fast," she said.

"Afore I came to the stables, I asked for bread and cheese to take with us. The stable boys knew to ready the horses for an early leave-taking. My men are already waiting near the front gate," Graemme said. He did not even look at her.

"But we must thank the good sisters for the night's lodgings." Magnus' gaze traveled from his brother to her face. "Ye dinna have other clothing with ye?"

"I have a bundle hidden in the stall with my horse." She cleared her throat. "Mother Cecelia's solar is in the main building."

"We know. We were there yesterday," Graemme's cold voice reminded her.

What was the matter with Magnus? He seemed to sway a little as he walked. Then she realized why when she looked down at his feet. Squat had clamped on the man's boot strings and tugged for all his might. Each forward step of his right foot, he shuffled with it low to the ground so as not to hurt the dog.

"This will take all day if ye dinna let me walk, dog."

Magnus bent down and gently pried his mouth open. On his way up with the dog in his hands, Squat filled his mouth again with the hem of Magnus' kilt. Magnus casually brushed his clothing down to cover himself.

Elyne averted her eyes, but not before she noted the brothers resembled each other in more ways than she would have expected. Men's body parts were not new to her. She'd seen more of them than most young women from her vantage point in the window opening at Raptor.

Graemme glared at her as if she'd been the one to bare his brother's treasures.

They found Mother Cecelia in the courtyard saying goodbye to two monks headed for Kelso. Elyne cringed when she saw a tall monk wearing a fresh robe with a piece of straw caught in the hem. If he knew he wore a robe sullied by bed sport, no doubt he'd have stripped naked on the spot! She breathed a sigh of relief when he mounted his mule and left through the open gate.

Elyne was next in line to say her farewells.

"Mother Cecelia, I thank ye for yer comfort and protection."

"Child, it is always an exciting diversion when you spend time with us."

The good Mother put her arms around Elyne and hugged her. Drawing back a bit, she studied Elyne's face.

"You are reconciled the Morgan brothers mean you no harm?"

"Aye. I suppose I must wed some time, and Sir Graemme is less disgusting than old Baron Hadley with his warty nose!"

Out of the corner of her eye, she could see Graemme stiffen with displeasure at her opinion of him.

"Far less disgusting!" Mother Cecelia burst out laughing and hugged her one last time.

The brothers gave their formal thanks and hurried her away.

Afore she knew it, they were in the stables. The stable boys had already readied the three horses and even had Elyne's bundle of clothing tied to her saddle. Graemme gave the two boys each a coin for their efforts.

She took the reins to her horse and led him outside to a mounting block by the horse trough. Her horse stopped for a long drink and sprayed water as he lapped. Far too soon, it was time to mount. Intending to mount by herself, she jumped when strong hands wrapped around her waist and effortlessly lifted her to the saddle. He frowned when she swung her right leg over the horse's back so she could ride astride.

"Chief Broccin allows ye to ride thus? 'Tis most unwomanly." Graemme's lips pressed together.

"Ye didna object to Muriele skill at riding, did ye?"

She directed her question to Magnus, who grinned. The man was forever surprising her. He looked so stern and quiet, like he was about to rail at someone for some minor mistake, and then he broke out in a broad smile.

"'Tis why she eluded me so easily. I didna expect her to be so adept at riding, much less at the hunt."

He looked at his brother, obvious pride in his voice. "She once speared a boar intent on ripping me a new, uh, new opening in my back."

"How did ye take her saving yer arse?" Graemme's eyes watched Magnus' face.

"I had her seized by my men for stealing a boar spear from

my squire. I thought she meant to deprive me of my guts. My foster father Olaf named her the best hunter of the day. I felt like a fool!"

Graemme laughed for the first time that day.

"Ye dinna know shame until ye get a nasty dose from yer bride."

His lips thinned to a white line. Shoving her foot into the stirrup, he adjusted the straps. He was none too gentle or smooth; his movements were hard and jerky. He had to be thinking about the humiliation of everyone knowing he couldn't walk for a whole day because he couldn't be away from a bucket. Had it not been for Aunt Joneta, he and Squat would still be heaving and spreading shite all over the castle grounds!

She felt some shame for doing such a thing to any person, but if she had her life to relive at this point, she'd do it again. But first, she'd make sure she locked Squat in her room.

"We should be ready to leave. Thank you, Brother Octavius, for your vigilance over my bride when she came."

"'Twas an honor to aid Brother Ranald's sister."

He turned a steely glare on Magnus. "It will be some time afore I forgive yer making an arse out of me and stealing the Lady Muriele from under my nose!"

Magnus nodded solemnly at him. "I would feel the same if it were done to me."

"Be watchful for brigands. Many homeless people prey on travelers."

"Aye," Magnus said as he put his foot in the stirrup and swung up into his saddle.

Bryan and Colyne fell in line behind him, the rest of the men followed. Graemme walked over, picked up Squat and handed Colyne the dog.

"Dinna forget to pay heed when he starts to squirm, else ye'll find a yellow stream travelin' down yer leg."

Colyne tucked Squat against his chest beneath the kilt draped over his shoulder and around to his belt in back.

Graemme mounted and nodded to the guard to lift the bars that secured the gate at dusk. The courtyard was busy with visitors continuing their journey after stopping for the night. Elyne's gaze searched out the good sisters and Mother Cecelia and waved to them. A lump formed in her throat. Likely, she would not see them again.

Before she had more time to think about it, Graemme led them out with a fast walk. When they were far enough from the gate, he urged his horse to gallop across the open fields. It would be slow going when they reached the hills on the opposite side. She rode behind him while Magnus followed her to see she didn't stray.

"We could have broken our fast afore we left," she grumbled. Her stomach was putting out its protest in growls worthy of Squat.

"When we get to the woods, we'll stop and divide up the bread and cheese," Graemme called back to her.

"How kind of ye," she said, lifting her nose in the air.

"We need to make as many leagues today as we can. I don't want to spend more than two nights in the woods."

Graemme's words were sharp and impatient.

They started to canter the horses for they were near up to the woodland path. Once they reached there, she started to shiver. The weather was gloomy to begin with, but surrounded by damp woods was not pleasant. The trees still held water from the light rain during the night. She felt a drop in her hair and wished she'd unbundled her cloak so she could pull its hood up.

True to his words, Graemme pulled over to the side, hurriedly dismounted and untied the bundle of food. He tore off hunks of bread and passed to her and Magnus. Cutting the cheese with the knife secured to his sword belt took a little longer. Her mouth salivated smelling the fresh bread. She put the food on her saddle between her legs so it wouldn't fall off. Looking around, she saw the sisters had given the rest of the men small bundles of food before they left.

She untied the bundle of clothing from behind her saddle and shook out her cloak. Surprisingly, Graemme pulled his horse alongside hers and helped spread it across her shoulders. While she tied the ribbons at her neck, he spread the heavy wool over the horse's haunches to keep the material from flapping around the animal's legs and spooking it.

Elyne nodded her thanks, but when she reached to take the reins into her hands, he kept her from it.

"Nay. I will lead the horse," he said.

"I'm not helpless. I can feed myself and ride too!"

"I prefer leading yer horse to plunging through the woods pursuing ye!"

She huffed and pulled hard. He didn't let go.

"Goat dung," she muttered under her breath.

He quirked his brow at her, defying her to elaborate further on what she thought of him. She shoved bread into her mouth to keep from yelling her opinion of him.

"It doesna matter what ye think of me. Ours is not a marriage of the heart." He snorted and shook his head. "'Tis a marriage of the sword. Likely Chief Broccin will have one trained on my back until the vows are done."

"If ye both would stop yer quibbling, we would be closer to our destination," Magnus said.

He put his food in the pocket of his cloak, but not before tearing off a small piece of bread and moving close to Colyne to give it to the drooling dog.

"Ye should have been a wolf! Ye near bit my fingers, ye ungrateful wretch."

Though his words were harsh, his tone was mellow. They began again, though her horse lurched a bit, unused to the rider not controlling the reins. Once its gait smoothed out, she found it was quite easy to nibble on her food and keep it from falling to the ground.

She huffed as she ate. So, he was afeared she'd take off through the woods, was he? Since she didn't have to pay attention to where they were going, she was free to look at the woods and the creatures living there. 'Twould be good eating tonight, for hares seemed to be everywhere, jumping around and showing off for their females.

True to her thoughts, when the sun started to wane, Magnus took up his bow and arrow. Soon after, he and several warriors had hares thrown across their horses' rumps and secured to the back of their saddles.

She was grateful they'd had at least one stop to refresh themselves. Her churlish husband-to-be didn't allow her much privacy. He had Magnus stand to one side of where she went into the bushes and he stayed close to her on the other.

When she'd stepped on a twig, he was there so quickly he couldn't have been but an arms-breadth away.

"What are ye doing, woman!"

"Turn yer back, ye disgusting piece of sheep dung! Cannot ye see I'm trying to keep my skirts unsullied?"

The eejit looked her over as if she was some strange creature. She flushed so hot she wished for a cold cloth to soothe her face. She thought she had felt shame when Magnus came upon them in the stall, but this was far worse. Later she could have used another break, but she decided to hold off until they stopped for the night.

The men had no trouble, though. When Magnus pulled off behind them to relieve himself, they kept going forward and he rejoined them. When Graemme needed to piss, he passed her reins to his brother and did the same. Being a man had its advantages. Many of them! She started ticking them off on her fingers.

They had no need to squat behind a bush. They stood and peed against a tree like the tree welcomed water!

They had control over their lives. Even the old, gaseous and toothless man could bring a young bride to his bed with little effort. Fathers thought nothing of how the young girl would suffer when a smelly old man had the right to stake his claim on her any night as often as he liked.

They seemed to answer to no one once they reached a certain age, which was quite young to her thinking. Of course, she wasn't thinking of squires and lower knights, grooms or any such.

She was thinking of men like the two brothers. Once they decided a woman should be their bride, the selfish churls didn't once think of what she desired.

To pass the time, she tried to picture men and how they'd be in similar circumstances.

She grinned and pictured Graemme as he laid in all his naked glory under a crisp, white sheet. In came an old woman with wrinkles on her face, a pot belly from having borne six children. She had knobby knees and missed having more than one tooth. Oh! And her hair was so thin and straggly it left bare spots where her scalp reflected the candlelight.

She wondered if they could make their precious treasures stand and pay attention. She giggled at the thought of the old woman throwing back the covers to feast her eyes on his hard-muscled body. Would she fall into a rage when she saw he didn't have a cockstand?

No doubt, his shaft would shrivel up until it hid itself in Graemme's flesh when the old crone put her lips to it.

"What has ye so amused ye've been snickering like a young lass looking at her first tarse growing hard?" Graemme had turned in his saddle and stared hard at her.

"Do ye really want to know?"

"I would," said Magnus behind her. "I've been watching yer shoulders shake and wondered what pleased ye so."

"I was picturing men having to put up with the same life women have now."

"In what way?" Graemme said in an impatient tone.

"Well, can ye imagine pissing and having wet yer shoes?"

"Why would we do that?"

"If ye had to be burdened with skirts and tunics, ye would have to stoop to piss. Likely one foot would be in the way."

"Huh! Our kilts are much alike skirts."

"Nay. They dinna sweep the ground. Ye are picking at useless things. They dinna hamper yer legs when ye walk, climb or sit down."

"Aye," Magnus joined in. "Like Muriele when she climbed the pine tree afore ye came upon us in the woods, Graemme. She near killed herself."

"Surely there's more to Elyne's mirth."

"For truth. I pictured Graemme sprawled in bed, displaying

all his glory. Ye awaited yer mate who had complete control over ye. Even life or death, if ye displeased her."

"If she's going to have her way with me, I think I would glory in it," Graemme scoffed.

"Ah, but what if she came through the doorway and was withered with age. She had not taken a bath in weeks. She kissed ye with fervor, drawing yer tongue into her toothless mouth then felt yer, uh, tarse to see if it was eager for her."

"Dinna be disgusting," Graemme replied.

"Why not? It happens to women every day. But their loving husbands land a fist on their jaws for not arousing them."

"Lucifer's foul breath, woman!" Magnus exploded behind her. "Ye are right."

"How can ye think so, brother?" Disbelief sounded in Graemme's voice.

"Because of Muriele. When she failed to give Feradoch a cockstand just by looking at her, he beat her and tried to kill her friend Esa because she also refused to do the same."

"Enough!"

Graemme's explosive word kept her from talking further. When he glared at her and blamed her for starting such a far-fetched conversation, she shrugged. He may be angry for the talk, but he'd probably think back on it each time he saw an elderly man with a wife younger than his numerous bastards were.

Her buttocks and legs began to ache from riding so long. She'd be much more comfortable not holding onto the pommel of her saddle for support. Funny, when she held the reins she balanced much better, knowing if the horse was going to swerve to avoid an obstacle in the road or lurch to a stop. A pox on the man!

The sun didn't go down fast enough for her liking. If they made an early night of it, the longer it would take to arrive at Raptor and their odious wedding.

When darkness finally crept up on them, Graemme grudgingly found a clearing where they made camp beside a small loch. Her anger flared again when the eejit had her sit on the ground then tied a rope around her and the tree.

"What does he think I can do, Squat?" She grumbled and began stroking the dog when he came over and put his head in her lap. 'Twas a comforting feeling. "Where in Hades does Graemme think I would go? I'm nay a fool! I'd not set out in a forest alone. Even two men wouldn't travel without a torch to light the way. It would be an invitation for every thief and blackguard in hiding to murder them!"

The last words faded when the men turned to look at her with grins on their faces. They may as well have reminded her she had indeed done such when she left Raptor. She flushed and clamped her teeth together before she made a further fool of herself.

After the men had fires going and hare's roasting over them, Graemme came to her to let her take a trip into the woods.

"Are ye going to be breathing down my neck, or are ye going to be sensible and give me room for privacy?"

"Ye'll get yer privacy. Just be quick about it," he said as they reached a sizeable bush that would shield her from sight.

He turned his back, giving her more confidence. She was near finished when she felt something drop on her head. Something wet. And since her head was bent trying to watch out for her feet, its warmth trickled toward her forehead. She jumped up and brushed at her head, but it spread the foul stuff even more. She had bird shite on her hair! The blasted bird must be a friend of the Devil.

"Lucifer's crud-filled ears," she yelled and came charging from the woods, her head bent as thouogh she intended to ram it into Graemme's chest.

"Ye willna curse, Elyne. 'Tis most unwomanly of ye."

Then he began to laugh when she was close enough to see the reason.

"'Tis no laughing matter! Get the soap," she grumbled while heading for the sound of a stream no more than thirty paces away.

His footsteps were right behind her. She skidded to a halt and turned, unfortunately, for it whipped the foul-smelling hair across her nose. She swatted it away and glared at him.

"We have no soap. Men never use it while traveling."

"Ye like yer own stench? Ugh!"

"Nay. We use sand."

She marched on to the loch's edge, aware the other men were watching her with amused smiles on their faces. She carefully tried to fasten her skirts behind her. She pulled them tight and clamped them with her knees. The sand was soft and didn't hurt her skin.

"I wouldna lean there if I were ye," Graemme said.

"If ye must stand there to see I dinna swim away, kindly keep yer tongue behind yer teeth."

"If ye say so."

She snorted in disgust for Graemme sounded amused. The hateful man was probably laughing at her predicament.

Pulling all her hair from in back to up and over her head, she leaned forward to rinse it. Her left knee wobbled in the sand and she reached into the water to steady herself. It didn't help. Afore she knew how it happened, she was in the water thrashing about.

Her clothing got in the way of her legs, but she finally rose on her feet. She spluttered and fisted her hands and wanted to hit something. Anything with more substance than water. She glared at Graemme, who didn't bother to look up.

He stood on the bank slowly unbuckling his sword belt and carefully laying it on the ground. Once the belt was gone, the kilt had nothing to hold it. It flopped to the ground like a wounded bird. In all his naked glory, he came toward her. She backed up. She didn't want his help. Especially his *nekid* help.

She backed up. The ledge she stood on ended with only one small step.

She plunged beneath the water. Squat started barking and stopped abruptly when Magnus' muffled voice told him to be quiet.

One of the men called out, "Ye'd best fetch yer bride afore she drifts into some water monster's big mouth. She would make him a tasty snack!"

She kicked her legs harder and fought the water with her arms. As before, her clothes hindered her. Normally, she was a strong swimmer. But then she had worn only her brother's leggings and bindings for her breasts or nothing at all. It seemed forever before her toes touched bottom and she tried to push up to the surface again.

She may as well have saved herself the effort. At first, she felt terror when something pulled at her hair. Could it be a water monster had hold of her? She beat around her hair, trying to find what had caught it. For her efforts, she received a particularly hard jerk. Her hands flew out again and came in contact with the hard corded muscles of a warrior's forearms.

As he pulled her up, he slid her against his body. She realized he'd removed the bandage around his thigh. His injury was healing rapidly. Finally, the air she'd been holding back exploded out of her mouth when her cheeks rubbed against hairy thighs. His cock bobbed not a finger's width from her mouth. Why, the cold water hadn't seemed to affect it much. Still, she clamped her lips together. She could see his belly button as he kept lifting, then his nipples, shriveled from the cold.

When her head cleared the water, she realized he was standing. Standing? He must have read the expression on her face quite accurately.

"If ye hadna panicked and curled like a helpless kitten, ye could have bobbed up to get air."

"Let go my hair afore ye snatch me bald!"

He did. She immediately went under again, but this time, she kept her legs straight. The bottom was not far at all. She wished it was. From where she was now, she could see him above her, laughing.

"I dinna think ye need to keep dunking yer head, lass." Magnus' face was as somber as it had been at mass. He leaned forward and studied her from his vantage place on shore. "Looks to me ye have had a thorough washing bobbing up and down. 'Tis the same way the laundresses rinse our clothing."

Chapter 19

Graemme doubted she needed his help. In fact, she resented it. But he couldn't let his bride drown. Could he?

He was tempted.

The daft woman was as hard-headed as a ram trying to batter down a wooden fence.

She was going to be nothing but trouble for the rest of their natural lives together. The only time she was anywhere near submissive was when he had her pinned beneath him. If he was to have any peace in his life, he'd have to assure she stayed hot and wanting.

If he could keep Elyne in the Highlands without having to chase after her every time she took the crazy notion to bolt back to Raptor Castle and beyond, he'd consider himself lucky.

He shook his head. Worried. If aught happened to her while she was in his care, Chief Broccin would likely remove his head. With a dull axe.

He winced.

When she came to the surface, he grabbed her kirtle and pulled her back to the shallow ledge.

"'Tis no way to bathe, lass. Has no one ever taught ye to take off yer clothing first?" He tried hard not to snicker, but the disbelief on her face made it difficult.

"Turn yer backs to the loch and face the fires, else I'll put my blade to yer arses," he bellowed at the snorting men. They promptly presented their backs, though he heard them taking bets on whether he was going to swive her in the water, being he was already naked!

With a few deft movements, her clothing floated atop the

water. He'd never seen her in all her bare skinned glory. The only times she was nude was on top of him in the bailey while her father loomed over them, in the dark room at Raptor and in the gloomy stable. Unfortunately, time and people had prevented him from exploring her body.

Before him was a creamy back leading down to two lovely dimples above her hips. The water lapped beneath them, but he caught glimpses of her beautiful nether cheeks.

"Come, brother, 'tis no time to anticipate yer pleasure in the marriage bed," Magnus said from the grassy shore.

Surely, Lucifer must be cackling though bloody lips at his predicament. His brother's eyes roamed where Graemme couldn't see. Elyne's arms flew up and folded over her chest, and she bent her knees to hide herself beneath the water.

"Magnus, turn yer back! It might help if ye saw the men properly cooked the hares."

"Already started the fires and the men are turning the hares on their spits. If ye dinna want her to get a chill, ye'd best hurry. The water is too cold for leisurely explorations."

"Warm my kilt to wrap her in." He turned to Elyne. "Hold yer breath."

Without further warning, he stepped closer and held her shoulders to make her bend. He dunked her head low so her hair was in the water.

"Stop struggling, lass. All I'm doing is trying to rid ye of the bird shite in yer hair. I have no interest in tupping ye.... At the moment!"

He was lying through his teeth, too. She knew it. How could she not? His cock was hard and begging against her soft back. If she wasn't more careful, she might possibly sheath the eager thing.

"Be still. All yer squirming and pushing back against me makes my cock think ye're inviting him in."

Elyne gasped so loud, he saw Magnus glance over his shoulder.

It worked, though, for she stilled and frantically swished her hair in the water, rinsing it as fast as she could. She straightened quickly.

"For truth, ye're intent on breaking my nose, aren't ye?" He backed away from her. "Stay there until I get my kilt."

He gathered her wet clothing and laid them atop the first bush he came to. Lifting his warmed kilt from sticks beside a fire, he took it back to her. He didn't miss seeing her suddenly avert her eyes. He didn't doubt she'd studied his back as thoroughly as he had hers.

"Did ye like what ye saw, wife?"

"Nay. And I am not yer wife."

"Yet! But ye will be."

Elyne might lie to him, but she couldn't to herself. He had a magnificent body. His shoulders were as wide as Ranald's with taut muscles marking him as a warrior who swung a sword with vigor. Below were smooth muscles on his tanned back, narrow hips with tight buttocks and lean muscular legs. When he turned toward her, her mouth went dry. Far from being an old, withered man with naught to offer, he had everything. A more than handsome face, virile chest with a hard, flat belly and muscled thighs that looked to have strength enough to control the wildest ride. Her skin heated at the type of ride she was thinking of making.

She tried to avert her eyes from his rampant sex. It drew her like a moth to the rushlights outside the keep's entrance.

Had Lucifer formed him just to taunt her? How could she be so drawn to a man she feared?

She shook her head. By the look on his face, he'd said something she hadn't heard.

"Nay, ye dinna want to cover yerself, or were ye gathering wool? Again?"

Graemme's eyes crinkled at the corners.

"Of course I want the kilt, you cocky oaf!"

"Once we are married, I must insist ye call me by more pleasant names."

He motioned for her to rise out of the water. She did, but when she read the anticipation in his eyes, she quickly turned her back to him. Finally, she felt the warm wool against her flesh.

"Now back up to me so ye will be out of the water."

She did and felt the water finally down to her ankles. She grabbed the sides of the kilt around her body and bunched the cloth at her chest and waist. Her boots squished, making a funny sound. Once she came to a sizeable rock, she sat and pulled them off. 'Twas amazing how much water they held.

"Is it time to turn around yet?" Colyne called out.

"Nay."

"Ye'd best hurry afore we all starve to death." Bryan's laugh started the others to chuckling.

Seeing she had dried herself, Graemme brought her bundle of spare clothes over to her.

"Thank ye. Now please turn yer back so I may dress."

"Why it's the first time ye didna issue a command like I was a serf who earned yer wrath." Graemme bowed to her and turned to walk over to the fire.

She watched to make sure they weren't eyeing her like she was some strange creature. Graemme pulled a dry kilt out of his leather saddle bag and wrapped it around his waist. By the time she cleared her head through the necklines of her dry smock and kirtle, he had already donned his heavy belt and sword.

She felt safer having the men wearing their swords. Strangely, when she'd been alone on her journey to the convent, she'd been too intent on escaping to feel fear.

Too, she'd not built a fire. Now, the sounds of fat dripping and causing sparks to crackle seemed loud enough for anyone to hear a league away. Not to mention the smoke it created.

Graemme walked over to make sure the men didn't burn their food for the night.

"Are ye not afeared smoke will alert any thieves or brigands in the woods?"

"Nay. Look upward, lass."

She looked upward and saw smoke was one useless worry. The trees created a dense canopy of wet, green leaves above, hiding everything below.

He poked a cooking hare with the tip of his eating knife

and saw it was moist but not bloody.

"If ye cook them any longer, Colyne, they'll be dried as last summer's apples."

'Twas not too soon for her drooling mouth. Magnus lifted one away from the fire and laid it on an oiled cloth to cool then divided it between the three of them.

When they finished eating, Elyne stood and headed toward the water. She skidded to a halt when Graemme called to her.

"Have a care where ye kneel, lass. If ye fall in after all ye've eaten, ye'll sink to the bottom." He shook his head in mock sorrow.

"If ye had warned me of the ledge, I'd never have fallen in the first place."

"Remember. It's too dark for me to chance drowning trying to save ye. Again."

"Churl!" Icy scorn coated the word.

Carefully, she kneeled and cleaned her hands and face.

When she returned, she saw Graemme piling pine needles on the ground near enough to the fire to keep warm but not so close to become dangerous.

"Yer bed, my sweet tempered wife-to-be," Graemme said.

She gritted her teeth to keep from snapping a response at him. Wrapping herself in a spare kilt, she stretched out on the pine bed. After a sigh of comfort, her lids began to droop. She heard the drone of voices but was too tired to heed what they said.

"Brother, I oft wondered why ye didna marry Elspeth," Magnus said in a low tone. "She seemed everything ye liked all in one lass." He ticked off her attributes with his fingers. "Her hair was so lightly blond it near appeared white. She was small, had a narrow waist and hips. Her breasts were plump and just the right size to fit a man's hand. And most of all, she hung on every word ye uttered. Why, she even sewed shirts for ye..." He stopped when he saw Graemme's stony expression and cleared his throat. "What happened between ye?"

"We spoke of marriage and she seemed pleased. After we

announced we would wed, she started shunning me."

"Hm. Seems a strange thing for a newly betrothed to do," Magnus said.

"I tried to learn what disturbed her, but she always turned away and refused to answer. Then, one day, she disappeared. Her father said he knew naught what happened to her. We formed search parties, but could find no trace of her."

"Was Feradoch there at the time," Magnus asked, his face grim.

"Nay. I thought it was Feradoch's doings, too. But he was on his way to Kinbrace for his time with ye."

"Did ye ever find what happened to her?"

"Aye." Graemme looked down and tried to control his trembling hands. "After the snows melted in spring, we found a woman's body. Or what was left of it." His jaw tightened and he gritted his teeth. After taking a deep breath, he continued. "The strands of hair were light. Nearby, we found scraps of cloth. I recognized it as a piece of her favorite kirtle."

Graemme jumped to his feet and went to the water's edge to splash his face. He didna want his brother to see tears, else he would think him weak to cry over a woman. Especially one who had run away rather than face marriage with him.

A man was a fool to trust any of them.

He startled when Magnus clamped his shoulder in a comforting gesture but didn't speak.

"It is a good thing I dinna love Elyne." Graemme shook his head. "'Tis the truth, I have feelings more akin to hate than tenderness. But now and again, she amuses me with her knotty-brained ideas."

"Not to mention she is as beautiful as Muriele," Magnus supplied. He suppressed a laugh so as not to awake Elyne. "Having her demanding ye make love to her in the marriage bed will be far different than with the old crone and the young man she described today." He snorted again and his eyes twinkled with mirth. "Ye willna have trouble producing a cockstand to rival all others!"

Graemme finally grinned. "There is that in her favor. She

seems to love bed sport more than most."

He stopped and thought awhile.

"Elyne isn't like other women of her class. They keep themselves busy stitching shirts for the men of the family, making tapestries for the walls or pillows to cushion a man's balls." He snorted on a laugh and ended up coughing. "If she ever makes me a tapestry covered pillow, I'll be sure to look for hidden needles!"

"Huh! Mayhap not," Magnus said. "When I was gone from Kinbrace for a sennight or more, I returned to find Muriele had made a cushion for the arm chair in my chambers. Until I sat on it, I never realized how hard the wood had been. Of course, she was quick to say she made it for herself."

Graemme nodded. The two women were far too independent for his liking. But then, they also drew a man's respect.

"Elyne is as adept as many horsemen. She kept herself balanced riding astride without having the reins for control."

"Aye. I wouldna be surprised if she uses a bow and arrow as aptly as Muriele," Magnus said.

Graemme cringed. "I dinna want a bow and arrow in her hands any time soon. She's likely to take the notion 'twould be an easy way out of wedding me."

On the third day, Graemme allowed Elyne the reins, making it easier for her to ride. They rode in single file, with Graemme in front and Magnus at the rear. Elyne was in the middle with Bryan and Colyne watching out for her. They made good time and Graemme expected they would reach the hunting lodge soon after dusk fell. When they came to a fork in the road, he slowed until Elyne pulled alongside him.

Graemme caught Magnus' eye and nodded. Magnus moved his mount up behind Elyne, assuring she couldn't turn her horse and bolt. Slowly, Graemme reached over like he meant to chase off a bug on her hand, but instead, he griped her hands and took the reins from her.

"I know my way from here. If ye remember correctly, Raptor Castle is *my* home."

"Aye, it is. But ye will need to hold Squat."

Graemme turned to his men and called Bryan and Colyne to join them.

"If ye dinna dawdle, ye will make Raptor by nightfall. Sir Magnus will be in charge." He took Squat and handed him to Elyne. She hugged him tight to her chest, a confused look on her face.

Graemme nodded at the men and clasped his brother on the shoulder. Elyne stiffened. When the men took the left fork and Graemme led them to the right, she shouted at him.

"Wait! Ye're taking the wrong road. Raptor is to the left."

"We're not going to Raptor tonight."

"Why not! We can easily make it in the moonlight!"

"We're going someplace quiet where we can get to understand each other better," Graemme said in a stern voice.

"Alone?" She tried to lean out to catch hold of her reins, but she couldn't reach them. She signaled her horse to halt, but a demanding pull by Graemme quickly changed the horse's mind.

"Aye."

"You rotting, stinkin'...."

He knew Elyne was so angry she couldn't think of a word bad enough to call him.

"Churl? Knave? Lout?" He supplied the usual ones which came to mind. They weren't good enough.

"... maggot-brained son of Lucifer!" She finished for him.

"Enough!"

He twisted in his saddle and fixed her with a lethal stare through smoldering eyes. No one dared called his father 'Lucifer.' Not and get away with it.

She must have read his look correctly, for she shut her mouth and returned his glare. They rode in silence until they came to the road Grunda had described to him.

"I thought the hunting lodge had fallen into disfavor after yer brother died?"

Elyne refused to answer him.

" 'Tis not overgrown like it should be. Someone has cleared the brush and made it passable."

Before long, they came in sight of a clearing. It didn't look abandoned but well taken care of.

"Do ye think yer father has put it to use again?"

Stony silence answered him.

She didna have to answer. It seemed all too likely. The man was as fit as his own father, whose sex drive was still lusty.

Graemme pulled his sword when he saw a thin plume of smoke came from the chimney. He glanced at Elyne. She stared at the building like it was familiar to her.

"Ye have seen the lodge afore, Elyne?"

Still silence.

"How did ye know of yer brother's, er, adventures here?" He didn't expect her to answer, so he supplied it. "Huh! Of course, ye knew. If ye were in the habit of leaning out of windows to observe men, then it is likely ye followed yer brother and found out where he went with his leman."

He took his time dismounting, not taking his eyes off her face. She returned his gaze with a frozen stare and lips thinned to a grim line.

Still holding the reins, he gripped his sword firmer. At the same time, Domnall opened the door. Graemme sighed with relief when he didn't have to chase thieves from the building.

"Old Grunda said you would be here by nightfall," Domnall said and nodded.

"Did she also say we would be hungry and tired?"

"Aye. Cook brought provisions for a sennight. There's a mutton stew over the fire and enough wine and ale to soften the most stubborn lass in Scotland."

"I'll not need softening, Domnall. I order ye to take me back to my father."

She thrust Squat at him and slid off her mount as though the saddle had burned her nether cheeks.

Elyne stomped into the room with Graemme following close behind. Squat streaked past them and started sniffing all over the floor, searching for the scent of the castle hunting dogs.

"I canna do so, lass. Chief Broccin said you were to stay

here with Graemme until you came to your senses."' He turned
to Graemme.

She turned to put her hands on her hips and glare at him.

"He suggests you tie her ankle to you, Graemme, in case
she should have one of her dreams and decide to wander the
forest." He grinned at Elyne. "He said 'twas far more likely you'd
get eaten by wolves there than by your betrothed."

Graemme had expected a small structure with pallets rolled
against the wall, enough for a couple men and their lemans. This
was far different. The lodge was complete with furniture and
facilities for cooking. A large bed stood against the back wall
between two windows with shutters to keep out the night chill.

High above the fireplace was an array of weapons. Out
of Elyne's reach. He nodded solemnly. Domnall had thought
of everything.

"Well now, I'll catch up with your men. I believe Sir
Magnus' wife will be at Raptor on the morrow." He rolled his
eyes. "According to Grunda, she saw Sweyn's red hair gleaming
in her vision."

Graemme's face lit with pleasure. "They must have
left Clibrick earlier than planned else they had very fortunate weather."

"Oh, and Graemme," Domnall said, "I will take the horses
with me. When Ranald arrives, he'll return for you."

He took one look at Elyne's face and didn't waste any time
leaving. The next thing Graemme knew, he heard the three
horses beating their hooves back to the main road.

"What am I expected to do here?" Elyne almost kicked the
door but knew it was a childish gesture. 'Twould be better to
treat him as if he were less than a worm in a rotten apple to
her. "The lodge is surrounded by the forest with naught but its
creatures for company."

"*We* dinna need others to fill our days. Have ye never been
without other people at yer beck and call?"

"I dinna have anyone at my beck and call!"

"Oh, aye. No lady's maid to help with yer hair and dressing.

No one to draw yer bath when ye want one. Hm. And certainly no hot water brought up from the kitchens."

"All you have named are expected by everyone at Raptor Castle!"

"Well, now, in the Highlands ye will have to learn to take care of your basic needs. Many winter days it is too bitterly cold to leave the keep. Some days, if ye dinna learn to do yer chores in a hurry, the wet snow turns to ice on yer nose."

"Chores? What chores?"

"Why, anything I may desire ye do for me."

A good-sized table and four chairs occupied the area immediately to the left of the door. Next to them was a large fireplace blazing with a pot hanging from an iron hook. 'Twas where the delightful smell came from.

Graemme turned his back and went over to sniff the pot of hearty mutton stew. He rubbed his stomach as if he was already savoring the meal.

"Eh? Chores? Like what?"

"I desire to eat now."

He pulled out one of the chairs and seated himself. She went over and did the same. Squat, expecting a juicy bit of meat at any moment, ran over to sit up on his buttocks and beg. He looked from one to the other and waited. Neither person moved.

Graemme tilted his head and lifted his left brow, questioningly.

"I repeat. I desire to eat, wife."

She didn't move but folded her arms across her chest. "If ye think I'm going to serve ye, ye'd best think again! Ye brought me here. Ye serve *me*!

A goodly time went by. When he nodded, she almost chortled. She had won this round. Opposite the fireplace was the kitchen area. A wide shelf built under a window contained a basin, pitcher, pewter cups and plates.

He stood and went over to pick up the only two bowls and spoons. He stirred the pot then filled the top bowl with the steaming food. She expected him to set it in front of her, but instead, he left the two bowls cuddled together and returned to his seat with them.

Why, he was eating what should be her bowl! So this was how he was going to be? She'd just wait him out. He didn't bother to glance her way but continued to eat until he was sated. Her mouth began to water. She looked forward to his eating his last and leaving the table to her. Instead, he took the second bowl, poured what he'd left in his own into it and set it in front of Squat.

"Here ye go. Ye are a good watch dog and will let us know if any wild animals come sniffing outside the door, right?"

Elyne had to clamp her teeth together to keep her mouth from falling open. At Raptor, she'd always taken food as her right without having to perform any special duties for it. Why, she was the Chief's daughter!

"A proper wife serves her husband without fail. When she doesna, she finds she eats last — even after the hunting hounds."

"I... am... not... yer... wife!"

"Get used to it! Ye are as much my wife after our betrothal as ye will be saying yer vows afore the priest."

Squat pushed the bowl all over the room, savoring each little droplet. Graemme surprised her when he got up, rescued the bowl and placed it with his in a basin beside a bucket of water. Without looking at her, he opened the door and called Squat to him. They both went out into the night.

Glaring at the dirty bowls, her mouth drooled so much she didn't have a choice except to clean one of the bowls so she could eat. She preferred the one Squat had licked clean. After washing it, she ate quickly, taking just enough to satisfy her hunger so she'd be finished before he reappeared. 'Twas not the smartest thing she had done this sennight, for the food was so hot she burned her tongue on the first spoonful.

Of course, she had restacked the dirty dishes to appear the same as he had left them.

When he opened the door wide to let the dog in first, the fresh air scented with pines made the fire flicker. Elyne had barely reached the bed before he came in and latched the door. In front of the fireplace, animal skins thick enough for leisurely bed sport looked warm and inviting.

Picking up the nearest pillow, she threw it on top of the furs, following it with one of the wool blankets. She expected him to protest. He didn't say a word.

Graemme stretched and yawned in front of the fire, enjoying the warmth on his chilled body. Unbuckling his belt, he let his clothing drop to his feet. Bending, he picked up the wool cloth and folded it neatly. He had no need of its warmth when a fire was at hand. After he placed his sword on the floor, he padded around naked. He went to the pitcher of water and poured himself a glass, not because he was thirsty, but so he could see what she'd done with the food bowls. At first glance, they looked the same, but since he'd put Squat's on top and it was licked shiny clean, he saw it now had remnants of food on the sides.

So, she had washed and eaten hurriedly. He had expected she would do so, since he'd given her plenty of time to appease her hunger and her pride. No doubt, she expected him to demand he share the bed.

He would not.

Walking around the big room, he inspected the different trunks along the walls. One held bedding, another spare wool kilts. In the kitchen area, a wooden box with a tight lid held bags of oats and barley, different herbs, root vegetables and bottles of ale and wine. Everything needed to sustain them for the sennight was there. He'd provide the fresh meat.

Her gaze heated his loins, but he forced himself to relax and pretend he was unaware of her scrutiny When he knew he had stretched and bent enough to interest any woman with blood in her veins, he pinched out the candles and banked the fire.

Still naked, he stretched out on the furs and breathed a long yawn of comfort. Making sure he could touch his sword with his fingers, he closed his eyes and pretended to drift off to sleep. It was hard to do when he could near feel her gaze traveling from the tip of his head down to his toes — with long stops along the way.

It wasn't long before she was tossing and turning in her bed.

For a lass who readily took to bed sport, she was as uncomfortable as he. To hide the evidence of just how uncomfortable *he* had become, he snored and turned over on his side, his back to her.

It worked. Not only did he eventually wilt but she finally went to sleep. He slept with his lids near open as he did when he was alone in the woods.

Somewhere in the wee hours of the night, he sensed she was awake and stealing out of bed. When she edged past him, she walked on her tiptoes and carried her boots. He waited until she thought she'd been successful before his fingers tightened around her ankle.

Elyne shrieked like a spider had wrapped his legs around her. It awakened Squat, who started barking and running around the room, searching for an intruder.

"Goin' somewhere?

"Again?"

Chapter 20

Elyne shook her foot, but Graemme held fast.

"I have need of a private place, ye lout!"

"A private place? Ye have all the privacy ye need."

"Ye well know what I mean! There are no, uh," she waved her arms to take in the whole room, "provisions for a woman's comfort."

"Ah. Ye need to piss?"

Elyne's face turned rosy as a ripening apple.

"It's the middle of the night. Ye canna go into the woods. There are all sorts of woodland creatures which roam close to a hut or lodge."

"I am not afeared of a stray dog or fox!"

"Ah, 'tis more than such mild creatures. Wild dogs and foxes become used to men throwing bones and uneaten food outside. One might think ye a rare haunch of mutton!" He released her ankle and sprang to his feet. "Wait here."

Sliding into his boots without lacing them, he went outside and returned quickly with a bucket. He banged it against the stone of the fireplace to rid it of creatures which had made it their home.

"No need to worry. There's a lean-to out back for horses. I guess this one held oats, since crawling things have tried to eat it clean."

Elyne watched in horror as he knocked several spiders out into the flames. Icy chills went up and down her back, making her feel as if the creatures were crawling over her. She shivered and pulled her clothing tight, trying to rid herself of the awful thought.

He peered in the bucket and nodded. She supposed he meant it was now empty? Taking a hand, he rubbed all over the outside, the bottom and then the inside before slamming it down in front of her.

"Here ye go. All empty and ready for ye."

"Ye expect me to use a bucket? Here?" She looked around, but there was no private place she could use except the back corner. It was in shadows.

His gaze followed hers. "Ah. Ye are no blushing innocent. I'll turn my back."

"I'll not use a bucket! 'Tis for an uncouth lout, not a lady!"

"Hm. I'm neither uncouth nor a lout, but the crone made it necessary for me use a bucket for a throne." He looked down at the bucket then up at her.

"Ye deserved everything the old crone did to ye."

His face tightened into a grim mask.

"Lady, consider yerself lucky ye dinna have to go into the woods where any sort of creature could come sniffing after yer arse. One as pale and ivory as yers would shine like a rushlight to a wild pig."

What was she to do? She could not do anything so personal in front of him! 'Twas bad enough in the woods, but at least outside there was a sizeable bush to help hide her. Here there was naught!

She plunked down on one of the chairs beside the table and crossed her legs. Could she possibly hold out until daybreak?

Graemme put his hands on his hips and watched her. When she wouldn't budge from the chair, he shook his head and sighed. Likely he was at the end of his patience. She refused to acknowledge him. If he was anything like her father and thought she was being a pain in his arse, he'd likely fly into a rage.

She focused her attention on Squat instead. He'd slept on the floor with Graemme and hopped up when the man did. Since then, he'd followed him everywhere he went. Was the dog hoping he'd be still long enough they could go back to sleep?

Graemme's footsteps didn't near, which was a good thing.

She heard him dragging something across the floor and dared to glimpse what he was doing. He pulled the chest with the bedding over to the corner of the room and placed it an arm's length from the corner.

Trying hard to ignore him, she lowered her head and stared at her toes. After a few breaths, she peeked through her lashes again. He had gone back for the smaller chest of extra kilts and woolens. When he bent over, he spread his legs and used them to help pick up the chest.

She made a strange sound when she spied his ballocks swinging between his legs. She cleared her throat and coughed a little in case he thought the sound had been one of interest.

He grunted when he picked it up and placed it atop the linen chest.

Bleh! She could tell he chuckled from the way his shoulders moved. Unfortunately, he turned as she was composing her face to appear unconcerned. She didn't think he would believe it for she could feel heat rising from her chin to her brows.

He walked over to the bucket and marched back to deposit it in the corner behind the chests.

"Now, my lady, ye will have privacy apleanty," he said with a courtly bow.

"Are ye going outside?"

"Do ye think I have no wits? If I were gone more than a breath or two, ye'd drop the latch in place and slam the bar across the door."

Elyne knew she didn't have time to argue. Even though she made a mad dash across the room, she barely made it. Sighing with relief, she was grateful she'd not left a trail behind her.

After they both went back to bed, Graemme had a hard time returning to sleep. She had surprised him with her modesty, for she acted like she was unused to having a man about when she was unclothed. And even though she had a reputation for watching men bathing at the well, she blushed and was surprised at his bare flesh.

Was she used to seeing men from afar but didn't have the same experience of them within touching distance? When he remembered the lack of any blood after their first bed sport, the thought made him frown. She had been so tight he'd expected to break through a barrier. Perchance, she'd had one encounter and didn't like the experience enough to repeat it?

He grinned, for she liked it well enough with him. Had he been standing, he'd have preened like a fool. Squat became tired of Graemme's tossing and turning, and once Graemme turned on his side, the dog used his paws and legs to scoot himself back firmly against the man's warm chest. Graemme automatically put his arm over the warm bundle and ruffled the hair on its head. It gave Graemme the peace he needed, for not long after he yawned and finally closed his eyes and slept.

Elyne was afeared to open her eyes, for she didn't know what the day would bring. Her life had turned upside down — not for the first time — and she needed time to adjust and put the changes in their proper viewpoint.

She winced, for it wasn't as horrible as when she'd seen her father near kill Ranald. Nor could she compare it to her fear when a foolish man kidnapped her, thinking her ransom would make him rich. When Chief Broccin threatened to behead the man, she near fainted.

Young women were married off all the time. At least Graemme had all his teeth and hair. And he was young. Bed sport wasn't a thing to dread and make her want to cover her face with a pillow. In fact, she had been pleasantly surprised to have liked it as much as the servant girls had at Raptor.

The lower classes had the freedom to make sport with anyone they liked. She didn't know many knights' wives who had a satisfied air. Since Ranald had returned from the Abbey and was a frequent visitor to Raptor Castle, no one feared rape. When he'd first arrived, he'd dealt harshly with any man who had taken a woman by force. Even their father knew better than to try.

She dared to peek through the lashes of her lowered eyelids

and breathed a sigh of relief. Graemme must be outside, for she didn't see him. Bounding out of bed, she took care of the necessities and quickly changed into her smock and kirtle.

Graemme must have relented, for two clean bowls and wooden spoons waited on the table and a pot of porridge sat to the side of the fireplace to keep warm. Since he had made an effort to be polite, she decided she would see if he was ready to break his fast.

When she opened the door and looked around but didn't see him anywhere, she decided to do some exploring of her own. Walking around the right side of the house, she passed the lean-to for the horses he'd mentioned. While she looked around, she heard a steady thumping she felt even through her boots. Was someone cutting down a tree? She glanced at the treetops but didn't see any movement out of the ordinary.

Cautiously, she darted from one tree to the next. What if someone other than Graemme was in the woods? She saw someone through the bushes ahead and crept closer.

Ah, it was Graemme. She could tell from his bare back. Sweat rolled down his muscled shoulders as his arms lifted a heavy axe and came down with a mighty thwack. Beside him, he'd stacked logs cut just the right size for the fireplace.

Twenty or so paces away was a lovely pool framed by trees with drooping branches, gleaming wet rocks and ferns growing close to the water. Likely, there were herbs she could pick, too. Sunlight filtered through the leaves overhanging it, making the light dance over the water.

There was something about him working beside the water that stirred her blood. Why would such a sight affect her? He'd bunched his kilt around his waist, so it wasn't as if he was unclothed. Though the muscles playing over his back was enough to make her breathing a little uneven.

What a fool she was to consider the man interesting.

Squat lay not too far from him, watching his every move. He followed him everywhere, the same as he used to do her. Either Squat was a stupid dog or else the man was not the horrible person in her dreams. Even so, she had to be wary of trusting him.

"Are ye going to come out or are ye going to hide behind trees the rest of the morn?"

Graemme knew she was up from the instant her hand had touched the latch on the door. Had she eaten the porridge or had she decided to wait until he came to share it with her?

"I am not hiding! I thought 'twas foolish to come barging into the woods afore I knew who was in them." She huffed and walked over to stand where she could see his face.

He finished his last log and rested the axe on the ground to lean on the handle while he looked her over.

"Ye look rested. I thought ye were going to sleep well past the noon hour."

She looked more than rested. Her lovely auburn-tinted hair curled around her shoulders and stirred with the breeze behind her, now and again blowing a strand to annoy her dark brown eyes. Reaching up, she unconsciously flicked it back only to have to do it again in a few breaths.

One thing for sure, he may not have picked her to be his bride, but he had to admit she was the most beautiful lass he'd seen since his unfaithful Elspeth. His teeth clamped together and he blinked.

They were complete opposites. Elspeth had been small with blue eyes, light skin and blond hair; Elyne was tall with dark eyes and hair, and sun-kissed skin.

Turning his back to her, he pretended he had drawn a black curtain over his memories and willed them to disappear. He went over to the water and splashed his face, head and chest. The water was cold. What little sunlight filtered through was not enough to warm it. He'd cleared a space about twelve paces wide to make it easier to get into the water.

He looked forward to swimming after his body cooled and he'd broken his fast. Hopefully, there was still something for him to eat. He wouldn't put it past her to throw it out the window if she was still vexed about last eve's meal.

His hands stopped to rub thoughtfully over his face. Was

he foolish to leave the food unattended? What if she'd already eaten and had dosed the rest with one of her nasty herbs? He couldn't let her know he was uneasy, for she would get pleasure from it. He snorted, disgusted with himself. She was a woman, after all, not a warrior he had to fear.

He straightened and wiped the water from his arms. Elyne was throwing a stick for Squat to fetch, but he sensed she'd been watching him. She turned and started walking back to the lodge. He would leave the firewood until after he'd eaten. Once he fetched it, he would be ready for a swim.

Watching Elyne's hips sway gracefully over uneven ground, he pictured her unclothed, her dark curls falling down her spine to rest on her creamy buttocks. He'd thought of her when he cleared the area, making it wide enough to stretch a blanket over the leaves. Before the sennight was over, he intended to make love to her there.

Elyne glanced back over her shoulder and saw the brainless look men get when their cockstand was about to burst through their kilts! She skidded to a halt and shoved her hands on her hips, looking pointedly at the evidence.

"Ye had best forget what ye are thinking!"

"Ye are a vain one. What makes ye think it was ye who entered my thoughts?"

"Nay? Then I hope your memories are keen enough to give ye comfort!"

"Aye, they are most keen, so I would thank ye to turn yer back and let my hands and memories comfort me in privacy!"

"Huh!"

Elyne's chin lifted as she swished her skirts and walked faster until she reached the door. Before he got to the bottom step, it slammed in his face.

His cockstand died a shameful death.

Graemme waited outside for a goodly time — time enough for her to believe he had comforted himself but not too long to make her think he'd had trouble finding fulfillment.

"Ye had best get all the frowning and door slamming out

of yer mind whilst we are here."

She stood in the center of the room tapping her foot and looking about to explode.

"What do ye mean?"

"Dratted Lucifer's pickled eyeballs, lass. If ye keep scowling all the time, yer face will forget any other expression. By the end of the sennight, people will truly believe I'm wedding an old crone with wrinkles from the top of her hair to her chin!"

She frowned all the harder, then the words seemed to sink in. He could see she mulled over his words for she stopped scowling and reached up to feel over her face.

"There's a new wrinkle right here," he said and put a fingertip between her brows. "Ack! In fact, there are two. One for each eye."

"Ye lie!"

Elyne pulled away and turned her back. He could tell from her movements that she felt for the telltale wrinkles.

"Rub them with mud paste. The women at Clibrick do such when they start to show their age. Ye possibly played the crone so often yer face decided to change early."

Graemme kept his features straight though he wanted to chuckle. Not a woman in Scotland was immune to fearing the ravages of time. He saw she worried by the way she stayed stony-faced when she turned.

"Bad humors also cause creases to form beneath the eyes."

He shook his head hinting he noted a change there, too. Her hands twitched, but she didn't allow them to feel her face again. He pretended to ignore it.

"Come, if we dinna break our fast now, I will drop from hunger."

Keeping his back turned, he spooned enough porridge to fill each bowl near to the top. Placing them on the table, he laid a spoon by each.

"I think I saw an earthenware crock of honey and one of butter beside the window. Likely, it keeps them cool."

Still not looking at her, he went to fetch them and placed them between the two bowls. He pulled out a chair and waited until she sat before he went to his own.

"I hope ye notice how helpful I'm being. Yer father never said yer age, but I reckoned ye must be getting up in years for him to worry so about yer future."

"I am much younger than ye are," she scoffed.

"Uh huh. It's what yer father said."

Graemme poured ample honey and spooned butter atop his food then licked his lips. Every spoonful he took, he savored as he would a gift from the gods. As hungry as he was, it wasn't hard to do. After the first bite, he knew she hadn't done any nasty tricks to the food, for she ate the same thing.

"Dinna expect me to have porridge made every morn ye decide to sleep in. From now on, ye will prepare all the food. I will do the hunting."

She gave him a disgusted look and kept on eating.

"I saw near six hares this morn while I was chopping wood. Curious creatures. They didna even seem afeard of Squat."

He looked down at the dog and put his bowl on the floor for him to finish.

"Dinna think to sneak away, though, lass. Ye slept so long I had ample time to set some snares around the grounds. I'd hate to think of ye dangling in the air until I returned."

"Heh! Ye think I am chicken-brained enough to believe ye and will stay cowering in this room until ye return?"

"Test me and find out for yerself."

Chapter 21

Elyne paced around the big room until she was near dizzy. She had nothing to occupy her mind, so she decided she may as well make her bed. How hard could it be? Pull up the sheets and blankets, flop the pillows atop them and she was done. He could take care of his own bedding.

The idea made her grin until she tripped over the corner of his pillow and landed on her face. She thanked God for the furs on the floor else, she'd have had a nasty bruise.

Mayhap even a broken nose.

'Twas not necessary to fold his blanket, for he never used it. The fool slept bare arsed and seemed to enjoy the cold. A grin played with her lips. After he was fast asleep this night, she would open the shutters and let the cold air sweep through the room. Let's see how hale and hearty he was then! She put the blanket and pillow at the foot of her bed and looked around.

She found washing the bowls was no great chore after she put her own bowl down and had Squat clean it. A quick swish with a cloth and soap and her 'chores' were done.

"Come, Squat. 'Tis too lovely a day to stay inside." She patted her leg and the dog followed her out to the lean-to.

The door was open on the small room at the end of the shelter. There were tools stacked against the walls and a fresh bale of hay. Everything for caring for a horse was inside. In the far corner, two buckets were stacked together. They looked in much better shape than the one he'd brought her to use.

Carefully, in case they were spiders inside, she leaned over to check their condition. No spiders of any kind, no webs showing the critters had been there! In face, nothing disgusting at all. Why, the randy goat had brought her the bucket used to clean the manure out of the stalls! No wonder it was so foul.

She would bide her time, but he'd find she didn't take kindly to his treatment of her. Leaving everything as she had found it, she wandered over to the pool. The water was calm and clear. She began thinking of the wrinkles he spoke about. Could they be true?

She lifted the hems of her clothing and fastened them high on her waist. Elyne approached the water, testing the ground with each footfall. It was solid, thank the heavens. Getting down on her knees, she peered at the reflection of herself. The light wasn't strong enough for her to tell. Was there a wrinkle between her brows? Or had the water moved? She gasped, for she was sure she saw more wrinkles around her eyes and lips!

Hopping up, she near ran back to the room and got a bowl. Someone had planted flowers around a big spruce tree and they bloomed. The dirt looked black and rich there. Using a spoon, she half filled the bowl with dirt, took it inside and added enough water to make it thick so it would dry easily. Without anything to look in, she used her fingers to take small gobs of mud and spread it between her eyes.

Hesitating, she looked at the dark mud.

"If a little is good, a lot should be better," she muttered. She scooped most of it out and spread over the rest of her face.

After she finished, she dumped the remainder of the mud outside and washed out the bowl.

"Come, Squat, let's find some sun to sit in"

She and the dog found a tree to lean against. As the sun dried the mud, she could feel her face tighten. She tried not to talk to the dog too much, for the mud cracked and crumbled to her lap. He kept looking back at her and sniffing her hand. She guessed to reassure himself she was still there beneath the wrinkle treatment.

The sun made her sleepy and soon her eyes closed.

Graemme was far more successful than he thought he'd be and had brought down three hares in a very short time. He expected Elyne would still be in the lodge, perhaps taking a light sleep after she'd broken her fast. But there she was slumped against a tree, snoring as loud as any blacksmith.

With mud on her face! She'd taken the bait, but didn't think he'd know. He half wanted to go back into the woods and wait until she awoke and washed the disgusting stuff off. He would have, but Squat decided to greet him with barks shrill enough to wake the dead.

Elyne jerked upright. Her eyelids fluttered but had a hard time opening. Finally, the mud broke and she brushed it away. With a horrified look at him, she jumped up and whirled to turn her back.

Graemme knew better than to do it, but he couldn't stop laughing.

"Ye big blob of moat scum! Ye lied to me, didna ye!"

He tried to stifle his laugh, but the harder he tried, the madder she became. She turned and dashed for the pool. He followed, not wanting her to go in before he'd tested it for submerged tree branches and things which could snag her hair and keep her below the water.

By the time he reached her, she'd whipped her clothing over her head and threw it on a rock. Sunlight came through and lit her body in a glorious golden glow.

Except for her face.

"Keep the Hades away from me, ye pox-minded buffoon!"

Graemme could swear she had tears in her eyes, for they glistened more than ever. He felt shameful as the lowlife she'd called him. Before he could stop her, she went further out on the rock and did a low dive into the water. He threw down his catch and jerked off his boots, ready to jump in to save her. Fortunately, she surfaced quickly, unharmed.

"Ye should not swim in waters where they have not been tested!"

"Tested? I'm sure my brothers swam here many times. And dinna speak to me!"

She turned her back and swam to the middle of the pool, refusing to look at him. The mud stained the water as she swam until it was gone. Her hair lost its pins and floated out behind her covering her lovely back down to the dimples on her buttocks. He tore off the rest of his clothes and followed her.

"Keep away from me, else I'll skewer ye in yer sleep!"

Whenever he came close, she dove under the water and changed direction.

Surprisingly, she was one of the best swimmers he had ever seen. He hated to admit it, but she swam better than he did. Once he saw he would be unable to catch her, he washed from head to toe, using sand to clean the filth off his arms and chest. When done, he heaved himself up on a rock, shook himself and sat in the sun. He'd wait until she tired and came out of the water.

'Twas then he thought to look at Squat. Graemme shot up.

"Blasted Lucifer's minion! Little hellhound! Ye've ruined the hare!"

Squat stopped tearing at the dead hare's leg and looked at him. He was thoroughly sated, for he shoved the side of a leg out of his mouth, yawned as heartily as any man and put his head on his paws for another nap.

Elyne snorted a laugh and swam close to the shore.

"The great hunter canna protect his game from one little dog? Any halfling knows ye dinna leave fresh game on the ground for the hounds to pick up."

"And any halfwit knows ye dinna put mud on yer face and bake it like a mud pie,"

Graemme had replied without thinking. He groaned as soon as the words left his lips. So far, their getting to know and like each other was suffering a sad fate. One look at her face and he knew he'd ruined everything he'd done since coming here.

Her eyes were icy with haughty contempt. 'Twas enough to chill him to the marrow of his bones. He thought of the weapons over the fireplace. If she pulled the table close and stood on it, she could easily reach them. He'd be wise to sleep with a shield over his body.

If he'd had one with him.

No doubt, she was as good at archery and swords as she was at swimming and riding astride. He cursed Chief Broccin. He knew as if she'd told him she'd secretly trained with Moridac and Ranald as youths.

He could no longer trust her during the night. When they settled to sleep, he would do as they'd told him. Tie her ankle to him so he'd know whenever she moved.

Graemme washed and salvaged what he could of his hunt, which was most of two hares, and let Squat finish gnawing on his prize. He would have to go out again tomorrow and hopefully find grouse. He was tired of eating hare since he left Clibrick.

Elyne stayed in the water and swam to work off her anger. She was not used to anyone making a fool of her. She didn't like the feeling. Ignoring the man on shore, she wished he'd go away.

When he glanced toward her, hesitated then went back to the lodge with the meat, he fulfilled her wish.

Seeing more smoke than usual coming from the chimney, she knew he'd built up the fire to cook the hares.

Taking her time, she got out of the cold water and stretched out on a rock. The sun would dry her. She near fell asleep again. Last eve she slept lightly, forever aware Graemme was too close for comfort on the floor. How could she trust a man who had a cockstand most of the night? Now, more than ever, she couldn't believe him. She should have known better than to have fallen for his tale. She felt her face and wondered if the mud would cause her to break out or something equally as ghastly. She near gagged, thinking there could have been worms in the mud.

Well, she would have her revenge when he least expected it.

While the hare roasted, she put water on to boil and added some turnips and carrots. Both were silent. They still had more than half a loaf of bread, so she placed it close to the fire to let it warm and make the crust crispy. Graemme kept quietly turning the spit, not wanting the meat to overcook on one side and be rare on the other.

When the food was ready, they both picked up a pewter plate and goblet. Graemme took a skin of wine out of the food locker and poured it into both their goblets. He carved the meat and looked up at her.

"Do ye prefer the upper parts or the leg meat?"

"Either is fine."

He gave her generous portions of both. She spooned out a turnip and several carrots and sat down to eat.

"The forest is filled with woodland creatures. Perhaps tomorrow I can bring down some grouse."

"Do ye fancy yerself enough of a hunter to put an arrow through a wily grouse?"

"Aye" He held a leg in his hand and bit off a chunk of meat. A little of the juice ran from the corner of his lip down to his chin. He used the back of his hand to wipe it away.

She gave him a scornful look.

He raised his brow at her.

The tension in the room was enough to strike sparks. She kept silent and was thankful to see the sun setting. Some type of married life they would have if they couldn't stand to be in the same room with each other!

'Twas a shame, for he was better looking than most men. In fact, she couldn't think of anyone who was more pleasing to look at than him. Other than the men in her own family, and his brother Magnus, of course. From what she'd seen of the man they called *Magnus the Ruthless*, he seemed far more agreeable in his disposition than Graemme.

Graemme thought about the day and wished he could take back what he'd said to her in anger. He had never treated a woman so harshly afore. But this woman seemed to nettle him at every turn. She forever scowled and never tried to be pleasant as other women did. Why, half the women of Clibrick tried to snare him for their bed partners.

How had the fates selected this one woman to fall into his

lap? For truth. She hated the very thought of marriage to him, and here he was forced to marry her in a few days.

By the time Ranald arrived for them, he'd be lucky if they were both able to stand and walk around! He stole a quick glance up at the weapons on the wall.

Should he take them down and hide them in the woods?

At nightfall, when he stepped outside to give her privacy to bathe and prepare for bed, he stood outside the door. His hearing was keen, and when he heard her soft footsteps immediately approach the door, he opened it so quickly it near knocked her over.

"Dinna try it!"

"Try what? Escape? With ye outside?"

She had one telltale hand behind her. Though she was tall for a woman, the bar he placed across the door at night for security was a scant bit taller than her shoulder. He looked pointedly at her right shoulder and held out his hand.

"What?"

"Give me the bar." His hand reached for it, but she held tight. He shook his head. "Would ye rather I stay to watch ye bathe in the basin? I relish the idea of seeing ye lather her lovely breast. Mayhap I could rinse and lap them dry for ye?"

"Take the bar, ye churlish eejit! But dinna enter till I let ye know I am finished."

Graemme shook his head, noting his new description as a churlish eejit and stepped back onto the porch. She slammed the door.

As she walked away, she called him everything from a boorish hellhound to a slimy worm.

She was rather inventive with her descriptions of him.

He studied the stars and looked for signs of rain, but he didn't see any. Likely, they would have another day of ideal weather, which was unusual. When he began to think she had gone to bed when she was through with her ablutions, she called out to him.

All the candles were out, but he didn't miss the faint light coming from the two opened shutters. She could not be hot, for she was abed with her covers up to her chin. And there was a chilly wind coming through the window openings.

Graemme was no fool. She attempted to make him as uncomfortable as possible, for his blanket was missing. Well, two could play at this game.

"I see ye are lonesome for someone to share yer bed."

He made his voice husky and sensual, a tone that caused many women to throw back the covers and invite him in.

"Ugh! What make ye think I desire yer scrawny bones in bed with me?"

"The open shutters. The missing blanket. The fire ye have near put out."

Graemme started taking off his clothing as he walked toward the bed. By the time he stood beside it, he was bare down to the thatch of black hair nestled around his sex.

"The fire died because ye didna build it properly."

"Aye. I did."

He put one knee on the bed and reached for the top of her covers.

She gasped, scrambled back and reached beneath to pull out his folded woolen blanket.

"Here is your blanket. I must have been careless making the bed this morn."

"And I suppose ye didna know the shutters were wide to the night air. 'Tis no problem for me. I prefer sleeping with the night air. Though at night, bats from nearby caves are drawn to search out any opening."

"Ye may close it, if it is yer preference," Elyne said as she glanced nervously toward it.

"Nay. I prefer it open to the clean night air. I can hear the owls when they catch their prey. The mice and small creatures put up quite a shriek when the talons dig into them. I counted as many as ten kills one night."

"I never heard any when we were traveling."

"Aye. The owls kept away because we had a camp-fire burning."

Suddenly, an owl screeched then a small creature cried

out in distress. He near laughed at the speed Elyne leapt out of bed and slammed both shutters closed and latched them. He doubted he could have counted to five afore she was back with her covers pulled up to her chin.

"If ye are through with yer yammering, I would like to sleep now." The frost in her voice could have chilled a flagon of wine.

He let out a long, mournful sigh. "I do hope once we are wed ye show more passion for bed sport. At this rate, it will take a sennight afore ye get with child."

Elyne snorted. Loud.

"If ye wait for me to invite ye to my bed, it will be years."

She pounded her pillow and turned her back to him. When his hand snaked under her covers and grasped a delicate ankle, she screeched as loud as the owl.

"No need to scare the night creatures out of their feathers, wife. Since ye had such a stressful day, I feared ye would have one of yer foretelling dreams and might wander into the pool and drown."

She jerked her leg, trying to free it. His grip didn't lessen as he knotted a thin rope around it. He sat on the furs and tied the other end to his left wrist.

Elyne decided not to give him the satisfaction of fighting over the rope. She had slept comfortably when Aunt Joneta did the same, so now should be no different. Besides, she had not had such a dream since he came for her at the convent.

For truth, she slept peacefully the night through.

Not that she didn't dream, though.

She did. In them, she swived the Highlander until he was so sated his cock fell limp as a stewed chicken's neck.

CHAPTER 22

"IT LOOKS TO BE a clear day for me to hunt those grouse I'm hungering for," Graemme said as soon as he saw she was awake.

He was already up and dressed. Porridge steamed in a small iron pot hanging from the hook in the fireplace. Oatcakes were baking in the side oven.

Elyne rose and stretched, refreshed from a good sleep. She cast an appraising look at him and wondered if she should warn him or not. He was such a hard-head know-it-all, she hesitated. Shrugging, she decided to tell him what she knew from her dreams.

"I wouldna go hunting today if I were ye. It is going to rain. Buckets of it."

Graemme grinned at her, opened the shutters and pointed out at the blue sky. He didn't say a word.

"If ye are telling me ye dinna believe me, go ahead. But ye will be wet afore the noon hour."

What little dreams Elyne had last night all involved rain and a drop in temperature. And for some reasons, buckets of mud kept flashing in her mind.

"Oh, and if ye insist on ignoring my warning, ye'd best take a heavy cloak with ye. There should be one in the clothing chest. The rain is going to bring in cold weather, too."

"Ah. So the old crone can also predict the weather?"

"Aye. And she's very good at it."

Graemme snorted a laugh and shook his head. Well, let him make fun of her. She didn't care. The weather was the one thing she never failed to predict accurately. When he returned from his hunt, he was going to be very wet and cold, while she was going to be warm and snug here in the lodge.

After he left, she went outside to collect as many herbs as she could afore the rains came. She found an old garden in the woods behind the lodge. Weed-grown as it was, in amongst them were carrots, wild onions, turnips and beets. The furry animals, mainly hares, had harvested most of the wild vegetables, but she found a few which didn't bear the marks of their nibbles.

'Twas lovely to have the time to herself. She used the new buckets in the lean-to's room to gather the food. After washing her find, she took the buckets, returned to the abandoned garden and used a spade from the tools inside the room. For what she had in mind, everything worked perfectly. She set the buckets behind trees near the pool. They would not be visible but would be close to hand.

"Why are ye following me around Squat?"

The dog looked up at her, perked his ear straighter and sniffed at the buckets. When he looked back up, his brows drew together and reminded her of a grumpy old man. His eyes demanded answers, too.

She imagined he asked, "Why did you pick those scrawny things? Now why are you putting the same dirt into the empty buckets?"

"Dinna give me such accusing looks, ye little cur. Ye just don't understand what I'm planning. Besides, ye didna help me when his *High and Mighty* convinced me a mudpack on my face was a good thing."

She sighed loud enough to make him lower his ear. "I suppose it's all right if ye disapprove — ye cannot tell Graemme what I have in store for him."

When the sky darkened, she already had a large pot of soup on to cook. Lightning began striking. Heavy clouds filled with rain opened up. She closed the shutters, wrapped herself in a blanket and sat cozy and warm in the middle of the furs. Squat must have forgiven her, for he curled up on her lap.

Elyne enjoyed her day, but she anticipated her triumph when Graemme arrived, soaked and without anything to show for his day of hunting.

Graemme had tramped near to the top of the tall hill behind the lodge. No matter where he looked, wildlife seemed to have fled.

"The blasted creatures are hiding from me," he grumbled.

Standing still for what seemed ages, he waited for game to venture out of hiding. When they didn't, he became fanciful and wondered if some fox had carried the news a hunter was on the prowl!

He sighed and sat with his back against a tree while he nibbled on a dry oatcake and thought of his day. Afore dawn, Elyne slept so deeply she hadn't even moved when he untied the knot at her ankle. He'd had a chance to study her lovely legs. He didn't regret taking advantage of the moment. His only regret was he couldn't strip off the blankets and gaze at her lovely body.

Of course, if he had, all thought of hunting would have flown out the window as fast as she was able to think up things to bedevil him.

He leapt to his feet and settled his bow and arrows across his back. He'd look for game until he became so tired he had to return. But he didn't want to return empty handed. He'd never see the end of her *I told you so* looks she was so good at giving.

What happened to the sun? It had blazed overhead when he sat to rest. He looked up to see clouds scurried across the sky, chased by heavy sheets of rain in the distance. He heard it coming afore he spied it.

He shouted and struck his boot into the ground until he dug up a patch of grass.

"Blast ye, Lucifer! Ye're the one responsible, ye wart-covered, rat-eating spoiler of all things! Why could ye not wait until I had a string of grouse hanging from my belt?"

Growling and kicking, mud flew through the air.

He wanted to bang his head on the nearest tree trunk for being so stubborn he'd refused to bring a cloak with him. It didn't take long for the downpour to soak him to his skin. There was no way out but to go back empty-handed and face Elyne's mockery.

Halfway down the hill, the rain stopped. He wished it had not. After falling and sliding in mud, he couldn't go inside to get warm until he washed off in the pool.

Squat barked to warn Elyne someone approached. She peeked out the door and watched as a very bedraggled Graemme looked around him and walked over to the pool. So, he was going to clean himself up afore she knew what a bad day he'd had.

He should save himself the trouble.

Leaving Squat inside, she slid out of the barely opened door and eased it shut. If there was one worthwhile thing in training to be a lady, it was being able to glide across any floor or earth without making a sound.

As he kneeled at the edge of the pool and splashed cold water over his face and head, she retrieved the two buckets behind a tree. So intent on grumbling to himself, he didn't even notice her.

Elyne upended one bucket of mud on top of his head. Quick as a flash, she placed her foot firmly on his exposed arse and shoved him into the water. When his head bobbed up, he didn't have time to yell before she threw the contents of the second bucket into his face.

"Try a mud pack, Sir Graemme. It will do wonders for yer scars. It may even add an attractive color to yer skin!"

He let out a howl of rage. Her heart surged so hard it bounced against her ribs. He sounded like an enraged wild animal about to kill his prey.

He ducked his head beneath the water and shook it like a shaggy hound. Powerful arms and legs beat the water and brought him close to where she stood. Mud streaked down through hair that near covered his face and shoulders. His furious black gaze looked as if lightning flashed from it. She was unable to look away. Fear held her a prisoner.

What had once been sensuous lips now thinned to a cruel line. A snarl rumbled from his chest as his lips curled, baring his teeth as though he was ready to rend her flesh from her bones. He started to push up with his muscled arms. Terrified at what she had unleashed, she placed her foot on his head and shoved him back under the water.

He made a quick grab for her ankle. Fast as a deer, she drew it back and turned to run. She grabbed her skirts in her hands.

Where to go? How to hide?

He would break down the door to the lodge easily enough with the axe in the lean-to.

If she was fleet, she could find a place in the woods! Mayhap a cave. She would head to the left where the brush was most dense.

Holding her skirts above her knees, she ran as fast as she could.

Footsteps pounded behind her.

She dared not take the time to look.

Fool! She did.

It scared her so much she sprinted in even greater strides.

"Elyne. I can run all day." His words came through a tight jaw, more growled than spoken.

"Ye will tire afore I do," he taunted. "In fact, I will stop to give ye a better start. I will give ye to the count of five."

The sound of his footsteps silenced. Quickly, she glanced back again. On a boulder, he didn't stand upright but crouched, head slightly forward. Fists on his knees, his fingers clenching and unclenching.

The picture of a wolf ready to spring flashed through her mind.

"By the count of ten, I will have ye in my hands. Ye had best run like ye never ran afore!"

"One!" His voice was soft, silky.

She gasped and leapt forward.

"Two!"

She kept running. When he came to 'Five', the air rasped through her throat. She didn't think she could run so fast, but when she heard his footfalls begin again, she near flew through the air. He kept counting aloud.

"Six!"

"Seven!"

Whatever possessed her to taunt this man's pride? She should know from the men in her own family, pride was all a man cared about!

"Eight!"

His voice near sounded in her ear!

"Nine!"

Ack! He was right behind her!

Was he going to kill her? Pray God, not. Beat her? She didn't doubt it.

She ran like a rabbit chased by an eagle.

"Ten!"

Elyne flew through the air with such speed she believed an eagle had taken her ankles in its talons. The ground quickly receded. Upside down, she rose towards the treetops. She screamed louder than she'd ever screamed afore.

Several times, she rose and fell, each time less than the other. Finally, she swung slowly. Her skirts hung down over her arms.

Cold rain fell on her bare legs and nether parts as she fought her kirtle and smock.

Graemme grabbed the hems of her clothing and hauled them away from her face. He bent slightly to look into her eyes.

His voice turned gentle as a kitten's purr.

His eyes belied the tone.

Menacing.

"Ye should have listened. I told ye at *ten* ye would be in my hands. I neglected to add *helpless*. But then, ye should have known ye would be."

Elyne was too dizzy to speak. Nay, 'twas a lie. Too frightened to speak!

She realized how she came to be hanging arse over head.

Graemme had set snares to catch her in case she ever tried to escape from the lodge and run away.

She was embarrassed and angry because she hung upside down — exposed to his eyes.

Embarrassment was futile.

Anger was good.

Graemme could not believe any woman could get away with what Elyne had done. She had taken him by surprise. Had she been a thief or a soldier running from his lord, he would have had a sword through his back.

"Well, now. I have learned much from today. Ye can walk without making the sound of a single footstep."

He dropped her clothing over her face again. His hands caressed her nether cheeks then his fingers dug into her flesh as he twirled her in circles.

Elyne squealed like he'd pricked her flesh with the tip of his knife.

"Stop, ye barbarian! Cut me down!"

"Oh? Ye want something of me, my sweet, obedient bride?"

"Ye heard me, cur! Cut me down!"

"Hmm. I dinna think so. When ye yell and give orders, yer face hardens and becomes quite unattractive. I have a much lovelier view of ye the way ye are."

She'd stopped spinning and was swaying gently back and forth. He ran his hands from her ankles down to the joining of her legs.

"Stop it, lout!"

"From barbarian to cur to lout all in just a few breaths! Ye astound me with yer knowledge of my character."

Elyne tried to swat out at his legs, but her skirts were in the way. All it accomplished was to make her jerk around.

"Ah! Thank ye. What a tempting view." His fingers raked through the auburn curls guarding her sex.

"Cut me down, ye miserable piece of goat shite!"

She shrieked, loud and piercing, when he tweaked her tempting curls.

"I thought I requested ye find some less, um, bad-tempered names for me? I dinna think goat shite is a good name. My father might take offense at his daughter-by-law calling his son such."

"My father will take more of an offense when I tell him how ye hung me like a pig ready for slaughter!"

Her lovely, exposed body slowly swayed back and forth. His view of her from every angle tempted him. Suddenly, he roared and shook his leg. Why, a woodland creature had attacked him!

He'd been so fascinated with her gleaming flesh he hadn't noted she'd gathered her skirts away from her face. She'd held them with one hand, grabbed his right leg with the other and bit his nekid thigh as hard as she could!

Reaching down, he seized her jaw in his steel grip and pressed.

"Open yer mouth, ye little witch!"

She didn't.

He straightened and swatted her bare behind with such force the loud crack echoed through the forest. Her flesh started to turn red as she opened her mouth and wailed loud as a harlot caught with her hands in her lord's silver coffers.

"Ye want down? Then down ye'll come."

He reached up and, with one swipe of his knife, cut her loose. He'd known he'd need it when he saw the direction she'd taken to escape.

Too late, Elyne saw the large puddle beneath her. She put out her hands to cushion her fall, but she need not have. With one arm around her, he lowered her into the mud. Turning her like a cook using a spoon to scrape off the sides of a cooking pot, he covered her with mud from head to toes.

When he finally released her, she sputtered and wiped at her face. It didn't help. Her hands were just as filthy. She didn't say a word. Just sat there in the rank mud and looked up at him.

She wanted to cry and wail.

But she wouldna!

Before he saw her shed a single tear because of him, she'd turn into a goat's arse!

Chapter 23

Graemme stood, legs spread and hands on hips, as he stonily stared down at Elyne. He recognized her inward struggle to hide her humiliation and hurt, her determination not to cry though her eyes were moist with unshed tears.

If she gritted her teeth any harder, they would surely crack. He suspected if she uttered a single word, she would break out in sobs.

Graemme's chest ached when he saw her struggle to be as hardened as any warrior.

Her eyes were the same color as the dark brown mud covering her, but they reflected how hard she tried to keep her composure. Their expression shamed him.

"Come."

His voice was soft as he bent and scooped her out of the puddle into his arms. Elyne's body was stiff and unyielding. 'Twas probable she feared the unknown. Would he beat her? Her father would surely have done so. How could he tell her he never would, when he himself didn't know how far he would go when she angered him? He grimaced remembering how his hand seemed to have a life of its own when it flashed out and smacked her nether cheek.

He faced a lifetime of yearning for happiness, which was never to be.

Neither spoke as he carried her out of the woods and up to the edge of the pool. He hesitated about standing her there while he removed her clothing. He didn't want to tempt her to further rebel and run again.

"Yer clothes can stand a little rinsing."

He walked into the pool and slowly eased into deeper water. He felt her start to shiver and tightened his arms.

"'Tis cold today, but we have too much muck over us to even go through the doorway."

He splashed water over her long, slender neck and wiped his wet hand over her face. At this rate, it would take him all day to clean her. He moved back toward shore until the water was at his nipples. She could stand with her head above the water there. He let her go.

"Dinna try anything foolish, Elyne."

She wouldn't look him in the eye but turned her back to him as she pulled her kirtle and smock over her head. When she hesitated, he reached around her and took her clothing. He dunked it up and down in the water until mud no longer ran from the cloth. After wadding it into one lump, he tossed it to a large rock on shore.

"Rinse yerself."

He ducked himself below the surface but was not so foolish as to take his eyes off her form in the water. Running his fingers through his hair, he kept rinsing it. When he stood again, he opened his hands and pressed from his forehead to the back of his neck, then gathered his black hair there and twisted it. He was as clean as he would ever be.

Elyne had cleansed her face but was shivering as she tried to do the same with her long curls.

"Let me," he said in a soft, unthreatening voice.

When she tried to pull away, he lowered her hands with a warning look.

"Close yer eyes and lean back as far as ye can."

When she did as he told her, he worked her hair through the water until it squeaked when he ran his fingers through it. Gently, he cupped her head and lifted it then twisted her long tresses as he had done his own. Satisfied, he guided her out of the pool.

"Stay in the water until I'm finished. We canna walk bare footed else we'll be as dirty as before."

Elyne opened her mouth to speak, but he stared her down

again. He stamped on his boots and gathered their wet clothing into one big bundle.

"Come," he ordered.

When she came out of the water, he had to stop himself from devouring her beautiful body with his gaze. He held the clothing level with his sex so she wouldn't see how she affected him. When she stood close, he dumped the bundle into her arms and swept her off her feet. He near ran with her to the lodge, for her body felt like ice.

Twenty paces from the door Squat's barking became excited. When he entered carrying Elyne, the dog near toppled him over.

"Down, fool. I must get yer mistress warm afore she freezes."

He kicked off his unlaced boots and carried her to the fireplace. Standing her on the furs, he took the wet clothing and threw it on the table. Wrapping her in the blanket from the bed, he spied his handprint on her creamy nether cheek. It was red and swollen. By God's truth! He never intended to strike her so hard. He swallowed and vowed he would guard his temper with her.

With gentle hands, he pushed her shoulders so she would sit on the warm furs. It wasn't long before he'd placed new logs on the fire and had it blazing brightly.

"What do ye intend to do to me?"

Surprised, he stopped behind her.

"What do ye think?" He was curious to know. What she thought he'd do told him how she viewed him as a man.

"Ye intend to beat me until I obey yer every command," she said.

"Is a beating what ye think I should do?" He closed his eyes a moment.

He had his answer. She thought he was as brutal as her heartless father.

Never before had he ever mistreated a woman.

Never had he laid a violent hand on one.

Until today.

"If ye do, some day ye'll find my blade in yer chest."

Her voice was near a whisper.

He tensed.

"I am not your father. Elyne. I dinna want a wife who is fearful whenever I come into a room."

"You struck me."

"Aye. I did. Do ye know why?"

"Of course. I pricked yer pride with the buckets of mud."

"I was angry, aye. But my anger would have cooled after I dropped *ye* in the mud. Ye went a step too far and I lost control of my temper."

Gramme moved to stand in front of her and turned his right leg outward so she could see it. "Do ye see yer teeth where they tore through my flesh? Eh? And the blood dripping on the floor whenever I take a step?"

Her eyes widened and her face grew pale when she looked at his leg. She must not even have remembered biting him. It was turning fiery red and swelling.

It didn't help that mud had splashed over it. Nor did it help when Squat kept trying to lick it as if he was cleansing a wound on his paw.

"Thank ye for trying to help, Squat, but I dinna think 'tis the best way to heal it."

He picked up the dog and deposited him in her lap.

"Here. Keep yer mistress warm while I see what smells so good in the pot."

He hadn't realized how hungry he was until now. The day was near gone, and so was the scant meal he'd had to break his fast.

In a short time, he threw a kilt around his middle and belted it in place. Not to keep warm, but to keep his errant member from bobbing up at every opportunity.

"Fasten yer blanket under yer arms so ye can eat," he told Elyne when he brought a bowl of soup over to her. He waited while she moved the dog off and secured her cover, then put the bowl in front of her.

"Ack! Squat, no!"

The dog halted with his tongue half out of his mouth, just dangling there. He'd been ready to lap up Elyne's food.

"I found this old pot. It's small enough for ye,"

Graemme offered the food to the hungry dog. Squat didn't wait for it to cool before he started to tentatively lap at it.

Before he got his own meal, he took a drying cloth from the kitchen supplies and tied it around his leg. He sat cross-legged beside them with his bowl balanced on his left knee, though it was awkward. But then, Elyne couldn't be too comfortable with her sore nether cheek, either!

He had not meant to hurt her. Well, maybe he did a little else she'd not heed him. But he'd never use his fist or a whip like most men. He didn't want to break her. He needed to bend her to his will. If not in all things, at least to his commands.

A woman without a strong warrior to protect her would soon find herself captured for ransom. Or worse yet, used as a whore until her captor tired of her. He shuddered at the thought.

His brother's wife would help her. Some strong women in the Highlands were as warlike as the men. But they knew their boundaries.

"The soup is very tasteful. I didn't see beets in the food bin."

Elyne voice was husky, so she cleared her throat. "There was an old garden out back. It still had a few things the hares hadn't found."

"Ye learned to cook at Raptor?"

"Aunt Joneta and I always made sure a garden was thriving near the kitchens." She looked sideways at him and said quietly, "We also tended the herbs and gathered those noted for healing."

"Ye have been taught to be a healer?"

"Aye." She cleared her throat again. "I found fresh betony this morn. I always carry packets of it with me. Aunt Joneta dosed me with the dried leaves of the betony soaked in hot water each night to make a tea. It's on the table. It's supposed to ward off bad dreams."

Interested, he tilted his head, his expression doubtful.

"Ye mean the purplish flowered plants on the table?"

"Aye." She flushed, bringing color back to her still face. "It didn't work for the dreams. 'Tis also called woundwort. For truth, fresh betony bruised to a green paste is a great healer of wounds."

"Yer dreams could be useful. I should have heeded ye about the rain. It happened just as ye said it would. I will never again doubt yer omens about the weather."

They spent the rest of the time without talking as they finished their soup.

Elyne felt much better. She was no longer cold, and though her nether part was tender, it didn't sting like bees had attacked her. And once his temper had cooled, she was not afraid of him. While Graemme was occupied playing tug the boot strings with Squat, she stood clutching the blanket and got a clean kirtle to slip on.

Once she was clothed, she went to prepare the betony poultice. While she was mashing it into a green paste, she had a pot of water on to boil. She took a sheet and used the kitchen knife to cut strips to use for bandages and cleaning. His leg looked like it needed hot cloths to make it bleed more and cleanse the small wounds.

"Come. Lay on the bed so I may clean yer leg."

"My leg is clean. It has no mud on it and the bleeding has stopped."

" 'Tis not a good thing. We have found bites are worse than sword or knife wounds. They are far more likely to cause fevers and infections."

"Aye. But animal bites are different. They lick their, er, hind parts and paws when they bathe."

Graemme's eyes glistened with mischief as he stretched out on the bed. He looked much younger and more carefree than she'd ever seen him.

"Have ye been doing such when I have not watched?" He raised his brow. "Hmm?"

"What?! I dinna think it possible!" She saw his grin and knew he was teasing her. "Now lie back so I can see what I'm doing."

She brought two candles over and placed them on the small bedside table. She needed to drag the other chair over to put the basin filled with hot water on it. The folded cloths rested beside him on the bed.

"Ye aren't going to do any stitching, are ye? Ye're liable to sew my cock to my thigh in this light!"

"All ye think about is yer cock, isn't it? Ye are fearful of somehow losing those wondrous dangling treasures?"

She motioned him to raise his right leg while she slid a drying cloth beneath it. Picking up a folded pad from the bed, she dipped it into the hot water and gingerly held the ends to twist enough so she wouldn't dribble hot water all over the sheets. When she placed the hot square over his wound, his leg jerked.

"Are ye trying to scald the skin off, woman?" He gritted his teeth until his jaw twitched.

She watched as his muscles strained to hold still. Several times, she repeated it with clean cloths, fearful when her teeth marks on his flesh became red and angry.

Each one swelled and was growing hot to the touch. They looked to still have dirty water trapped beneath the swelling. She gulped. If she didna do a good job, in the next days they might swell with ugly, yellow fluid. Though she tried to squeeze them with the hot cloths, they didn't empty all the way. When she'd done all she could, she spread a heavy layer of the betony poultice over it and wound the bandages around his thigh to keep it in place.

When she got up to clean and put away the things she'd used, he tried to get out of bed.

"Nay! Dinna get up. Ye must be still for at least two days else the poultices willna work."

"Two days? Lucifer's monstrous arms couldna keep me abed for two days for such a trifling wound."

He pulled his kilt down to cover himself. Nothing looked so unmanly as a warrior with a bandage too close to his private jewels!

The night turned colder as Elyne washed the dinner dishes and prepared for breaking their fast when the sun rose again. She laid out the bowls and spoons, measured the oats in a cup and got dried fruits from the food storage chest.

She worried her lower lip wondering if she should share her bed with him. It seemed like a good idea for she could keep track of any fever he might have. But she was still leery of him. What if he became angry because she caused him to become sick?

When his skin flushed and he seemed listless, she yawned and pretended she yearned to sleep. As she walked toward the bed, she swept up his pillow off the floor and the extra blanket. She put the pillow under his leg and spread the blanket over him.

"It is so cold tonight I dinna think I can sleep alone."

"Ye want to make bed sport tonight?" His brows rose in disbelief. "Lady, yer timing is truly off."

"Did I say anything about swiving? I thought only to share our body warmth. Ye built up the fire, but during the night, it will die down and we shall be cold."

His eyes were beginning to look shiny and lifeless. She made him a strong tea from the betony hoping it would bring his fever down. He wouldn't drink his until she also had a cup.

"I canna chase ye through the woods and check each trap if ye have one of yer crazy dreams, lass. For truth, ye should have two cups!"

He leered at her, but it was so lopsided she laughed for the first time since she'd left Raptor.

Finally, she had him tucked into bed with cold cloths on his forehead. She doubted she'd get much rest this night.

For the next two days, Elyne found little time to sleep. Graemme's fever raged. She kept poultices on the angry wound with hot compresses atop. By the third night, his fever broke and he slept quietly.

The next morn, she rose early and made a thin gruel for him when he woke. She had time to freshen herself at the small loch. There was nothing like cold water to make a person feel lively when they are about to drop from lack of sleep. Too, she was tired of smelling of sweat and smoke from the fire. Carefully, she laid a blanket to wrap herself in after her hurried bath. She shivered even looking at the water, but she didn't have time to wait until the fireplace was clear to heat water and bathe in the small basin. Graemme needed food and hot water as soon as he awakened.

Taking a deep breath, she stripped her clothing over her head and jumped into the water. She wasn't brave enough to walk into it.

Ice! She could be covered with snow and not be as cold as she was now. She took a gulp of air when she broke the surface and started rubbing her arms and chest as briskly as she could. Can a person freeze solid in just a few breaths?

Well, drats! She was clean enough. It would have to do.

She heaved herself out of the water and was reaching for her blanket. It was gone!

Of a sudden, all Hell broke loose!

Graemme awoke feeling uneasy. The bed was no longer warm and comfortable. What had startled him? He remained still and listened.

Ah! 'Twas Squat's low, throaty snarls at the door. Graemme struggled out of bed and limped toward it. He peeked through a slight crack in the wood. A short distance away stood two men.

"Shh, there be a dog inside," one man whispered.

"So? He isna a problem. Kill him." The second man was larger and dumber, for his voice rose.

"And warn the nekid lass? Best ye quiet yer flapping tongue. We'll hide in the woods. When she gets out of the water, we'll grab her."

"Aye! I dinna want to go in after her. I took me bath not two months ago. Not time for anither."

"Ha! I'll swive her first. I dinna want yer filth rubbing off on her and then to me." He sniggered and heartily scratched his crotch where his hardened cock bobbed with his efforts. "Ye can watch and learn!"

The dumb lout snorted. "She'll welcome me after she sees yer little prick. While ye ram yer bitty thing in her, I'll kill the dog."

They moved away from the door with little regard to secrecy.

Bile rose to Graemme's throat. He couldn't bear the thought of what they would do to Elyne if he didn't summon enough strength to kill the men. All his pain and weakness left as energy surged through him.

Reaching above the fireplace, he grabbed a mace hanging from a nail. Spying his broadsword on the floor beside the bed, he swooped it up. He ignored his boots. They'd make too much noise. He gritted his teeth as he climbed out the back window. Circling around the woods, he drew near the water. He waited and scanned the trees surrounding it.

Two men in filthy kilts tried to hide behind the bushes. One clutched a blanket in his hand. He recognized it as one Elyne had wrapped herself in as she sat in the chair beside the bed last eve. Their faces picked up interest as she started to move in the water. One man, the dumber of the two he supposed, drooled so much that dirty streaks ran down his chest.

He glanced toward where they stared. The desire to gouge their eyes out near overcame him. They had no right to feast their eyes on his bride as she was!

When Elyne rose from the water, no goddess could be more beautiful. The sun finally broke through the clouds above and turned her hair's amber highlights to molten gold. The two fools sprang out from behind the trees, tripping on their feet in their eagerness. It gave him a little time while they picked themselves up. He had to reach them afore they could grab her. If they did, he would have a hard time killing them without harming her.

And kill them he would!

He wouldna let them lay their filthy hands on his beautiful, feisty Elyne

As Elyne stepped out of the water, Graemme ran toward her screaming a battle cry which terrified her. Long black hair whipped back from his face. His eyes blazed with blood lust. The veins in his neck stood out in livid ridges. With lips contorted in a grotesque snarl baring his teeth, he looked ready to pounce and rip out her throat.

Rising fever had made him berserk!

He intended to kill her, just as she'd feared!

Elyne screeched when he raised his sword and started his backswing.

"Down!" he roared at her.

Did he mean to behead her on the ground?

Strange. He didn't look at her but at something behind her.

Though terrified of him, her instinct told her to obey his command.

She huddled on the ground and made herself as small as she could.

The sword swooshed as it cut the air. Her hair fluttered. A strange sound followed. Something fell and rolled in the leaves. A scant time after, a body hit the ground beside her.

Warm blood splattered her. The man had no head! She didn't scream. If she had, she would have choked. She heaved until all that came from her stomach was yellow, bitter fluid.

It was not over.

Another man howled and tried to run. Gramme swung the mace with his left hand. It bashed into the back of the lout's head. Its iron studs embedded in his skull.

With a loud thump, the filthy churl fell like a log.

Graemme leaned over, his hands steadying his knees as they wobbled.

Still filled with blood lust, he growled, "Are ye harmed, lass?"

"Nay. I had no warning they were here."

"Do ye see any other's lurking in the woods, wife? Since I see two of ye, I dinna trust my sight.

He could not see clearly! He blinked his eyes and shook his head. Hopefully, there was only one of her now.

She swiveled her head, her gaze searching for anything unusual.

"Nay, no one."

Saints help her! Was he going to fall?

Elyne jumped up and paid no heed to the gory scene around her. She tried to put her shoulder under his left arm so he could lean on her. They took one step together. He used his sword as an aid to walk, but it wasn't enough.

Graemme slithered to his knees, but kept an iron grip on his sword hilt.

A horse thundered toward the lodge, scaring Elyne so much she ran back to the dead man and grabbed the blood-soaked handle of the mace. Giving it two mighty tugs, it released the man's skull. She jumped, spreading her legs wide to avoid the spiked iron ball near hitting her legs.

A single horseman came down the path. They were ready for him should he belong to the other two. Elyne ran to stand beside Graemme, her nostrils flaring and eyes blazing murderously. They could not see the horse or its rider from where they stood.

Squat barked ferociously.

The man banged on the door. It squeaked when he opened it.

CHAPTER 24

ELYNE EXPECTED TO HEAR Squat fighting the intruder, but his frenzied barking changed tone. He sounded excited and happy, happier than he'd ever greeted her!

Relief washed through her. Squat knew the visitor.

She near fell to her knees in relief when Ranald, dressed in his usual black clothing and robe, came around the lodge and turned toward the wood. Squat followed so close, he looked like he wanted to lean into the walking man.

"Elyne! Graemme! Where are ye? If ye're swiving in the woods, get yerselves back! It's time to return to Raptor and wed, whether ye wish it or no."

When Squat saw Elyne and Graemme, he came running and yipping, as happy as a dog can be on finding its owners. By the time Ranald reached them, the crazy dog was sniffing the corpses, then turned his back toward them and dug with his rear bowed legs, raining dirt down on the bodies.

"By God's brows, sister. Ye look like a Valkyrie ready to swing that bloody mace to dispatch another soul to Hell and not Valhalla." He looked her over closely. "Are ye hurt? Do ye know ye're blood-splattered?"

Unable to form words, she shook her head for his first question and nodded for the second. She'd started to shiver and her teeth chattered, which was strange. She should be relieved now her brother was here to protect them.

"Do ye also know ye are both nekid?"

She looked down and flushed.

He spoke low and soothingly as he walked toward her. Gently, he pried the mace from her hand. Removing his black cloak, he spread it around her shoulders, uttering soft soothing sounds.

"Ye are safe, now, love. But we must see to Graemme. He looks the worse for wear."

"I am fine. Take care of her." Graemme's voice was strained and weak. "I think she hasna seen a man beheaded afore."

"Aye. Being set upon by those two would ruin anyone's day."

Graemme didn't have the strength left to swing a weapon. He was relieved when Ranald helped him to rise then took his sword and laid it on the ground with the mace. He felt near to passing out, so maybe he imagined what he saw.

Ranald looked around the clearing, ignored the dead bodies but fixed his gaze on the leaves and small branches. His eyes held such determination Graemme wondered for what he searched. Suddenly, a wind started to blow. Leaves and branches lifted and hovered above the bloody weapons then fluttered to the ground until they hid them from view. It happened so suddenly Graemme blinked.

Ranald grinned at him. "That should keep them out of sight until I get you two inside."

Walking over, he put his arm around Elyne's shoulder and led her inside the lodge then turned to be sure Graemme was still behind him.

"Did I tell ye, ye look like Lucifer had hold of ye and dragged ye around the woods this past sennight? What happened to yer leg?" He stopped and eyed Squat. "This little beastie doesna look ferocious."

"A little mistake."

"Little? Dinna tell me ye set a trap and caught yerself?" Ranald's dark plum-colored eyes crinkled at the corners.

He settled Elyne in a chair at the table and put water on to boil.

"Ye both look like ye need a bit of care. Elyne. If ye feel up to it while I get my bag from Satan's Spawn, wash off the bastards' blood and dress yerself. Graemme, sit on the bed. Get yer leg up. It's swelling."

"What about the bodies," Elyne asked in a quavering voice.

"They dinna mind waiting until after I've finished caring for the living."

He picked up Squat, turned and strode out the door.

Elyne poured water in the basin, smeared a glob of soap on a cloth and scrubbed her body so hard she near took the skin from it.

"I wish ye had not seen what ye did today, Elyne."

For truth, Graemme sounded sorry she had.

"Ye took his head with one swing," she said and gagged. Covering her mouth and closing her eyes, she tried to wipe the memory from her mind.

"Aye. One swift act is merciful. Two is torture."

"When you readied to strike, how did ye know I would drop down? My head could be out there in the dirt."

She rinsed the cloth and thought she'd cleaned off all the horrible blood splatters. Dumping the soiled water out the window, she refilled the basin. She almost screamed when Graemme's hand reached around her and took the cloth.

"Hold still while I wash yer back. The louts were behind ye, so ye got more blood and, er, other stuff, on yer back than front."

He sounded almost out of breath with the effort. She spun around and tried to take the cloth from him.

"Ranald said ye should be on the bed!"

He raised his hand high, out of her reach. "I will after I've soaped yer back. Be still, else I'll fall. Ranald will think ye tripped me in my pitiful state."

How could he try to joke at such a time? She felt guilty enough. She sure as Hades didna want him fainting at her feet. Ranald would scold her for even allowing him to walk around.

When he rinsed the cloth of its soap, she was startled to see the water turn so red. He threw it out the window and poured a fresh basin full from the pot heating at the fireplace.

"Ranald's cloak will need washing. It wiped most of if off yer back," he muttered.

His hands got slower and slower as he wiped off the soap. Finally, he was done and dropped the cloth in the basin.

She turned and put her arm around him to help him back to the bed. On the way, she started to tremble again thinking how close they'd come to being dead. They would have killed Graemme, then after taking their turns raping her, 'twas probable they would have slit her throat.

"Ye didna say how ye knew ye'd not lop off my head instead of his."

"I knew ye would obey."

She almost stopped in her tracks, but the faster she got him to the bed the better. He might be losing strength, but his injury didn't seem to lessen his thoughts of swiving. She had ample evidence. Whenever his left hand *happened* to brush against her breast, he hardened further.

"Are ye daft? Ye *knew* I would obey ye?" She drew his thoughts away from sex. "How? Do ye think ye have tamed me so I will respond to yer voice?"

"Tame? Ye?" Graemme snorted. Loud. "Ye responded to the command to drop down. It was not a request. 'Twas the urgency in my voice. It made ye do as I said to keep yerself safe."

They had reached the bed. When he sat, she grasped his ankle and helped lift his leg onto the bed. He eased back on the pillows, looked up at her and winked.

"Mayhap ye had best dress now, unless ye'd like a tussle between the sheets?"

How could he sound so hopeful when he was near to passing out?

"Ha! Not likely," she made her voice as firm as she could, since it still quavered a little.

She turned her back to Graemme and hurried over to a peg on the wall where she'd hung a green smock and kirtle at dawn. No sooner had she pulled it on than Ranald called out he was coming in.

His body filled the doorframe. Squat squeezed between Ranald's legs, near tripping him. Not only did her brother have his supplies from his horse, but he carried Graemme's sword and the mace. He had washed the gore off both.

Ranald's gaze took in everything in the room with one quick sweep.

"Nothing has changed. 'Tis as if Moridac will walk into the room at any moment, bragging about his hunt for the day," he said.

Elyne's heart tripped seeing the beauty of the left side of his face lit in a wistful smile. 'Twas indeed as if his twin was there. Had Moridac lived, their appearance would be identical... except for the scars on the other side of Ranald's face.

He placed his large leather pouch of healing herbs on the table then hung the mace back on the empty nail. Carrying the sword over to the bed, he propped it against the wall near enough for Graemme to reach it easily.

Elyne went over to open the pouch and spread its contents on the table, selecting the jars, stoppered bottles and crushed herbs she knew would heal wounds. She rinsed the basin with hot water then half-filled it. On the small table beside the bed, she put it and the cloths she kept washed and clean for dressing Graemme's leg.

"Well, now, let me see what ye have been up to," he said as he started unwinding the bandage. When he had bared Graemme's leg down to the skin, he looked up in surprise.

"Teeth marks? And not from Squat, nor yer departed friends, eh?"

He looked from one flushed face to the other.

"Well, 'tis not likely ye bit yerself. Ye do remember ye were here to learn to know each other so yer marriage would be calm and peaceful? Looks to me ye decided to go at each other with tooth and hand." He raised his right brow, the scar crossing through it making him look even more quizzical.

"From the mark of a hand on yer right nether cheek, Elyne, I would say ye either started or ye finished an argument?"

"He started it! He told me packing mud on my face would smooth the wrinkles I've added to my face from frowning."

Ranald glanced up and studied her face then shook his head. "What wrinkles?"

She gasped and felt over her face. "Between my brows and

around my eyes!"

Her brother ducked his head. Still, he couldn't wipe the grin off his face.

"Lucifer's wagging tongue! Watch her else she'll dump another bucket of mud over me!"

"A bucket?"

"Aye. Not one but two! After I had hunted all day trying to find grouse for her dinner, I was bathing in a pool of ice water. She tried to drown me, too."

"It served you right. Ye were pig-headed and didn't heed me when I told ye it would rain and ye should take a cloak."

Ranald shook his head as he kept changing one hot cloth for another. Finally, he probed around the cleaned wound. "This can only be yer work on his leg, Elyne. I recognize yer bite from the time Moridac teased ye saying yer tits were getting bigger than yer head!" He stopped to look at her. "Did ye do it underwater?"

Graemme answered for her. "Nay, she did it whist swinging upside down!"

"Hmm." After putting another hot compress on the wound, Ranald sat back in his chair. "Whilst I wait for this to cool, I think ye'd best tell me all."

When they both started talking at the same time, he held up one finger. They shut up.

"One at the time." He pointed to Graemme. "You start."

Graemme told of his miserable day and of her giving him the mud bath. He admitted he had mayhem on his mind when he started to chase her.

She interrupted him to tell her brother the miserable man she was to marry had put snares around the woods to catch her like some wild game. Then he let her twirl and struggle until she was dizzy. Naturally, she wouldn't let him treat her like some pig held up for bleeding, so she grabbed him. The only spot she could reach was his thigh.

"If yer precious parts ye are so afeared of losing had been in reach, ye would be one short of a pair!"

"See! Yer sister is begging for a beating."

"Begging? Ye already struck me."

"Before or after the bite?" Ranald quirked his head to the side.

"After." Elyne flushed and lowered her eyes.

"Well, now, then ye are even. Mud for Mud. A hand print for teeth marks." He shook his head. "The two of ye are worse than my twins. He pulls her hair. She cuts his in his sleep. We will see what Grunda has to say about yer sennight together."

Elyne gasped when he lifted the hot compress off Graemme's leg. Two of the marks on his leg had swelled even more, the flesh leading from them red and angry. They looked filled with putrid fluid near to bursting the skin. Ranald stood and took a thin knife from amongst his things then put it in the boiling water. She busied herself getting more clean squares of cloth and spreading a thicker drying cloth beneath his leg.

Walking over to the food storage box, she looked at each bottle before she selected one slightly different from the others. It wasna wine but a potent drink the Scots brewed in caves close to waterfalls where they could collect the purest water. She poured a generous amount in a cup and brought it over.

"Ye're going to pour this on yer handiwork?"

"Nay, fool! 'Tis for ye to drink so ye dinna squeal like a girl getting her time of the moon."

She lifted his head and held it to his lips. After the first tentative sips, he rolled his eyes.

"Why have ye not offered this afore? 'Tis our favorite in the Highlands. Ye canna get cold after a few cups of it."

"Believe me, 'tis Chief Broccin's favored drink, also." Ranald came over holding the handle of the knife with a padded cloth and sat down. "This will hurt, but I have to release the poisons else they will spread through yer blood and kill ye."

Before Graemme could worry about it further, Ranald quickly cut through the two spots. Graemme grunted through teeth gnashed together. Elyne had wet cloths ready to catch the fluid as it spurted out of the wounds. A few squeezes from Ranald, and the flesh emptied. After he cleaned out the wound, he inspected the ugly smelling fluid.

"As I suspected. Elyne's teeth forced dirt into the wounds. Luckily, I always carry jars of creams and waxes made from chickweed wintergreen. The good Brother Cadfael came through Kelso Abbey several times and taught me much about wounds. It should heal quickly now."

While Graemme caught his breath, his new brother-by-law placed a heavy poultice of the ointments on his leg and held it with clean bandages.

"I dinna want ye on yer feet until the morrow. Unfortunately, we canna delay longer. Raptor's guests are getting restless. Chief Broccin threatens to bring everyone here to have Father Martin perform the wedding vows."

"Brother, he's marrying me off to a man who will beat me every time I thwart him. Ye saw the bruise!"

"Ye're the one who first angered me. I told ye once our family motto is *With a Strong Hand*."

Graemme snorted and chuckled. No doubt, the strong drink had made the man mindless.

Ranald looked at him and grinned. "I think ye got the better end of the fight, Elyne. Ye should watch yerself, though. He might decide to take a hunk out of yer arse the next time ye decide to act like a man." He stopped and studied Graemme. "Be wary, Graemme, if she picks up a sword. 'Tis more lethal than teeth."

Elyne was near as exhausted from the morning as Graemme. Whenever Ranald moved, Squat followed him. He seemed to want to know what was going on and was suspicious of the salves and elixirs. Every time Ranald stopped for something, Squat laid on his back, inviting him to pet his stomach. He declined until after he was through treating Graemme. Then he bent over and ruffled up the dog's fur and, putting one big hand on his underbelly, rocked him back and forth until Squat's tongue lolled out with joy.

She was grateful when her brother led her to sit her down at the table. Squat stood on his barrel legs and begged to get in her lap. She picked him up and he was snoring in a short time.

Ranald went over to inspect the gruel. "It has been on for a while, but a little extra water will thin it out," he said as he added some and stirred. "I picked some wild fruit on the way. With butter, honey and nuts, it will help make a filling meal."

"Nay. I have not found any nuts. I already checked the food bin." Graemme volunteered.

"Ye didna know there is a storage area under the floor?"

Ranald pulled the bins out of the way. Beneath them was a trap door with a hole in the top to open it. When he pulled it up, he reached inside and took out several jars of preserved apples and pears, crocks of mixed nuts, a salted ham and more flour.

Seeing Elyne's surprised look, he spoke up.

"Domnall must have thought ye knew everything about the lodge, else he would have shown ye where the storage area was in case hunting proved scarce."

Before long, he had made oat cakes and put them in the fireplace oven. He sliced ham which soon sizzled in a pan as he explored another treasure trove with enough bowls to feed eight people.

After Ranald made sure the two had eaten enough to help bring back their strength, he felt over Graemme's body. He had cooled from his fever but would bear watching when night began to fall. He expected it would go up again. Hopefully, for the last time.

They had to leave in the morning. Though he had joked about his father bringing the wedding guests here in the woods, he didn't doubt the Chief and Father Michael, along with members of their family, would appear by another day or two to see the union tied tight and proper.

"Graemme has fallen into a much needed sleep, Elyne. I suggest ye do the same."

He was glad his sister didn't argue but gave him a grateful smile and went to curl up on the bed as far away as possible from Graemme.

Ranald grinned. She was defiant even when the man slept. Poor Graemme would have a time taming his strong-willed sister!

Scooping up Squat, he eased out the door and proceeded to find a proper burial place for the two louts. They didn't deserve to rest for eternity in the lovely surroundings. Deep in the woods would be more appropriate. He no sooner had cleared the area when Colyne and Brian came trudging through the bushes.

"When we approached the door, we heard Graemme's snoring so loud I wondered how yer sister could sleep through the noise," Brian announced.

"Aye. 'Tis best they sleep it off. They look like they've had a pitched battle here this past sennight." Colyne grinned. "Saw two buckets out there. Did she poison him again?"

"Quiet, Squat." Ranald pointed to the ground, and the barking dog immediately quieted and spread out on his stomach, his head resting on his paws. "Nay. They had a difference of opinion. I'll tell ye of it while ye help me get the bodies beneath the ground."

"Magnus and Graemme do the same. They leave no bodies above ground by nightfall."

The three men dug a hole large enough to hold both bodies and had them covered in record time. Ranald stood at the head of the grave and said prayers for the dead with as much dignity as he had as Brother Ranald at Kelso Abbey.

When they finished, they stripped off their clothes and jumped into the water. Brian and Colyne were their usual playful selves but respected Ranald's restrained personality. They were still enjoying the chilly water when Elyne came around the path, rubbing yer eyes and yawning. When she saw the men, she blushed and turned her back.

"I see yer husband-to-be has already cured ye of spying on men, little one," Ranald said with a laugh.

"He hasna *cured* me of anything. Nor will he." She boldly turned around and glared at him. "I have seen ye nekid afore, brother."

Ranald chuckled under his breath, for he saw she avoided looking at the other two men. Mayhap Graemme had indeed begun to tame his bride!

Soon after dawn the next morn, Ranald redressed Graemme's wound and pronounced him ready to travel. After Graemme finally answered his two friends prying questions, Elyne threw up her hands and stalked out of the building. She had to. Had she heard one more request to see her bruised nether check, she'd have taken Graemme's sword and chased his teasing friends all the way back to Raptor Castle.

Ranald insisted everyone have a meal to break their fast, for they would arrive at Raptor after the sun passed westward. With all the people at the castle to witness the wedding, there might be next to nothing left from their noon meal.

When Graemme helped her to mount, she steeled herself not to wince. Never would she have believed a simple wallop on the arse could cause discomfort for more than a day. But then, it hadn't been a simple wallop at all. Furious, Graemme had used all his strength. Since all eyes but Ranald's watched her to see her reaction, she acted unconcerned and near bounced down on the saddle. She almost gulped and regretted her pretended unconcern. Rather than have them think Graemme had been able to punish her to where she minded it the least bit, she'd rather parade around with mud on her face.

"Why are ye not ready to ride? Ye stand around staring like ye expect to see a court jester ready to make ye laugh."

She urged her horse up beside Ranald and didn't wait for Graemme to mount and follow. Brian and Colyne were still arguing over who should carry Squat when she entered the forest road.

Her hair flew out behind her and the dew wet air on her face felt refreshing. She rode to the left of Ranald, for she knew he never allowed anyone on the right. 'Twould hinder drawing his claymore from the sling on his back.

Watching him, she could easily see why everyone from the northern Highlands to the south of Northumbria called him the Black Raptor. He ignored a helmet this day. His midnight black hair flew freely around his face, his black cloak lifted from his body and flapped on either side like huge wings. He preferred black breeches and shirts or black tunics, unlike his twin who had worn only bright, colorful fabrics.

Ranald felt her gaze, for he glanced at her and flashed a smile. She would miss him deeply, but he had promised he and his family would come to visit her at Clibrick Castle. If ever she needed him, she knew he would be there.

Graemme couldn't believe a mere woman could ride astride and keep up with the man beside her. He was glad it had rained the day afore. If not, he would be riding in the dust behind them. The hunting lodge was closer to Raptor Castle than he had realized. Once they cleared the forest path behind the castle, Ranald slowed his pace so Graemme could ride to the left of Elyne over the open countryside.

When guards on the wall walks spotted them, the castle piper shrilled a welcoming tune. By the time they reached the drawbridge and slowed to canter across it, the front bailey filled with people waving and calling out their names. Graemme was surprised at the welcome, for they called his name as well as Elyne's and Ranald's.

They rode up to the foot of the keep's steps. Chief Broccin and Aunt Joneta stood on the second step with Magnus and Muriele beside her aunt on the right, and Ranald's wife Catalin beside her father-by-law. Eager to see her family, Elyne stood in the stirrups and slung her leg over the hind end of her horse. Bracing herself with her hands on the saddle, she slipped her left foot out of the stirrups and sprang to the ground afore Graemme could help her. The women quickly surrounded her. She hugged Muriele and leaned back so she could run her fingers through Muriele's gold and amber colored hair.

"It has grown back even lovelier than it was afore," Elyne said.

Catalin laughed and kissed Elyne's cheek. "Aye. We did a good job, did we not?"

"Well, lass, are ye ready to obey yer father and marry young Graemme here?" Chief Broccin interrupted.

"Do ye give me a choice?" She looked guiltily at Muriele.

After greeting Elyne, Muriele had moved into Magnus' embrace and leaned into his side. 'Twas readily apparent she loved him, though Elyne couldn't understand how she could after all he'd put her through.

"Child, ye have added gray hairs to my head," Aunt Joneta said as she squeezed her tight. "I had a messenger from Raik. He and Letia couldna come for the children suffered from bad colds in their chest."

"I will miss them, but they canna take a chance with the children. The weather turns cold one day and warm the next."

"Aye. Grunda says I am not to worry. She says they will be bedeviling their father in less than a sennight."

Glancing around, Elyne saw many people from surrounding castles. 'Twas a surprise, for Chief Broccin had never been a friendly sort. But after Ranald had returned from Kelso, when someone required help to fend off marauders, he had always responded. He had helped most of them at one time or the other, either with his healing skills or fighting prowess.

Elyne felt eyes boring into her and turned to look upward. Beside the doorway to the keep, Ysabel and Grunda stood, watching everything below. Ysabel gave Elyne a hesitant smile then her gaze searched through the throng of people until she found Colyne. Why, her eyes lit up and her cheeks flushed like a young maiden!

Grunda stirred, bringing Elyne's gaze back to her. The old crone looked from Elyne to Graemme, who had been so close to Elyne's back since they'd arrived he might as well shackle her to his ankle! She glanced at him and was alarmed seeing his face was so pale. She frowned at Ranald, who had finally finished talking to Catalin. He glanced at Graemme and immediately came over.

"Father, we are tired and hungry. Let us retire to the Great Hall and have ale and something to appease our hunger."

"Retire to the Great Hall?" Chief Broccin snorted. "Ye all may retire to yer rooms to freshen up. Father Matthew has been waiting at the church since Grunda said ye were on the way."

"What! I am not ready to wed today!" Elyne had a hard

time keeping her jaw from flapping open.

"Ye will be. Yer mother and I wed hours after we met each other. Ye have had a sennight and more to get to know Sir Graemme." His jaw squared and he glared at her, defying her to offer any more resistance.

When he turned and started up the stairway, his voice floated back to her. Though she was but two steps below him, he spoke as loud as if she was some distance away.

"Anyone can see yer groom is tired. From the way ye were going at it by the well, ye've already wore his arse out. He needs to get the wedding over so he can get some rest."

CHAPTER 25

SURELY 'TWAS THE STRANGEST wedding in the Lowlands of Scotland!

Everything was ready and waiting for them, from the festive decorations of the Great Hall to her wedding attire spread out on the bed. When she learned she had Grunda to thank for it, she wanted to swat the old lady on her nether parts. The old seer had told Chief Broccin three days earlier exactly when the couple would reappear.

Everything became a blur from the time they entered the great doors of the keep until she arrived at the door to the church. Aunt Joneta, Catalin and Muriele giggled and lifted her spirits, while Ada and Ysabel helped her in her bath.

"I had time on my hands since Aunt Joneta and your Father played with the children and kept them from under my feet," Catalin said, holding up a light blueberry-colored kirtle with long flowing sleeves.

On the square neckline and the edges of the flowing sleeves, she had embroidered butterflies sitting on branches with vividly colored threads. They rivaled the beauty of Catalin's striking hair which was either gold or red, depending on the brightness of the sun.

"'Tis beautiful! But I thought ye hated needle-work."

Catalin grinned. "I like peace and quiet more than I hate needle-work! 'Twas a good exchange, I believe."

Elyne tried to prolong her bath, but after her father sent Domnall to rap on her door and tell her the Chief was beginning to be ill tempered, Elyne surged out of the tub. The women refrained from commenting on the bruised outline of a man's hand on her nether cheek. Once she was dry, they slid her smock on then the lovely kirtle. Aunt Joneta selected a belt made of silver rings and tied it low on Elyne's hips. A matching silver band held her unruly hair back from her eyes.

Still, she practically drug her feet until Chief Broccin himself banged on the door so hard she feared he would crack the wood.

"Get yerself out here if ye dinna want to be escorted to the church nekid, daughter!"

"Hault yer scolding, Brither!"

Aunt Joneta frowned at the door as if her brother could see her. He didn't need to. She had trained herself to speak as their neighbors did to the south. When Joneta's Scottish brogue became thick, all of Raptor knew not to prick her temper. She took Elyne by the shoulders and peered into her eyes.

"Now, child, delay will nay change the day. By nightfall, ye will be married. But ye'd best not make yer groom wait. Ye didna slip him a draught which will make him unable to, er, perform, did ye?"

Muriele gasped so loud it caused Elyne to glance over her shoulder at her. Her friend looked horrified.

"Graemme is a gentle man, Elyne," Muriele said. "He threatened Magnus with bodily harm did he learn Magnus had mistreated me. He made his brother explain the cuts and bruises covering my body were not his doing, but my own for falling out of a tree!"

Elyne snorted. "Huh! Ye all got very quiet of a sudden when ye saw my nekid nether cheek. He wasna so gentle then!"

Aunt Joneta's hands dropped from Elyne's shoulders and her lips tightened disapprovingly. After all, she knew Elyne better than anyone else did.

"Did ye break yer vow not to poison Sir Graemme again?"

Elyne groaned. "Nay, I didna. I'm sure Grunda can give ye an accounting without my saying a word." She stamped her foot and marched toward the door. "Well, come on, then. We'd best get the vows done. The men will drink themselves into a stupor if they dinna get food in their guts."

When she reached the door, she gave a mighty tug and it flew open to bang against the wall. She almost got her forehead rapped, for Colyne stood outside with his knuckles raised.

"Well, I am pleased I dinna have to break down the door," he said with a silly grin.

"Why would ye dare to do such?" She raised a brow and waited for his answer.

"Graemme said I was to take an axe to it if ye had barricaded yerself inside." Colyne looked only too happy to relay his information. "He seems impatient to consummate the wedding. I think he longs to sleep," he said with a light snicker.

He hiccupped then slapped his hand over his mouth. 'Twas obvious he'd had a few swigs of the strong Scottish drink distilled from rye. They called it *usquebaugh* the 'water of life,' but why, she didn't know. It seemed to make fools of even wise men.

"Keep yer tongue behind yer teeth, fool," Brian said as he came up behind him. "She is dressed and ready for the wedding, not the bedding."

"But they already had a bedding. In the woods. Remember?" Colyne looked confused. "Oh! Squat wanted to be in the wedding, too, but yer brother willna let him."

"Squat knows nothing of weddings." Elyne said with disgust.

"Does too. He scrambled, uh," he took his hand and swirled it in the air, "ye know, what was in big pewter pitchers is now on the steps? Ate some, too."

"Flowers?" Aunt Joneta supplied.

Brian nodded. "Made him spew all over the floor. Servants are cleaning up now."

"Aye. 'Tis why the Black Raptor wouldna let him attend the wedding. Had to give him a tonic to quiet his stomach."

Brian rolled his eyes then near fell over when it made him dizzy. "I know ye are eager and wish to run to yer groom, but 'twould be better if ye walk... slooow."

Colyne grinned now they'd relayed what was going on below. Two very large hands separated the two men. Ranald quietly turned them around and pointed to the stairwell.

"Go and tell Sir Graemme his bride is on her way."

They bobbed their heads and tussled with each other as to who was going down the spiral stairs first. If they weren't careful, they'd both end at the bottom with broken limbs.

"I am sorry, little one. The Chief grew tired of waiting and brought out the barrels too early. Now half the men are tripping over their feet. Including him."

He held out his arm and Elyne tried to still her trembling when she placed her hand on it. He covered it with his own and gave her a gentle squeeze of encouragement. Aunt Joneta arranged the ladies in pairs and they followed the brother and sister down the stairwell, through the Great Hall and out into the bailey.

"Dinna worry. The servants will set the room to rights afore we get back," he said as they walked through the Great Hall. Servants were frantically straightening the white table cloths, replacing the pewter goblets with clean ones and picking up the tipped over benches.

When they went through the great doors, everyone had gathered on the sides of the stairs leading down and along the path to the small church in the corner of the bailey. The women all cheered but the men were busy belching and weaving.

Elyne saw wives pinching husbands' arms, forcing them to be quiet and stand straight. Elyne couldn't hold back a giggle.

"'Tis a wonder they dinna tweak their ears. The warriors dinna look to have touched a drop," she whispered to her brother.

"They know better than to drink afore I have released them from duties," Ranald said with a smile down at her. "We need 'sober' witnesses, after all."

Elyne clutched his arm as they walked between the people lining the path. She spied her father waiting at the foot of the stairs to the church. By his blurry eyes, he must have been the first to toast the coming wedding. When they drew near, Ranald relinquished her arm and placed her hand on Chief Broccin's arm. Ranald stayed behind her as they walked up to the steps to meet Graemme.

Graemme and Magnus stood together, both sober and

dressed in beautiful wedding attire. They wore forest green bonnets, green, black and blue woolen kilts held at the shoulders of their creamy white shirts with the Morgan Clan pin. Her nether cheeks had good reason to believe the motto etched in Latin on it. Their white stockings had black tassels above the tops of their shiny black boots.

Though Magnus looked relaxed, Graemme's face was still pale and drawn. She was grateful when he gave her an encouraging smile and looked at her with eyes that said she was beautiful beyond what he had expected.

From there on until the end, the ceremony passed in a blur. Father Matthew must have had orders to keep it brief for he nearly flew through the vows and had a short mass afterward. She did not remember repeating the vows after Father Matthew until it was over. When he said "promise to never give him concoctions to disable him in any way," she heard herself repeating the words though she had determined beforehand she would not.

Graemme's kiss afterward was stunning. She found herself enfolded in a warm embrace, his mouth slowly lowered to hers and he bent her backward over his arm with an enthusiastic kiss which left her breathless. Her heart beat to a wild rhythm like someone in her chest played an ancient Celtic Bodhran with its bone tippers.

When they straightened, her father was the first to grab her in his arms. She was shocked to see tear tracks down his cheeks. Never once in his life had he said "I love ye," but she felt it in his bear hug and heard it in his whisper, "If ever yer dreams prove true and he harms ye, I will tear him limb from limb."

He released her for the rest of the crowd to greet her as Graemme's wife. Men looked toward the Black Raptor and restrained their drunken ardor. They didna want their ears singed. Others not familiar with Ranald's strange gifts looked to old Grunda and quickly sobered. Everyone knew the old seer could cause a man's precious parts to wither and become useless!

The Great Room's rafters flew banners honoring their guests. Whoever had a hand in hanging them had done a fine job, for each one complemented the colors of the first and so on throughout the room. Colorful tapestries were spaced apart on the walls, some depicting events in the lives of Raptor Castle's families; others were of the mountains and scenery around the Castle.

An impressive array of weapons filled in where tapestries wouldn't be appropriate. Chief Broccin's tunic, cape, shield, helmet and sword from the Crusades were on a corner stand, made specifically to display a warrior's armor.

On the opposite corner, Elyne was startled to see Ranald's monk's clothing displayed the same way, though it seemed strange to see a shiny Claymore claymore strapped across the back. She glanced at her brother and saw he stared at it. Did he ever miss being a monk?

Certainly, life was more peaceful at Kelso, except when raiders crossed the borders and tried to steal everything of value. Once he became the Abbey's Protector, the raids soon ended. When he left, he made sure another warrior monk, as well-trained as he had been, took over.

The family banners hung above the fireplace. Out of courtesy, Ranald had hung Magnus' banner next to his brother's. The ferocious faces of the two wolves often drew her eyes. They seemed to watch her, which made her more than uneasy.

Large pottery vases painted with woodland scenes and filled with all types and colors of flowers were on pedestals throughout the room. At the high tables, etched pewter plates, goblets and spoons sat near folded cloths to wipe the juices off chins.

Graemme seated her at the center of the high table then took the chair beside her. They were in the place of honor with the Chief and Aunt Joneta beside them.

A rousing round of toasts started the feasting. If it continued along these lines, they would soon all be sliding off their benches and snoring beneath the tables.

"Ye dinna have to keep yer hands touching me every minute, pest," Elyne whispered to Graemme as she tried to pull her hand out from beneath his.

"Ah, but I find ye so soft and silky, my sweet mannered

wife," Graemme said and squeezed her hand.

"I dinna like to be handled like I am yer new possession." She frowned at him to make her point.

Graemme must be keeping an ear on the toasts, for he never missed raising the chalice high and then brought it to her lips until she drank before taking a swallow himself. He leaned toward her, put one hand on back of her head and pried her lips apart with his own. She near coughed when a flood of wine filled her mouth. He drew back and grinned at her when she could do naught but swallow. He put his cheek to hers, causing the men to applaud.

"But ye *are* a new possession, my affectionate one," he whispered. "I want to touch ye all over. Taste ye, too. It would please me if ye signaled yer women half-way through the food courses."

"Why would I do so?"

Her words were louder than she'd meant, for people looked to them awaiting his answer. They were disappointed when they couldn't hear his reply.

"So ye could go above and prepare yerself for me. 'Twould please me most to come into the room, throw back the covers and find ye nekid and yearning for my tarse. Why, it near takes my breath away just thinking on it."

"Ye may as well save yer breath, for it will never happen, ye swell-headed lout!"

"My lovely, docile bride, we have never made love with complete privacy and leisure. I can guarantee Magnus, Brian or Colyne won't be listening for yer moans of pleasure."

She flapped her hand in exasperation and ignored him.

As at many festive occasions, there were five courses to the meal. The first was a salad of chopped greens, along with shredded carrots dressed with oil and wine; fresh herbs and cheddar cheese, poached beets dressed with vinegar; bread and various butters; and to end it, a spiced honey and breadcrumb confection. Elyne barely picked at the food on her side of the silver wedding plate.

Ada had given her a review of the courses while she'd washed Elyne's hair, so she would know when Cook would serve her favorite foods.

While they awaited the next course, a tall, skinny man amused them by skillfully juggling ripe fruit. At the end of his act, he deliberately let each one land on his head, splattering himself with their juice. Thanks to the heavens, Graemme was amused enough to leave her alone.

Roasted pheasant was the main dish of the second course, along with diced turnips cooked in apple cider and butter, a variety of cooked greens, spiced pears in sweet wine syrup and sugar-glazed currant cookies.

They listened to a strolling minstrel singing tales about the great loves who made men as strong as the monster in Loch Ness when their lady loves were threatened.

Graemme snorted in disbelief. "They likely ran in the opposite direction so they might take a second wife. Of course, she'd be younger than the first." He looked sideways at her. "How old did yer father say ye were?"

She picked up her eating knife and aimed it at his hand. He was too quick for her and soon had the knife out of her reach. Chief Broccin looked at her and scowled.

Even though Elyne took the smallest bites of each course, she was soon full. Graemme's appetite seemed as hearty as Ranald's and the rest of the men, for when the third course arrived, they all cheered.

Her interest in the food picked up, for this course was her favorite. Roasted pork in wine and coriander sauce, mushrooms and green onions in creamed broth, broiled asparagus topped with roasted seeds and baked rice with apples.

"Return my eating knife, spineless husband."

"Nay, my evil-tempered wife."

Graemme selected the juiciest pieces with his fingertips and held them up to her lips. When he refused to take his hand away, she took a dainty bite, careful not to touch his fingers with her lips. He rubbed the juices on his fingers over her mouth, bent over and nibbled and licked her lips clean afore he kissed her. Of course, his actions caused a loud banging of cups and goblets on the tablets and cheers for 'More!'

When acrobats ran and tumbled into the room, it distracted the guests. But not long after, when it looked like the man atop nine others was about to fall into the hot fireplace, she near screamed. It wouldn't have mattered, for other women shrieked and covered their eyes. A heartbeat later, she realized it had been part of their act.

Would the eating and toasting never end? 'Twas impolite not to respond to a toast, so Elyne wet her lips and pretended to sip. Graemme was sparing on his own swallows, but when there is one toast after another, more than one groom had found himself not remembering fulfilling their wedding vows the next morn.

"Watch what ye drink, wife," Graemme said softly. "I dinna want to awaken a snoring wife so I may consummate the marriage! I like my women screaming and urging me on with lusty vigor!"

"Best ye watch yerself, husband." She snorted in scorn. "The rate ye are swilling the stuff, ye will be sleeping afore ye reach our bedchamber."

"Ach! Have ye not heard I have been known to swive comely lasses in my sleep and not lose a stroke?" He waggled his brows at her with a wicked look in his eyes.

Elyne snorted. Loud. And with scorn.

Domnall couldn't have done a better job.

CHAPTER 26

ELYNE FELT A STREAK of jealousy when she pictured Graemme, fast asleep and still swiving a woman. She brightened when she thought of the likelihood he would pass out from drink. She would keep to the edge of the bed or even sleep on the floor.

If he was unable to perform this night, she could have the marriage annulled the next morn stating he was not the virile man he appeared.

She didn't consider it overlong when it struck her mayhap she was already breeding. It had been two weeks from her courses the night she unfortunately gave herself to Graemme thinking to delay his capture of Muriele. Unfortunately, her courses had never occurred on schedule. Aunt Joneta claimed it was because she was overactive and worked as hard as many men did.

She scowled, for her sacrifice had been a total disaster... and unnecessary. In fact, all their bed sport had ended in her embarrassment. Magnus thought it amusing when he had come upon them in the stall. She was sure he thought her ready to swive whenever the breezes blew up her skirts!

When a balladeer, older than most, took a stool and began to strum a lute, her scowl turned to interest. He sang of Chief Broccin and his battles with the Turks, was careful in wording his sad lyrics about the twin who perished the day afore his wedding and of the other twin who came from God to fill his place.

The banners hanging above began gently swaying as if the great wooden doors had been propped open. Ranald had a tight reign on his feeling, but Elyne could see the strength it took. His lips pressed near white in concentration to hold back any reaction. When the man sang of the exploits of The Black Raptor, he relaxed a bit, a wry smile on his lips. It amused him when people imagined he could turn into a huge, black raptor when his anger peaked.

When the balladeer began a tale about Magnus the Ruthless and his brother, Graemme the Relentless, Ranald leaned back and grinned, relieved when the subject of the ballads had changed. The teller of tales sang about the lonely youth Olaf treated harshly until his squire, Sweyn, with hair as bright as fire, taught him fighting skills even his foster-father couldna equal. Only then did the harsh treatment stop. Elyne's ears picked up every word, hoping to learn more about the family who now was also hers.

She had not had enough time to talk to Muriele to learn what all had happened to her before she showed up at Raptor. So when he sang about how Muriele first was drug to the Gunn stronghold by a rope around her neck, Elyne near jumped up from her seat. Graemme's arm around her shoulder kept her from erupting in fury.

She had been so engrossed in the ballad her new husband had taken advantage of it to nibble on her neck. He stopped long enough to whisper to her.

"Nay, wife. I will tell ye the whole story when we are alone."

Gille, Graemme's new squire, was a gift from Magnus. Elyne liked the young blond boy who was so intent on pleasing Graemme. She would have to ask Graemme's brother about the young man, for though Magnus said he'd come from a small village near the Gunn's fortress, he looked to be some lord's bastard. No serf could be so comely with silky hair, fine features and eyes the color of the sky on a summer morn. The young man was diligent in refilling the etched silver wedding goblet she shared with Graemme, a gift from Ranald and Catalin.

Elyne stilled when Magnus' foster-brother, Feradoch, came into the song. Described as a golden angel, it made her itch to look at Gille. Had Magnus or Graemme ever thought mayhap he was this Feradoch's bastard? Well, of course they had! They were not fools, though sometimes she was quick to call Graemme one.

Though Cook displayed each course in a way to tempt even the daintiest appetites, she lost all interest in food. Neither the figs with red grapes in a crust nor the stewed apples with mint looked inviting to her.

The more Graemme drank, the more ardent he became. Why, the lustful goat would be happy to push aside the chairs and swive her on the floor!

"I grow impatient, wife, to feel ye hot and weeping for me," Graemme whispered in her ear.

"Hold yer tongue! If I had my way, ye'd sleep in the pasture with the sheep this night and not in the keep."

"Ah, do ye not remember screaming my name when I pleasured ye with my tongue?"

"I ne'er screamed!" She glanced from the corner of her eye and realized not even the table's cloth could hide his growing erection.

"Aye. Ye did." He smiled with confidence.

"I would scream with pleasure should ye sleep curled around a four-legged critter."

"Think of what ye would miss if my nekid body wasna next to yers."

When he nipped her plump lobe and blew a light breath into her ear, shivers coursed from where his tongue had dampened her ear down to the center of her body. She squeezed her legs together to ease the emptiness she longed to have filled.

It didn't help.

Nor did it help when Graemme's hand beneath the table's cloth kept inching up her skirts trying to bare her thigh to his touch. She'd pinched his arm so many times he should have bruises from his wrist to his elbow on the morrow. When he started pinching her in return, she gave up.

At the close of the fifth course, the feasting ended with creamy loaves of white bread, and sharp cheeses with sugared walnuts.

After Elyne had responded to a multitude of toasts, she began to daydream about the times she and Graemme had made love. Nay, not 'made love' but swived. It made her hot and needy, until she remembered each had ended in a fight. She scowled down at the sugared walnut in her fingers then began to nibble viciously at it until she near bit her own flesh.

Graemme leaned close, took her hand and placed it on his lap, then pressed her fingers around his hard shaft. When he released her hand, probably expecting her to be overjoyed because his special treasure was so lengthy and eager, she slid her hand up close to where his tarse nested. By his gasp, he anticipated a continued caress. Instead, she felt around for a few breaths gathering his tunic in her fist. Assured she also had hold of the hair around his shaft, of a sudden, she pulled as hard as she could.

Elyne grinned when he let out a squawk worthy of the finest rooster. He near crushed her wrist until she released him. She continued to look at her plate as if nothing had occurred. When the room erupted in a cheer, it startled her. Graemme had stood and stretched, like a man longing for his bed.

They quieted when old Grunda came up to him. He startled and turned to her. She put her right hand on his head and her left on Elyne's. Before the seer spoke, she waited a moment and looked at the ceiling as if she could see the sky above.

"This husband and wife will make a bairn this night. But if he is not careful of those who would try to draw him away from her, he will lose all. Take heed to two who say they love ye, for one is yer worst enemy." She stared straight into Graemme's eyes. Satisfied that he'd heard her words, she withdrew and seemed to flow through the tapestries behind Gille. The young squire looked like a ghost had just touched him.

The women at the table followed Graemme's lead and stood, ready to take Elyne above and prepare her for the marriage bed.

Graemme had other ideas.

This lass to whom Graemme was now forever bound to, tested him at every turn. If he didn't prove he was her master, not her servant, she would believe she could lead him around by his balls whenever it suited her.

He stood behind Elyne's chair and abruptly pulled it back before she knew what he intended. While still trying to get her balance, he scooped her up in his arms as if she weighed less than a child.

The guests hooted and hollered advice, ready to follow them up the stairwell and usher them to their bed.

Elyne spluttered, ready to argue.

"Ye will be silent, wife, else I'll dump ye on the middle of this table and swive yer brains out!"

She stilled.

With a bright smile, he glanced around the room then at the women who stood to help her prepare for him.

"I find I am too impatient to explore my beautiful bride's body to wait for the bedding ceremony. Excuse this impatient Highlander, I beg ye."

When she started to struggle, he loosened his grip and jiggled her in his arms. She grabbed his shoulders to keep from falling.

He leered at the crowd and said loud enough for all to hear, "She grows impatient! Wait a short time then lend an ear. Ye'll hear her screams of pleasure!"

"They'll hear screams all right!" Elyne was so furious she hissed like a cat. "They'll not know it isna a lass when I take a knife to yer ballocks!"

"Think of all the pleasure ye'd deny yerself for the rest of yer life. If aught should happen to cause me not to harden, ye willna ever have the pleasure again."

"Any man can provide the same service!"

"Nay. Ye willna *ever* have another man betwixt yer legs but me! If ye dare to attempt it, ye will find his severed head in yer lap."

Seeing movement at the high table, Graemme glanced to see if someone sought to halt him. 'Twas Ranald. But he had no intention of stopping him. He and Magnus were helping reseat the women and soothing them.

Magnus grinned and nodded at Graemme. Having seen Elyne enough over the past month, he would know if Graemme didn't get the upper hand, he would be forever plagued with a wife who thought to command his every movement.

Chief Broccin raised his goblet in a new toast. "Drink to the one man who can finally tame me spirited daughter! He will give me many strong and valiant grandchildren!"

The guests cheered, only too happy for another round of drinking.

Elyne didn't make it easy for Graemme to carry her up the spiral staircase. She stiffened and put her feet out to bump against the wall. He stopped and turned near sideways. Halfway up the stairs, he stood her two steps above him then shoved his shoulder into her middle, carrying her draped over him like a big bundle of laundry. When she started kicking in earnest, he slapped her behind.

Gently.

She squealed.

Men hooted from below.

"Nay. 'Tis but a minor feel!" Graemme called down to them. "She will bring down the walls when she reaches her peak!"

By the time they arrived at the top and turned toward her bedchamber, his patience was at an end. He kicked the door open, slammed it shut with the heel of his boot and stalked over to the bed. Reaching up and grabbing her by the hips, he bent forward and dumped her on the bed.

Rose petals flew in the air as Elyne sank in the down mattress. The bed rocked when he fell on top of her, holding her down while she ranted and raved. He needed to grasp her wrists above her head to keep her from scratching his face.

Never had he seen such a temper in a woman. Why, she had more rage stored in her mind than a whole keep full of women.

"Ye foul-mannered cur!"

"Call me dear husband and I might let ye up."

"Ye maggoty horse's turd! Get yer body off me."

"Ah, ah! How about loving spouse, my dear sweet-tempered bride?"

She bucked under him and near had the strength to throw him off. He did what any sane husband would do.

He started kissing her. Every time she opened her mouth to speak, his warm lips clamped on hers. He finally felt her softening beneath him. He slanted his mouth, molding and kissing her lips, nibbling and tugging at them.

Her clamped teeth denied him entrance.

His lips slid along her cheek to her ear, where he nibbled and kissed around it and finally whispered, "Please."

She ignored him.

He reached between them and pushed her skirts close to her body so his knees wouldn't rip the lovely fabric. Being careful, he moved one leg at the time to straddle her then lifted onto his knees. He wriggled his hips and settled lightly down on her.

Her eyes spat fire at him. He ignored it, for his right leg gave a slight twinge, reminding him of the healing bite marks and the bruise covering most of his thigh.

His kilt settled around his thighs. Her heat came through her soft clothing onto his bare flesh, making his cock even more eager. He looked down and wondered if it peeked between his kilt and her soft linen kirtle.

Elyne surged up with her hips. He almost missed seeing her hands flash up to push him off, but he gripped her wrist before she could unseat him.

"Tsk! Ye would shove yer husband to the floor on his wedding night? What would Father Matthew say if it cracked my skull like a goose's egg?"

"A rotten egg, ye mean?"

She struggled and twisted her arms and, though strong for a woman, she was no match for him.

Graemme stared down at his lovely bride. Finally, she stopped struggling. He reached to smooth her hair back from her face.

"'Tis beautiful," he said as he removed the circlet from her brow. He placed it beside him.

He lifted his right leg and moved to her side. When she would have sat up, he put his hand on her shoulder and shook his head. He untied the silver chain from around her hips and spread it out on both sides. Tilting his head, he studied the dress.

He stood and held his hands out to help her to stand.

"Ye can scream yer hatred of me till the cock's crow at dawn, but it willna change a thing."

"I didna want a husband."

He studied her face and saw the conflict there. He tried to see things as she would. It would be hard for her to leave Raptor and her family behind. Especially Ranald. And Lady Joneta, who must have been like a mother to her. A memory flashed through his mind and gave him a start. 'Twas when he was but five years old. He had stood watching as his seven-year-old brother Magnus swore a blood oath with Feradoch while their fathers stood behind their sons.

When the oath was final, Graemme had cried out when Chief Olaf rode away, taking Magnus beside him. Until then, he'd not understood how being a foster brother worked. He didn't want Feradoch for a brother! He wanted Magnus to come galloping back to them. As the tears had run down his face, he remembered the disgusted sneer Feradoch had turned on him.

"Aye. I understand. But we are married now, for good or ill." His strong hands were firm as they turned her so her back was to him. "I will be yer maid for the night, wife."

"I can tend to myself," she said and tried to turn around.

"Up," he ordered with a light pressure on her elbows.

She surprised him by lifting her arms. He bent to take the hem of her kirtle and was careful when he lifted it over her head then draped it across the back of a chair. Her smock followed before she had time to think about it.

The loveliest back in all of Scotland peeked through the curly brown hair flowing down to her hips. He studied at leisure her lovely, ivory back peeking between the dark tresses. He noted she had folded her arms in front of her.

Why, his bride was shy on her wedding night. Strange, for

'twas not the first time they'd had bed sport.

He came close behind her, reached around to cup her full breasts and whispered against her velvety neck, "We may fight over everything else, but ye have to admit, we make passionate bed sport together."

As he kissed her shoulders, he watched his tanned fingers brush over her rosy nipples. When they jutted with interest, his calloused palms rubbed them afore retreating. He cupped her breasts and kneaded them, sighing, for they swelled in his hands.

"Ye are beautiful, wife. Never did I think any lass could be so lovely and so skillful at the same time."

"Skillful?"

Did she know she was thrusting her breasts into his hands, begging for more attention?

"Aye. Skillful. Someone who knew nothing about weapons couldna dislodge a mace the way ye did."

By Lucifer's crooked toes! The last thing he wanted was her thinking about the blood and gore of dead men. But since she hadn't jerked away, mayhap she wasna listening.

He redoubled his efforts. As he nipped and kissed his way down her neck below her right ear, he breathed in her fresh heather scent. She caught her breath and stretched her head back, offering more of her flesh to his kisses. He suckled the tender skin there and then lapped it with his tongue to soothe it.

All the while, his impatient cock pressed against her back, hot and throbbing. He wanted to rip his clothes off so they could be flesh to flesh, but he forced himself to wait.

"Come, sit on the bed so I may remove yer stockings and shoes," he whispered in her ear.

Her jaw tightened against his cheek afore he pulled back. She was still resisting him, but at least she wasn't swinging her fists! Leading her by the shoulders over to the bed, he removed the chain and circlet to the table so she could sit. He'd had ample practice removing a lass' clothing, but never had it seemed so slow!

When he pulled off her left stocking and held her foot in

the palm of his hand, he stroked up and down her leg. He lifted her foot and nibbled the tips of her toes. It must have tickled, for her leg muscles jerked. After he'd treated her other foot in the same way, he stood.

"Stand." He held her hands and brought her closer to him. Reaching around her, he grasped the covers and jerked them back, leaving the bare sheet. He started to lift her in his arms, but she pulled back.

"I am nay a child. I can get into the bed by myself."

"If ye were a child, we wouldna be here."

He turned away. Not wanting any curious viewers, he went over and latched the door. If anyone tried to enter, he'd hear them afore they raised the latch.

Someone had lit a brace of candles in the room. Between them and the fireplace, it looked near daylight. He pinched them all out, thinking she would prefer the darkness. Most women he'd swived liked the light, but he sensed Elyne wasn't interested in watching his cock bob around like a curious puppy when he walked toward her.

He moved to the other side of the bed and made sure his sword was near to his hand, should he need it. Not like most men, he was methodical at undressing. He removed and folded each piece of clothing until he was as naked as she.

When he slid onto the bed, the bed ropes made the mattress rock and sway. He braced himself so he wouldn't roll atop her.

Elyne surprised him by her next question.

"Ye didna want to marry me, either, did ye?"

"Nay."

"Then why did ye return? Ranald would have protected me from Father's wrath."

"The night I first came here, ye were afraid of him. He wouldna have scarred ye like he did Ranald, for the value of a female is marrying for gain. But he was angry enough to pick the oldest, meanest and vilest of men for yer groom." He shook his head in disgust. "He'd keep it a secret from Ranald until the deed was done. Oh, aye, he would have regretted it after ye were gone, but he didna think far ahead."

"Oh."

He almost didn't hear her, she spoke so low.

"And, I vowed I'd return. I couldna shame ye by breaking it."

Elyne stilled. What thoughts had caused such sadness to flash over Graemme's face? To look so lost? She stilled, and watched as he composed his features. Was he as unhappy about marrying as she was? No doubt, he had thought his love, Elspeth, would one day be his bride. Instead, he was married to a woman who angered him at every turn.

At least the fire had gone from his eyes. But the coldness wasn't such a good thing, after all. She'd rather have him angry at her than to show no emotion at all.

Delicious warmth spread over her when his bare flesh pressed against her side. When had he started teasing her breasts?

And when had he started kissing her again? She sighed when his lips nibbled at hers, begging for her to open. She did. His tongue surged inside to explore, to dance over and around his 'till he teased and coaxed it into joining him. His large hand came to rest atop her stomach, near spreading from one side to the other. Its warmth felt like the sun on a hot rock after ye'd been swimming in an icy pool. How could something so calloused be so gentle when it smoothed over her body?

She murmured deep in her throat when his palm rested above her secret spot and his long fingers delved through her hair to play with her nether lips. He teased her with his fingers, each touch bringing moisture there. When he touched her nub, she arched against him, hoping he would enter her. He didn't but cupped her instead, moving his hand up and down her slick center until she reached for his wrist, held it still as she ground herself against his palm.

So empty! She spread her legs wide, inviting him. After he removed his hand, he thrust his right knee between her thighs and rocked it against her center. His fingers returned to tease her nub, gently tweaking then retreating. Each time she built to a burning peak, he distracted her with a touch somewhere else until she cooled. He brought her ardor to near ecstasy. She heard herself moaning and begging him to give her release and clamped her tongue with her teeth. Unable to bear the hot need, she tugged at his arms, urging him to cover her. When she felt his warmth and weight over her whole body, she sighed with relief.

Balanced on his left arm, he lifted his weight off her. His tarse rubbed up and down her slick opening. Each downward thrust, he entered slightly then retreated to slide the silky head of his tarse over her sensitive nub.

Clamping her legs around his hips, she tried to force him to enter until he filled her. He was too strong for her. She screamed out in frustration. Only then did he plunge to the hilt and begin to rock. He built a rhythm, slow at first then several hard thrusts 'till she was sure if she didn't find her release she would explode from the mounting tension.

Each time Graemme felt the slight tightening of her stomach muscles preceding a climax, he distracted her with a murmur or lifted his upper body off hers until the quivers calmed.

She had challenged him to pleasure her to ecstasy in the Great Room. He wouldn't stop until she screamed for him. Every woman deserved a wedding night she would remember until she was old and gray. Though they might test each other from dawn to dusk, he determined when they were abed they would find a common ground in bed sport.

When she banged her heels against his nether cheeks and pulled his hair near out at his temples, he reached between them and feathered his fingers over her swollen nub. She tightened all around him, arched her back with her head pressed tight to the bed and gave a lusty yell of pleasure. Only then, did he stop thinking and let pleasure build until he thrust so deeply he needed to hold her shoulders to keep her in place.

He wasn't sure who had yelled the loudest.

Elyne? Or himself?

CHAPTER 27

THE NIGHT HAD GONE too quickly, Elyne decided, when she awoke at dawn. Why were her thighs aching when she stretched? 'Twas like the first time she'd spent hours riding astride. Her eyes widened and her vision cleared to see amused near-black eyes watching her.

"Sore, wife?" His smile suddenly stilled. "'Tis sorry I am I couldna get enough of ye last night."

"'Tis sorry I am when ye didna let me sleep more than a few heartbeats between yer assaults."

"Assaults? Was I wrong and it was the old crone cackling and making noises I thought were cries of delight? I must admit I added mine to the tumult."

"When did ye get up?" Elyne asked when she realized he was already dressed and ready to travel.

"Ye were snoring so loud ye didna hear me when I slipped from the room afore first light."

"I dinna snore!" Insult stiffened her body, only bringing the sore muscles more stress. She forced herself to relax. "A lady doesna snore. Only men snore."

"Ask Ranald. He came to scratch on the door thinking Squat had stolen into the room."

"I will prove ye wrong by asking him."

"Chief Broccin was there, also. Best ask him, too, while ye're at it."

Ada spared her further embarrassment when she came into the room, scolding him. "Lady Joneta told ye to let her sleep. She had a hard night." A mischievous light came into her eyes. "Screaming and begging wears a woman out, ye know."

Elyne pulled the sheet over her head and ordered in her most commanding voice, "Get ye both from the room. If Muriele and Catalin are about, I would appreciate their company."

"Can't leave yet," Ada said, "the servants are outside the door with a hot bath yer new husband requested for ye." She shook her head. "If they hold the tub much longer, they are liable to get tired and leave it in the passageway."

She went to the door and threw it wide, letting them in. Elyne crawled down in the bed, mortified knowing everyone in the castle had heard her last night.

"Ye look like a mole. Best watch out if Squat does come in. He's likely to take a nip out of yer hind end afore he realizes 'tis ye."

Elyne stuck her hot face out and scowled at him.

"Has no one taught ye the proper way to greet yer husband when we get to the Highlands?" Graemme looked at Ada and saw her blank expression. He sighed. "'Tis the custom to start the day off with a kiss and fervent thanks for giving ye a robust swiving during the night."

When Elyne's eyes widened in disbelief, he explained further.

"The Highlands are bitter cold most of the year and we retire to bed when the light lowers. The only way to stay warm is by vigorous bed sport." He shook his head solemnly, but his eyes sparkled. "We have many bairns in the castle come early summer."

"Ye are telling a mistruth, and I'll not thank ye for something ye enjoyed even more than I."

"Fair enough."

Graemme crawled on the bed, lifting his kilt to give his legs freedom. His weapon of pleasure drew her gaze only to see if it was as worn out as her pleasure center was. It was not. She put up her hands to keep him back, but he didna come closer.

Cupping his hands on her cheeks, he gazed softly into her eyes until she looked back. In a low voice, he began. "Thank ye, wife. Ye have pleased me greatly. 'Twas the most gratifying night I have ever spent with a woman. Yesterday was hard on ye and I am sorry. I hope I made up for it a little by giving ye an enjoyable night to remember."

He rose up on his knees and took a box from the pocket in his kilt. The wood was deep brown with amber streaks and was beautifully hand-carved with Celtic symbols of eternal love knots. He moved back so she could sit up and take the box on her lap.

"The wood reminded me of yer hair. Esa helped by knowing a Welsh trader who specialized in wedding boxes. 'Twas fortunate he was at Clibrick when I arrived. Look inside."

Elyne opened the box to find a scarlet cloth cushioning a lovely neck chain with clear green stones embedded in twists of thin gold around them. Surrounded by the curled up chain, a gleaming ring caught the light coming from the window. It flashed shimmering green lights around the stone walls. 'Twas the most beautiful thing Elyne had ever seen.

With great tenderness, Graemme picked up the ring and put it on her ring finger alongside the gold wedding band he'd placed there yester eve.

A knot formed in Elyne's throat, for his expression was tender and he was as gentle as handling a bairn when he placed the ring on finger. He couldn't have been more sincere looking if he'd truly loved her. Her heart gave a twinge and she realized how very handsome Graemme was. Far more than Magnus or even Ranald. 'Twas strange, for she had never thought anyone more pleasant to the eye than her brother.

"Thank ye, Graemme. Yer morning-after gift is most beautiful."

"It should be. Ye have pleased me so greatly ye deserve everything beautiful I can give ye."

Aunt Joneta interrupted by coming into the room like a summer breeze. Ada followed close behind her. She seemed excited to be moving to the Highlands with her mistress. Her adventurous spirit was the reason Elyne had chosen her as her personal maid.

"Have ye not allowed the poor lass her bath? Get, Graemme! Go below. Magnus needs ye to help form the line of horses and wagons. There are three wagons now. One for Clibrick's tents and chests of clothing, one for Elyne's things from Raptor and the third filled to the hilt with food from Cook.

"Oh, and Ranald packed a box of special herbs, unguents, and salves. We selected what we thought ye would have a hard time finding in the Highlands."

"But I dinna want to empty yer own medicinal preparations."

"Pfft! Girl, you know my herbal hut is filled to overflowing, so 'twas a good time to clear room there."

Turning around, Lady Joneta flicked the backs of her fingers to Graemme and smiled at him. "She canna prepare for a journey if you keep looking at her like she is a fruit pasty and you are starving."

Graemme laughed and turned to leave the room. He looked back when he reached the door and found she'd thrown off the sheets. The sight near made Graemme tell her aunt to leave the room or else be shocked, for he wanted to swive his wife again. She was incredibly beautiful with her sleepy eyes and curling hair falling all around her face. Her rosy nipples peeked between locks of curling hair, and her skin looked like light cream above the curly dark hair guarding her woman's place.

When he gave her his most passionate leer while looking at her nekid torso, she turned rosy red.

Her aunt chuckled as he eased the door closed.

Never had Elyne seen Raptor Castle so busy. She peered out the heavy doors into the Great Hall to see guests were still riding out through the barbican while others were sitting on the keep's steps while grooms prepared their horses. The men held their heads in their hands, trying to stop the pounding from too much drink. Their wives didn't give them any sympathy, but instead seemed to talk extra loud, considering the men's wincing faces.

Catalin, Muriele and Ysabel were still at the table breaking their fast. Elyne hurried over, thanking the good Saints because two of them would be with her when she left. 'Twould be less hurtful to leave, knowing she would have friends in the Highlands.

She grabbed Aunt Joneta's hand when she came into the room.

"Come, Aunt. Have ye broken yer fast?"

"I waited to eat with you, dear one." She blinked and turned her face as she busied herself making sure the servants brought out hot food for the travelers.

An empty pit formed in Elyne's stomach as she saw men begin to file into the room. When her father and Ranald arrived with Graemme and Magnus behind them, she began to feel a panic she never thought could happen to her. Where were all her brave feelings? She'd thought she would welcome the day she left the heavy-fisted control of her father. Instead, she longed to throw her arms around him. And leaving Ranald was like losing him again the first time. She could still see the cart and hear its squeaky wheels when it carried her brother across the barbican to be lost in Kelso for the greater part of her life.

Ranald must have known her thoughts, for he came and put his arms around her. She knotted her fists in his black tunic and held him tight.

"Lass, we are not going to be lost to ye. Young Graemme and his brother both have promised to bring ye for a visit once a year when the weather permits. And knowing the Morgan's, they will keep their word.

"But a year is such a long time," she said in a broken whisper.

"Nay, sweet lass. A year from now ye may be bringing yer son or daughter to show off to Father. Dinna worry. I will continue to check on him often to see he doesna do anything foolish. Aunt Joneta plans to return to Raik and his family, now ye are settled."

"Ack! Are those tears in my sweet wife's eyes? They must be tears of joy, since I heard it from her own lips she ne'er cried!"

Elyne stiffened her back, and in the protection of Ranald's chest, swiped her fingers over her eyes.

"Huh! Ye see things which are nay there."

When Graemme came over, Ranald released her with a

somber smile. Before she could turn, Graemme wrapped his arms around her and snuggled his face in her neck and sniffed.

"Mmm, ye smell sweet, wife. Did ye roll in heather whilst my back was turned?"

"Ye have done yer job, Sir Graemme," Grunda's gravelly voice said. "'Twas the right time of the month to plant yer seed." She chuckled. "From the sounds of it, ye plowed the field enough to bear fruit afore a year is out."

Embarrassed, Elyne pulled back. She had tried to be quiet after the first time she climaxed, but she must have failed. She felt Graemme's chest moving in silent laughter. She glared at him, daring him to speak. Thank the good Saints he held his tongue. She sighed with relief when her father came charging into the room.

"Dinna forget to take this misshapen dog with ye," he roared. "The hellish little hound tried to send me backwards off the landing."

As he came through the doorway, an impatient Squat scampered around him. His tail whipped against Elyne's skirts as he tried to tunnel between them.

"We thought to leave him with ye so ye wouldna miss Elyne," Graemme said.

His tone sounded so wistful Elyne shoved him away.

"Dinna fear, Father, we thought no such thing!" Bending down, she scooped the dog into her arms and went to sit beside her aunt.

Who knew a night of bed sport would make anyone so hungry? She near drooled seeing her aunt had already put honey and butter on her porridge. She broke off a piece of warm bread and gave it to the dog when she put him down. Before she finished eating, she glanced up to see everyone watching her and grinning

"What?"

"Ye look about to eat what is left in everyone's bowls, lass," Graemme said. "If bed sport makes ye this hungry, ye will be twice yer size in near a month!"

"Swiving hasna anything to do with it. In fact, the mere

thought of bedding with ye takes away any desire to eat another bite."

She dusted off her hands and made a quick survey of the table. Everyone else had finished and was waiting on her. How had the time passed so quickly?

Their leave-taking was so swift she suspected Graemme and Magnus had planned it that way. When she descended the stairway leading down to the front bailey, she saw mounted warriors patiently waiting. Magnus and Graemme's mounts were at the front with Brian and Colyne, several warriors were between them and Muriele and Elyne's waiting horses. Gille was to ride close to the women to relay any messages between them and their husbands. Behind them was a cart with soft pillows, blankets and padded benches on each side for Grunda, Ysabel and Ada. In the middle was a square wooden form around a small pallet covered with sheepskin for Squat. When Gille had learned the dog was going back to Clibrick, he'd made a bed saying the little beastie couldn't survive the trip bouncing around on a wooden cart.

Toward the end were several large carts carrying Elyne's things and those going with Muriele to Blackbriar Castle. Between each section, armed warriors rode for protection.

Before she knew it, she had hugged and kissed her family until Graemme led her away and lifted her into her saddle. She was glad to have Muriele riding beside her. When she looked back and saw her family waving, she blinked and swallowed.

Not until they cleared the drawbridge did the squires unfurl the two gray Morgan brother's banners with the black wolves. Graemme's with the wolf leaping down off the rock, and Magnus' wolf baring his teeth in a mighty snarl.

"'Tis added protection, Elyne. When traveling through Scotland, the wolf banners warn everyone the Morgan Clan is not to be trifled with."

"Aye." Elyne grinned and lifted her left skirt to show Muriele her leg. She had strapped her dagger there. Her short sword hung from a strap on the pommel of her saddle.

"We think alike." Muriele laughed and flicked up the side

of her own slit skirt to show she also had worn her weapons. One on each leg. "I dinna travel without them."

"Do ye feel like we are overrun by women on this trip?" Graemme looked at Magnus somber face and winked.

"Aye. From the looks of it, ye'd think we will be slow in making our way to Clibrick."

"Dinna fear. Elyne is as good a rider as Muriele. They'll not hold us up. My fear is the carts will break down or some such thing."

Squat's shrill bark reminded him not only did they have the women to consider, but someone would have to stop each time the dog needed to relieve itself. His stubby legs wouldn't allow him to run alongside the horses. Poor misshapen thing would collapse within a league away from Raptor.

Turning in his saddle, Graemme signaled Gille, who in turn dropped back beside the women's cart. He reached out and Ada passed the squirming dog to him. Before long, he returned the dog to the women's cart and pulled in behind Elyne and Muriele.

"Magnus?" Graemme called.

"Aye?"

"Have ye learned who Gille's father is? Chief Olaf or Feradoch?"

"I dinna know. I tried to find out when his birth month was to see if Feradoch may have been spending his weeks at Kinbrace, but no one in the village recalled when he arrived there. I suspect it was Feradoch, though."

"Why?"

"Chief Olaf didna care who knew he'd fathered a bastard. So many of them were in villages close by, he seemed proud of the fact. Gille was at an outlying village. I think he was meant to stay hidden." He frowned. "The day we cleared Gille's village of raiders, Feradoch was scornful when I'd killed the man holding a knife on the boy. He said the young man wasn't worth killing a man over. I insisted on bringing Gille back to Kinbrace. Later, I found he had a brown birthmark on his lower belly."

"What has it to do with the boy?" Graemme glanced at

Magnus, who seemed to be considering his answer.

"Feradoch would never acknowledge he had a son who wasna perfect. He'd have killed him at birth, so the mother must have hidden him at the village." Magnus shook his head. "The man was obsessed with his own beauty."

Surprisingly for Elyne, the day passed quickly. When they stopped for the evening, she was surprised at how tired she was. The men had ridden hard to come to a clearing next to a loch where they had stopped before. 'Twas large and surrounded on three sides by dense woods.

"Sweyn, Brian and Colyne, see to the camp. Sir Magnus and I will take the women to a place where they may bathe without fear of men hunting firewood coming upon them."

Sweyn, being the most experienced took over, ordering Brian to see to the men gathering firewood and building the fire. Colyne was in charge of rounding up the game caught during the day. As they had ridden through the woods, hare scrambled to run from their horses, grouse had taken to the sky and deer were fleet of foot.

Sweyn had Gille and some of the younger men putting up tents. The one for Graemme and his new wife was on the fringe of the camp, Magnus and Muriele's was closer in. Ada, Grunda and Ysabel shared one closer to the warriors for they had no man to share their sleeping arrangements.

The women were anxious to wash the dust from their bodies and wondered what took Graemme so long to take them to the loch. When he joined them, they found they couldn't walk as swiftly as they'd thought, for banging their behinds on their saddles or bouncing on the cart benches had made them stiff and sore. Grunda, the eldest by far, seemed the most rested.

"I think ye are lost, my careless husband," Elyne announced as they made their way through the bushes.

"Nay. 'Tis on the other side of this stand of trees. Canna ye hear the waterfall?"

"Be patient. Once ye see this part of the loch, ye will want to spend several days here just to be able to swim." Magnus hiked a brow at the three unattached women. "Ye can all swim, canna ye?"

"I can keep myself afloat. My brothers tossed me in a loch every chance they got," Ada spoke up.

Ysabel simply nodded. Grunda gave him a look conveying several things. Among them was how did he think she lived this long without being able to swim? Loch's covered the Highlands. Though drowning was frequent, they were mostly people who feared the water and had eventually fallen in, or some man wanted one less mouth to feed and had tossed them in.

"Graemme and I will stand guard just inside the woods. If anyone is in distress, ye have but to call out and we will be there."

Elyne stood on the edge of the water and looked around her, amazed at the beauty. They were only one day from Raptor, but she could see a change in this sparsely populated area. Great trees overhung the loch and from the mountain they had descended, a waterfall cascaded down, making the water foam and sparkle in the sunlight. A large flat rock stood close where they placed their clean clothing.

Graemme was right. She'd like to stay here for days. Judging from the delight on Muriele and Ada's faces, they would also. The women threw off their clothes and tossed them atop branches nearby, then raced to stand in the water, tentative with each step they took, testing the ground. When they waded out to their waist and didn't feel any drop-off they jumped up and down like lasses at play.

Even Grunda's eyes shone with delight. She looked years younger. While Elyne stared at her, she could see the beauty hidden by age. Why, she must have been quite beautiful as a young woman! Elyne felt Muriele watching her and nodded. She seemed to have thought the same thing, for a tender smile touched her lips.

Grunda astounded them all by plunging to the bottom of the pool and coming up with sand clutched in her hands.

"Ye dinna need scented soaps out here. The sand will wash the dust off yer bodies and leave ye feeling cleaner than ye have afore."

For those who had never done it, she put a little in their hands and they copied her movements as she rubbed it on her arms, chest and neck. When 'twas gone, she showed them how to dive deep. Muriele helped, for after Magnus had besieged and captured Blackbriar Castle, Grunda had taught her and her mother when they had escaped to live in the woods.

"If ye stay in the water any longer, ye will be shriveled near to nothing," Graemme called.

"Get back into the woods, ye uncouth churl! Dinna spy on women when they have asked for privacy."

"Why not?" Magnus cut in. He, too, stood in the clearing watching them. "'Tis a charming sight to see mermaids. I begin to think Grunda was first born a fish, for she is the strongest swimmer I have e'er seen!"

"Turn yer back, please, husband," Muriele ordered.

He did. But Graemme, with a soft smile on his lips, continued to watch them.

"Did ye not hear Muriele, ye randy goat?" Elyne called to Graemme.

"Aye. I did. Did ye?

"Of course, fool. I asked ye first."

"Well, then, did ye not hear how nicely she said *please* and *husband*?"

Elyne near ground her teeth together. The women watched her, hugging their arms across their chest, whether in cold or modesty, she wasn't sure. When her gaze met Ada's, she seemed to see her for the first time as she truly was. Why, she was quite pretty! She had large blue eyes and curly red hair even though weighted by water. Her lips were near blue from the cold, but it didn't hide their laughing curves.

Elyne stamped her foot, for all the good it did her. The water barely moved.

"Dear sweet, loving husband, would ye please go back into the woods with yer brother?"

"Was being nice so difficult?" Graemme immediately turned and walked back into the woods with Magnus.

Elyne stuck her tongue out and made a face at his back.

"Best ye heed yer husband in all things once at Clibrick. If ye become careless and dinna listen to his caution, ye will be in great danger."

Grunda's voice was for her ears alone for she stood so close no one else could hear. The old seer surged out of the water and walked over to her clothes. She seemed to have grown, but 'twas because she didna slump or bend. It amazed and caused Elyne to wonder about her real age. Now, she seemed no older than her mother had been. As she watched Grunda dress and tend her hair, she realized the seer deliberately gave the illusion of great age.

When they returned to the camp, they were delighted to see everything looked as if it had been there for a long time. Elyne was especially glad they had provided tents and hoped the women would share two and the two commanders would take the third. She knew it was a useless hope when Graemme led her to the farthest one. Gille had finished putting pillows on the pallet and furs for warmth.

"Thank ye, Gille. Ye have made a pleasurable sleeping spot. 'Twill be very comfortable."

He bobbed his head, a shy smile on his lips as he bowed and left the tent.

"Well, now, ye took so long we have no time for a quick round of bed sport," Graemme said, a hint of disappointment in his voice.

"Ye canna be serious! The moon isna even up, and everyone is about. Forget it, husband!"

"If ye refuse to be adventurous, then there is no choice but to dine, since the food is near finished."

Food had never tasted so good. Elyne could only believe it was because they were outdoors all day and she had become especially hungry. Even Squat had more than his usual share, since Gille shared his food with him.

When she could put it off no longer, since all the other women had already retired, she finally allowed Graemme to lead her to the tent.

She should not have protested, for there followed the most

delightful night of her life. Graemme was right. They might fight by day, but the nights were devoted to sensual bed sport — of the most wonderful kind.

By the end of a fortnight, Elyne was sorry the trip was over.

CHAPTER 28

ELYNE AND MURIELE HAD spent part of every afternoon in the wagon with the other women. Muriele was like a sister to her, and Ysabel had become a good friend, though reluctant to speak about her past. Grunda had promised to help Elyne to understand and read her dreams. Each day, when they stopped to eat or when Elyne and Muriele sought rest from the horses, Grunda had Elyne start with telling her first foretelling dream and what she'd thought it meant.

Elyne's mouth gaped when Grunda shook her head and told her the true meaning. The seer knew nothing of events which had occurred many years ago, but for each dream she interpreted, her foreseen outcome had happened as she predicted.

Whenever Graemme or Magnus required Gille, they whistled loud and shrill to summon him. Shouting would have gone unheard, due to the long row of horses and talking warriors. She grinned, for the first time she had signaled him thus, he had near jumped in his saddle thinking his lord had somehow circled to come up behind him. On the last day of their trip, the young squire pulled alongside Elyne when she whistled as skillfully as any man.

"Will we reach Clibrick soon, Gille?" Elyne asked, standing in her stirrups trying to get a glimpse of her new home.

"Do ye see the shimmering light through the trees ahead? 'Tis the sun on the waters of Loch Naver. There is a level spot on the other side of the trees where a watchtower stands. After Chief Olaf approached around the Loch instead of the hill, Chief Angus posts a guard to warn the castle which way raiders are coming. Ye can see the castle from there."

Elyne settled back in her saddle and waited patiently. Muriele had told her about Chief Olaf's raid and the fight between his son Feradoch and Magnus.

Excitement welled in the pit of Elyne's stomach. Never before had she been this far from Raptor Castle. At first, she had missed the lands around Raptor, not to mention all her family there. But now, she was becoming used to it.

She didn't have long to wait. Within twelve heartbeats, they rode out onto the level ground. A small, round tower stood close to the edge of the hill, where a guard could watch both the shoreline and the road coming down from the top of the hill. He stood atop it now with a square of polished metal turned to catch the light and bounce it down to the guards atop the corner turret of the castle below.

Once he had an answering signal, the guard in the hill tower scrambled down and burst out the door to greet Magnus, Graemme and his friends. After a few words, Graemme turned in his saddle and motioned for the two women to join them. When she edged her mount alongside his, the sight took her breath away.

Clibrick Castle was every bit as huge as Raptor, but where her home looked more like the dark fortress it was, this had a softer glow from the sun shining on the surrounding great walls and keep.

"Are there always tall grass and wildflowers on the open grounds?"

"Nay. Winter takes its toll. The wind is icy coming off the Loch. But in months as warm as this, the land seems to glory in it."

"Look! Someone is coming over the drawbridge," Elyne said. She shaded her eyes with a hand and stared. "It's a woman with long black hair."

Sweyn let out a war cry and kicked his horse into a gallop.

"Well, cruddy Hades! Why is he yelling at her?" She poked Graemme on the arm. "Stop him afore he hurts her."

Muriele chuckled. "I dinna believe Sweyn is mad. Watch."

Elyne caught her breath, for the two horses looked like they would collide, surely killing both riders. To Elyne's amazement, the woman was riding without a saddle and scrambled to stand on the horses back. At the last breath, Sweyn's horse skidded to a stop, digging its hooves into the earth. The man stood in his stirrups and the woman leapt off her horse into the air. Sweyn's arms reached out and plucked her to his chest.

"Oh," Elyne whispered, amazed.

'Twas easy to see they were kissing like they'd never let each other go.

" 'Tis my friend Esa who I told you about. Only a Welshwoman can ride a horse like a demon and sing with the enchanting voice of a Siren." Pride in her friend sounded in Muriele's voice.

As they raced down the hill, Elyne's heart pounded. The warriors followed at a slower pace taking care not to upset the cart of women or the wagons. Elyne slowed down halfway to the greeting party spilling out of the barbican. Sweyn and Esa stopped kissing long enough to look sheepish as they caught up to them.

When an imposing man with gray on the sides of his temples rode ahead, she knew she was seeing Chief Angus, her new father-by-law, for the first time. The three looked so alike there could be no doubt Magnus and Graemme were his sons. Age had softened the sharp angles of their father's face and etched small lines beside his eyes and lips.

The three men dismounted and clasped each other's shoulders. She watched their eyes and faces and noted the difference in how they viewed each other. Never had she seen the same expressions on Chief Broccin's face when he greeted Ranald or herself.

This father clearly showed love and respect for his sons.

Graemme breathed a sigh of relief for they'd made the journey without any unexpected attacks. Thieves and louts had spotted them, for truth, but thought better about attacking when they saw the wolf banners known to belong to the sons of the chief of the Morgan clan. They may have been stupid louts, but they were not so stupid they had a death wish.

"Well, now we have greeted each other, I should like to greet my daughters," Chief Angus said.

His eyes had already picked out Elyne riding astride beside Muriele. Magnus and Graemme went to help their wives dismount. Elyne surprised Graemme by waiting politely for him to aid her. Knowing her, he realized she was following Muriele's example. He didn't know whether it was relief or pride he felt for his new wife. She seemed to be on her best behavior. How long it would last, he didn't know. But he could hope she wouldn't do anything foolish — at least for this first day.

Magnus helped Muriele down from her spirited horse. She immediately went to Chief Angus and put her arms around him. He hugged and patted her on the back.

"I am pleased to see ye, Father Angus," she said as she kissed him on the cheek.

'Twas obvious she was already fond of Magnus' father.

"Graemme has married one of my best friends! It will be like home having her within a day or two's ride," Muriele said.

Graemme near held his breath, wondering what mischief Elyne would get into. Still, he couldna help but tease her. She looked so tense in trying to be the reserved lady.

"Father, this is my comely and dutiful wife, Elyne."

As his hands closed around her waist and he lifted her from the saddle, her muscles tightened in rebellion.

"She wishes to please me in all things and vows to obey my every wish," he said as he near dragged her off the saddle and stood her in front of him.

Elyne put her hands on his shoulder and shoved. Hard. He nearly rocked back on his heels. Not being a fool, he released her. Instantly angry, she raised her hand to swat at him, but his father intervened.

Chief Angus caught her upraised hand, bowed and brought it to his lips to kiss.

"I am delighted to meet ye. Graemme didna disappoint me by bringing some vapid plaything as his bride, but another spirited lass like Muriele."

Elyne's eyes opened wide as an owl at midnight when the chief wrapped her in a hug. Graemme had seen Ranald give her affection and love, but he wondered how many times her own father had shown her he loved her other than the day she rode away.

Squat brought everyone back to the present by barking and charging across the ground ready to pounce on the man who held his mistress in an embrace. Chief Angus dropped his arms, turned to the running dog and patted his thighs. To Graemme's surprise, Squat jumped at the last minute and his father caught him in his arms. Never had he heard his father laugh with such abandon. After rubbing the scruffy head, he turned sparkling eyes to Elyne.

"This must be yer companion. Aye?"

"Aye. His name is Squat." She looked at Graemme, a smile fighting with her lips. "Yer son named him."

He had never seen Elyne show a touch of shyness afore!

"'Tis true. We could not go around calling him *Dog* or *Ugly Cur*. But be careful. He tends to do, er, strange things now and again."

Chief Angus bent and placed him on the ground, giving him one last pat. "Come. Everyone has been waiting with great eagerness for my sons and daughters to return."

As they walked through the barbican and into the massive front bailey, women and soldiers called greetings to the brothers. They didn't ignore the women, either. Some knew Ysabel and went to greet her. Ysabel held Ada's arm and introduced her to everyone as Elyne's friend and helper.

Grunda needed no introduction, for they respectfully whispered "the Seer of Blackbriar" amongst them. They all eyed her as if she would climb to the top turret and declare some prophesy at any moment. Instead, her gaze roamed amongst them, sometimes stopping to study and then moving on. She seemed most interested in a lass who hung back from the crowd, the hood of her cloak pulled low over her face. Before long, the unknown young woman edged backward to disappear amongst the servants standing near the orchard.

Graemme wondered who the girl in the cloak was, but soon forgot about her. Elyne stood amongst the women with Muriele. The other women seemed most interested in whether she carried as many weapons as Muriele did. When they became too bold, he walked over and put his arm across Elyne's shoulders.

"My sweet tempered bride can handle a mace, a sword, bow and arrows and, er, some herbs which will cause grown men to cry out in anguish."

She gave him a look that would crush most men, but not Graemme.

"When I'm in my cups, remind me to tell ye about the curse she put upon me the first night we met."

When they all asked him to tell them immediately, he laughed and grabbed his bride's fist to lead her away afore she could show them just how good she was at hand-to-hand combat.

Elyne pulled as hard as she could, but Graemme didn't let her go. He walked companionably beside his father with Magnus and Muriele on the other side. Once inside the keep, a serving girl led Ada to Graemme's bedchamber so she could start making the room comfortable for her mistress. Men were already carrying in clothing trunks and trudging up the stairways with them.

"Well, now, let our travelers settle in. My sons will have five days to catch up on everything here at Clibrick afore Magnus leaves for Blackbriar this coming Monday. They must rest, for we have a grand banquet to prepare for on Saturday."

With no further words, Chief Angus took both brothers into his solar, along with Fergus, his commander, Sweyn and Brian, who acted as chief squires to Magnus and Graemme.

The door no sooner shut than Chief Angus' body became stiff with tension. His eyes took on a worried look and his brow furrowed in deep thought.

"Magnus, I think 'tis best ye leave at first light. I have heard rumors about someone planning to waylay ye when ye leave for Blackbriar. It will take their spy a day at least to advise him ye are here. He willna expect ye to leave so abruptly since I said ye'd be here 'till Monday."

"Who could wish me dead? Feradoch was my only known enemy."

"Someone who covets Blackbriar perhaps? Or Muriele?" Sweyn asked.

"Guards have warned me someone has used the postern gate, though they have tried to cover their tracks on the ground," Fergus said. "I have doubled the sentries along the wall walks."

"Tell the men to pretend they have no time to remove my things from the cart tonight, since dusk will soon be upon us. We will leave before first light on the morrow."

"Ye've traveled the same route for nigh on twenty years, on returning to Kinbrace. They will not expect ye to change," his father advised. "Go south to Loch Choire then south-east through the Ben Armine Forest and circle down through Strath Skinsdale. 'Tis wide and shallow and easy riding. Ye'll come up south of Blackbriar."

Graemme rubbed his chin, trying to find a reason for anyone wanting to kill Magnus. He was well-feared by most of the Highlands, so whoever it was had to have a terrible grudge. What it was, he didn't know. Though the Highlanders called his brother Magnus the Ruthless, he was always fair in his dealings with people. 'Twas only vicious men who brought out the ruthlessness in him.

The Clibrick men all offered suggestions, and finally Graemme pulled them all together to make a workable solution.

"My men and I will rise afore ye," Graemme said. "I'll send out two patrols, one to search yer old route to catch anyone hiding to waylay ye. Another will trail behind ye to be sure the ruse works."

"Thank ye, Graemme. Will not yer new wife suspect something when ye leave her bed afore she is sated?" Deviltry gleamed in Magnus' eyes. "Ye are usually swiving until the wee hours of the morn!"

"Do ye never get sleep?" Brian teased. "'Tis no wonder yer eyes have such deep shadows beneath them. Yer tent near turned over more than one night on our way here."

"Would ye like some lessons on pleasing a lass 'till she begs for more each night?" Graemme's lips lifted in a wide grin.

"Mayhap 'tis not pleasing her but lack of it? She must try again and again to reach her peak?"

"Humph! Ye heard her caterwauling loud enough to wake all the forest creatures. And even when I had my hand o'er her mouth!"

"The proof if whether yer seed took root will be in the harvesting come nine months from now," Chief Angus laughed. He stood and put his arms across each son's shoulder and led them to the door. "We had best show up else anyone watching will get suspicious. All of ye take note of any uneasy diners or anyone who leaves afore the food and drink are gone."

He squeezed each son's shoulder. "Both of ye be on yer best watch on the morrow. I dinna want harm to come to either of ye."

They left the solar acting as if they'd had a good chat and several pitchers of ale.

During the evening meal, mead, ale and wine flowed freely. Everyone seemed quite the worse for it by mid-meal. In conversation, Chief Angus became boisterous about his two magnificent sons and mentioned again, come Monday, Magnus would be leaving for good to take over Blackbriar.

"Who do ye search for? Is there someone ye wish to see?" Elyne asked when his gaze roved over the diners.

"If I said an old leman, would ye be jealous?"

"Ye'd best not! If I dinna satisfy ye, say so now. Two can play at this, ye know. If ye fail to satisfy my needs, I will also look elsewhere."

Graemme's hand shot out and grabbed her slender wrist. Her gaze met his, and what she saw there must have shocked her for she stiffened and her eyes widened. Hot rage broiled through his gut, thinking of her with another man between her long, muscular legs. She could lock them around his waist until he was nigh unable to move. He smiled wickedly, sending her a message of unspeakable consequences if she dared betray him.

The roaring in his ears eased enough to hear someone's light shoes whispering on the floor. 'Twas Grunda. She put her hand on Graemme's shoulder.

"Hsst! Follow me!"

She motioned to the doorway hidden by a tapestry on the wall behind the Chief's chair. Once they had entered the dark hallway, she looked around to be sure they were alone.

"Did ye note a woman in a gray cloak when we arrived this day? She kept to the edge of the crowd. She slipped away when ye drew near."

"Only a glance. A village lass?"

"A village lass also attending dinner this night?"

"What are ye getting at, old seer?"

"She is not what she seems. She tries to disguise herself. When Muriele fled Blackbriar, I did the same for her. The lass' hair isna brown, but blond. She isna stout but is slender as Elyne, though not tall."

"Ye have a feeling about her?"

"Aye. 'Tis evil. She left as soon as she heard the Chief repeat about Magnus leaving on Monday. She kept her back to the wall and edged toward the door. When the crowd got rowdy, she slid out of the keep like a cat stalking a mouse."

When Graemme began to speak, she pressed her fingers to his lips.

"I followed. She was alone. The guards didna even see her disappear through the postern gate." She gave a disgusted huff. "They didna see me follow, either. A horse awaited about fifty paces into the woods. I cleared my mind and closed my eyes to feel her movements. She made her way up the hill south of the watch tower where we approached the castle. She has gone to tell her master what he longs to hear."

"Do ye know who her master is?"

"Nay, not as yet. I will go atop the tallest turret. The moon is full this night. I will take a white crockery of water and see what occurs in it."

"A basin of water? How can water help?"

"I will clear my mind of all thoughts. If there is something afoot, a vision will appear in the water."

Graemme shook his head half believing the old seer was demented. But the other half told him she had always been right about her other predictions. He nodded and started to make his way back into the great hall, but stopped. Her eyes held him steady.

"Ye must know where yer heart lies."

He frowned, wondering what she meant when she turned and faded into the shadows of the dark passage. As children, he and Magnus had wandered the hidden passageway many times and found it led to the top of the keep. Other than his father, he didn't know anyone who had ever explored its darkness.

He waited until he heard laughter bursting from men's throats and knew it was safe to enter. Everyone watched tumblers dressed in outlandish clothing and fanciful makeup as they pretended to fall, one after the other, until the cleared space amongst the diners became so cluttered the next acrobats had to straddle those on the floor.

Slipping into his seat, he gave just a slight tip of his head to Magnus, sending a silent message he would meet with him when he left in the middle of the night. Leaning back, he stretched his arms out at the sides and gave a huge yawn.

"Father, I fear I am near falling asleep at the table. We all need a good sleep to make up for the days of travel."

Magnus agreed right away, with a lurid smile at Muriele. "A down mattress and soft sheets, love. I may be sleepy, but not enough to take my mind from swiving!"

He laughed at her flushed face and helped her to rise at the same time as Graemme had hold of Elyne's elbow. Neither woman protested, for they too were tired from their travels. Chief Angus nodded and called for the next entertainers to come into the room, and for the servants to bring in another barrel of ale. If the drinking and eating continued, no one would note the warriors who would quietly slip away, one by one.

Elyne was no fool. She had seen the looks passing between the two brothers and their father. Also, Bryan and Colyne had already left, wriggling their brows, each leading a lass out of the keep.

When their bedchamber door closed, Elyne twirled around and confronted Graemme.

"What is going on tonight? I saw the looks passing between ye men and know ye are up to something."

"We have learned someone is going to waylay Magnus when he leaves. Grunda and I both saw a woman who appeared to be listening for information about when that would be. Father announced Magnus would not leave until Monday. Afterward, the woman slipped out of the castle by the postern gate and headed to the east. Magnus really plans to leave in the middle of the night, soon as everyone is abed."

"Will they not be riding into a trap?"

Elyne began to wring her hands and pace about the room. Graemme followed behind her, quickly plucking at all the ties holding her kirtle together in back.

"Nay. Magnus will not return over his usual route, but will go southeast and come up from below Blackbriar. The raider who waits to waylay Magnus' party will be empty-handed."

Elyne had been so engrossed in this news she was barely aware Graemme had already removed her kirtle and was determined to swiftly make her as nude as the day she was born. She didn't mind. Magnus' suggestion of a down mattress had been tempting. To make it even better, Graemme's bed was huge. They could roll and thrash about to their hearts content and not end with bruised bodies on the floor.

When the cold air hit her skin, her eyes widened with surprise.

"I am nekid and ye are still clothed!"

"I dinna have time to undress. Grunda is foreseeing where the spy has gone and will surely come to let me know."

She crossed her arms, covering her breasts, and refused to back up to the bed.

"See?" He grabbed the hem of his kilt and lifted it high.

His rampant cock was ready and eager. "Clothing doesna hinder me!"

He came close and thrust his hips at her. His cock felt enticingly warm and, er, very interesting on her bare stomach.

A few short breaths ago, he had been the aggressor. She took over. He found himself backed up to the bed and sprawled across the mattress. Before he could blink his eyes twice, Elyne straddled him, took his hot weapon in her hand and promptly began to rub it over her already slippery entrance.

His gasp of pleasure was all she needed for encouragement.

Rising on her knees, she nestled down on him until the head of his tarse broke into her hot sheath. When he expected her to seat herself firmly, she grinned slyly and popped up, leaving him wanting.

"Lucifer's crooked eyes, woman! Ye tease when ye should be rocking away afore Grunda appears."

His breath came in gasps, but she resisted when he tried to push her down again. She leaned forward, pulled his plaid over his chest to the side and latched like a starving bairn onto his left nipple. She played with him the same as he had always played with her. Bringing him to a peak where he thought he would explode, and then retreating until he caught his breath.

She started over, and each time, he became more aggressive. But Elyne's legs were strong and he feared if he used more force, he would bruise her lovely thighs. Finally, he surged upward. Now he had control. He rolled until she was on her back and began to plunge into her like he couldn't get deep enough or fast enough to suit him. Finally, her nails scratching on his back warned him he'd best bring her release or else he'd look like a wildcat had mated with him.

He thrust his tongue deep into her mouth to keep her from crying out.

When she finally could think again, she giggled.

"Funny? I guess I did not do it right else ye wouldna be grinning like a simple lass."

"Look where we are, husband."

"Graemme raised his head and everything looked out

of place.

They had wrestled themselves across the center of the bed until they slid onto the floor. From there, the ceiling was higher than usual and the bed appeared huge.

Panting for breath, they sprawled twisted amongst sheets and wool blankets atop the wolf skins on the floor.

CHAPTER 29

GRAEMME LAUGHED SO HEARTILY Elyne squealed and slid to his side, afore she, too, saw the humor in it.

"Hsst!"

They both stilled.

"Was that ye?" Elyne lifted on her elbow and looked down at Graemme's surprised face.

"Nay! Of course it wasna him. He was far too busy thinking on his pleasures than heeding my scratching at the door," a gravelly voice whispered.

"Grunda?"

She answered with a snort.

"Ye'd best straighten yer clothing and get below. If ye had been quieter in yer loving, ye would have heard Magnus and his guards gathering in the bailey."

Elyne's head popped up above the bed when she rose on her knees. Seeing the old woman's look of satisfaction, she grabbed her kirtle off the floor and tugged it over her head by the time Graemme adjusted his kilt and stomped on his boots.

Picking up his sword, he whispered loud to Grunda on his way to the door, "Lace her for me, old one. She'll want to wish Muriele Godspeed."

He was gone in a flash, only taking time to ease the door shut without a sound.

"Come girl," Grunda said as she twirled her fingers in the air, "I didna wake Ada to tend ye. She and the blacksmith's son had a long night of it."

Elyne presented her back so the old woman could pull the ribbons tight.

" 'Twas kind. Thank ye." Elyne said over her shoulders as she held the bodice up around her breasts and wriggled until the kirtle fitted comfortably. A few more quick moves and she had her shoes on and ran out the door and down to the front bailey.

When Elyne burst through the keeps doorway, Muriele smiled and waved.

"Ye have a rosy glow of a well sated wife, Elyne," she teased.

"Bleh! 'Tis no such thing. The glow ye speak of is naught but from running down the staircase!"

"Oh? When I passed yer bedchamber, I must have imagined yer voice telling Graemme he was killing ye with pleasure." She grinned and enveloped Elyne with a loving hug.

"We will be within days of each other, Muriele. 'Tis only a half-day longer than traveling to the convent! We should see each other often."

"Well, now, my bonnie ladies. We must leave," Magnus said.

As the portcullis squeaked up and the drawbridge lowered, Graemme put his hands on Elyne's shoulders and moved her back from the horses. With a solemn nod at Graemme, Magnus threw Muriele up into the saddle. Once she settled her feet in the stirrups, she arranged her slit skirts to cover the knives strapped to her calves and adjusted the short sword belted at her waist. She looked the ideal warrior woman, a fitting mate for Magnus the Ruthless.

Elyne felt a sense of loss seeing her friend waving as she crossed through the barbican and rode out over the drawbridge. After the long line of warriors left, they were barely a shadow moving through the night.

"Why are more warriors coming out of the stables leading their mounts? And their standard bearer carries Magnus' banner?" Elyne's stomach turned, knowing the answer afore she asked. She drug her feet as he led her back into the keep to the great hall.

"We have laid a trap for anyone looking to capture Magnus. Father sent a patrol to hide in the woods a few furlongs away, the perfect spot for an ambush. Closer to the sun's rise, I'm taking more men up the hill. They'll think I am Magnus. When they attack, they'll be surprised."

"Won't they know ye are not Magnus when Muriele isn't with ye?"

Graemme shrugged and didn't say anything. By the way he didna meet her eyes, she knew what he'd planned!

"Dinna tell me ye are using Ysabel as a lure!"

"'Twas her own idea. She went to Father and asked we do this for her. She said it would soothe her conscience for having pretended to be Muriele afore."

"I canna believe ye'd do this! What does Colyne say?"

"Colyne? What right does he have in this decision?"

"Fool! He loves her." Elyne snorted and put her hands on her hips.

"Ah. So that is the reason he insisted on arming her and having our best men surrounding her."

"'Twill work."

Grunda had appeared so silently when they entered the great hall she seemed to be made of smoke.

"Aye. After ye looked into the bowl of still water and told us what they planned."

"Their surprise will be their undoing." She heaved a sigh. "Though, their master will get away. Again. He is near mad. His leman believes he is pure and ye and Magnus are evil. He keeps his body and face hidden."

Elyne had no stomach for breaking her fast this morn. Though the sun was not yet up, the great room was crowded with hungry men. All too soon, Colyne came into the room with Ysabel. The resemblance was unnerving, for Elyne had to look at her up close to tell it was not Muriele.

Why was she so uneasy about Graemme's leaving with them? Grunda assured her all was going to work out for the best. But what if the *best* made her a widow? Why should she care? Hadn't she wished more than once Graemme would disappear from her life? Why, she'd even disliked him so much she'd bitten him!

When had her feelings changed to worrying about his safety? Too soon, Chief Angus nodded his head at Graemme. 'Twas time. The darkest part of the night was gone and the bailey filled with warriors anxious for a fight.

It seemed like a repeating dream to Elyne when she hugged Ysabel and saw Colyne help her onto her mount. Worse was when Graemme smothered Elyne in his arms and kissed her so heartily his father chuckled. She gave him an accusing glare. What if Graemme never came back? She was near to crying.

And she never cried! Chief Angus immediately came close, and she went from her husband's arms to his father's. Grunda stood on her other side, murmuring softly.

"Dinna be troubled. If he does as I told him, he will return unscathed."

'Twas three days of being in Hades before Grunda announced the men would return when the sun was high the next day. When she awoke the next sunrise, Ada helped her with her bath. Elyne was so tense she spewed before she even had a chance to break her fast.

"'Tis normal," old Grunda pronounced from the chamber doorway.

"How did ye know I was going to be sick? The pork last eve must have been old. Did it upset ye too?"

"Nay. The pork was fine. Ye'll find out soon enough what troubles ye."

Grunda bustled about preparing hot barley water to settle Elyne's stomach.

Soon, she went below to have a small bowl of porridge. 'Twas all she felt like eating afore she went atop the castle's wall walks to watch the hill for any signs of movement. She wanted so badly for the warriors to return that several times she imagined she saw something when 'twas only wind in the trees.

Afore the sun was directly overhead, she saw flashes of color, and the guard at his post on the hill flashed a light twice with his polished pewter square. She watched the castle guard return two flashes.

"Two flashes means 'tis castle patrols returning with a victory," Chief Angus said with a huge grin. "Looks like we will have time for a celebration this eve!"

Headed for the stairs leading down into the bailey, Elyne barely heard him. Squat, who had been unusually quiet since Graemme had left, set up an earsplitting series of barks and tried to squeeze through the teeth of the portcullis.

"Come, ye silly dog. Ye'll get yer head stuck, and then what would I do?" She grabbed him up in her arms and held him close.

The horsemen came thundering over the cleared land. She shaded her eyes with one hand and saw Graemme galloping toward her, slightly ahead of the rest of the men. Her heart finally calmed knowing he seemed not too much worse for the fighting. Blood splattered his clothing near from head to toe, but he rode upright and strong.

All the men wore big grins and none led horses with men slung over the saddles. When Graemme leaned over and pulled her up in front of him, Squat and all, she was happy to feel his warm body against hers. Until she became aware of the stench of blood.

Her stomach turned and saliva gathered in her mouth.

"Graemme! Stop, quick!"

With a puzzled look, he did and waved the men past them. His face drained of color when she leaned over his arm and spewed her porridge, soiling not only her own garments but him from his knees down to his boots. Squat huffed low in his throat as if admonishing her for squeezing him too tight.

"Ye are ill!"

"Nay. I thought so, too, but Grunda says 'twill pass."

"Aye, it will," Ysabel's voice said close by. She and Colyne had drawn up beside them when they saw Elyne was in trouble.

"'Tis naught but worry," Elyne said, trying to wipe her mouth with the sleeve of the ruined kirtle.

"Nay. She's ailing from lack of bed sport!"

Ysabel giggled. Colyne grinned and Graemme flashed a big smile. How could they be so carefree when she felt so unsteady?

She raised her bent left arm and hit back with her elbow into Graemme's ribs. Hard.

"Ouch! See, ye are not so ill I couldna prick yer temper!"

He laughed aloud when she gave him a look that would have warned another man to silence.

When they rode through the barbican, everyone in the bailey was excitedly chattering on how they had outsmarted a band of outlaws awaiting them in the forest. All but their leader had died in the skirmish. He had stayed off in the distance then disappeared in the thickest part of the fight, galloping off when he knew all was lost.

Grunda waited at the keep's wooden stairway. Without a word, she took Elyne's elbow and guided her up to her and Graemme's bedchambers. Graemme was unable to follow, for men grabbed his arm and insisted on hearing about the fight.

"Ada, bring hot water so we may clean this smelly girl from head to toe.

While Grunda helped Elyne strip without soiling her hair, Ada tended to having a bath brought up. When it arrived, Grunda was gentle as a mother cat tending her kittens. While she had Elyne lean her head on the end of the tub and close her eyes, she washed Elyne's face and insisted she relax and let the warm water soothe her. Within a short time, Elyne's stomach settled.

"See, I told ye it was naught but a slight sickness from the pork."

Grunda rocked back on her heels and laughed. "Lass, with all the bed sport ye've reveled in for the past month, didna it occur to ye a bairn could take seed?"

Elyne sat up so quickly water sloshed over the sides of the tub. "A bairn? But only people who are happily married produce bairns! Look at Ranald and Catalin. She even had twins!"

"Aye, but look at yer cousin Raik and Letia. She near hated him when he got her increasing."

Before they could argue further, Graemme barged through the doorway smiling from ear to ear. He must have bathed elsewhere, for not a bloody splatter remained, and his clothing was fresh and clean.

"Are ye through spewing?"

"Of course. 'Twas the stench of blood and sweat. It turned my stomach," she bluffed.

"Sure and it was! If ye had beheaded and chopped arms off bandits, ye would be covered in slimy blood and guts, too."

She did what any increasing woman with a good imagination would do. Turned green and gulped to keep from spewing over the side of the tub.

"Well, piss and shite! If ye are intent on upsetting an unsettled stomach, get yerself gone from the room!"

Graemme's laughter rocked off the walls.

"I see ye will not mellow whilst ye carry a bairn." He shook his head and gave her a disapproving look. "Ye must watch yer words, else when ye pop the bairn out he will yell, 'Piss and shite, 'twas tight in there!'"

Elyne eyes widened. He ducked and made a quick retreat afore the soapy cloth could reach him.

Graemme was truly happy for the first time in many years. His brother was safe from the Gunns, his father was in robust health, but most of all he had a bride worthy of a Morgan.

She would be a strong mother for their sons.

He turned the last step descending the stairwell when he glimpsed his father going through his solar door with a knight. He didn't recognize him, but something about his profile caused his heart to trip. Frowning, he tried to recall the face, but thinking of Elyne breeding distracted his thoughts.

No sense wasting time trying to draw forth a memory when he had to see to his men.

"Now Elyne is settled for a short nap, take me to the wounded men," Grunda demanded behind him.

"Do ye think my wife will mellow now she's to be a mother?"

"Ye dafty man. If naught else, she will become even more fierce. She will have a young one to protect."

"Protect? I will do the protecting. Her duties will be to feed and nourish my son until he's big enough to start training with a wooden sword."

"Eh? Where are yer brains? She is in more danger now than at any time in her life."

"Ye have seen trouble with the birthing?" Graemme's stomach clenched in sudden fear.

"Nay. The birthing will go well enough. If she makes it that far."

"That far? Ye just said the birthing will go well."

"'Tis not all. There is a long time afore she births, ye impatient disbeliever."

Graemme halted and turned back to her.

"There are other things far more dangerous than birthing the bairn. Dinna let Elyne out of yer sight. She may wander the walls during the night. Above all, dinna let her leave the castle grounds. In her condition, she is ripe for waking dreams."

"How am I to stop something within her head?"

"By keeping her calm at all times. Her dreams lead her astray when she is upset or angry."

They had no more time to talk, for Grunda began making order of the chaos in the men's barracks. She soon had the warriors separated according to their wounds. The less serious she left to the men's squires to attend to. The others, she treated herself.

He stayed to help, amazed at how fast the old woman could clean, attend to the wound and place the stitches before going to the next man.

When all the men were treated and comfortable, 'twas time for their evening meal.

The great hall was festive this night, for they celebrated knowing Magnus and his people would arrive at Blackbriar unscathed, and the diversion party led by Graemme had been successful.

Chief Angus had barrels of wine brought from the storage rooms on the first floor of the keep. Elyne felt refreshed and better than she had in weeks. She refused to dwell on the reason — Graemme has returned safe from harm — and preferred to believe it was because of the bairn.

Mid-way through the meal, Chief Angus stood and announced his son's wife would provide him with a son come next spring. She felt herself flush when everyone stood and yelled all manner of advice for making sure she birthed a son. Some were so ridiculous it made her laugh.

"Put a fresh pulled carrot with the stalk beneath yer sheets each night. 'Twill assure the bairn has a hearty tarse and hair to nest it in when he reaches his father's shoulders!"

"Plump turnips will provide hearty ballocks!"

"Nay, beets will cause his tarse to fill with blood for a hard cockstand," another shouted.

"Yer mither likely used withered beets afore ye were born! Ye have a crook in yer cock whenever it tries to rise."

Now and again, someone's fist hammered another's jaw. Chief Angus stopped it by rising to make another announcement.

"Sir Colyne has asked my permission to wed young Ysabel, who came to us from the Lowlands. She has no living relatives, so I shall stand in for her deceased father this coming Saturday."

Ysabel and Colyne had to rise and go through the same bantering Elyne had borne, only theirs was advice on swiving to keep yer wife happy and content.

They took it in good spirit, and Elyne laughed with the rest. She was still grinning when she felt an uneasy scrutiny. She lowered her head and studied the room until she found the source. An older knight looked at her with pity. Her brows knit wondering why. She glanced at Graemme, and he too, had felt the man's gaze. Suddenly, recognition flashed on her husband's face.

She didn't like what she saw. So many expressions in such a short time. First shock, then excitement. Of a sudden, his shoulders slumped. Then he straightened, his lips thinned and a look of determination hardened his jaw. When she looked back at the knight, he was gone.

Elyne turned for Graemme to help lift her kirtle over her head. She had sent Ada on to bed earlier, for by the looks passing between Ada and her soldier, 'twas apparent they craved time together.

"Who was the knight who studied us like we were strange bugs to be pitied?" She asked when her head cleared her skirts.

"He's been in father's service since I was a lad."

"Then why did he study us so closely?"

"He has been gone for a long time and just returned today. I guess he was surprised to learn I had wed."

"Why should your taking a wife be a surprise?"

When Graemme didn't answer, she started to think of reasons why the man would think this unusual. The only one that made sense was such a shock it caused her nape to feel like cold fingers creeping up her neck.

"He is *her* father?" The words exploded like they were arrows shooting from her lips.

"What do ye mean by her?" he asked, his head lowered as he started taking off his kilt.

"Ye sure as Hades know who! The lass ye loved who disappeared. The one ye were still in love with when we wed," she shouted.

"He was her grandfather. There is no need to announce to the whole world ye are jealous of a dead woman!"

"Jealous? Are ye daft?"

For answer, he thrust her on the bed then straddled her. With his knees on either side of her, she sank into the down mattress. He stripped off the kilt still flapping around his waist and threw it on the floor. When he lowered his body atop her, her legs clamped around his waist, holding him tight.

Time and time again, his mouth ravaged hers. It wasn't for pleasure, she knew, but because he wanted to silence her. She twisted her head until he clamped his hands in her long hair and held her still.

She bit his lower lip. He bit her back.

She scratched his back. He flipped her on her stomach and nibbled down from her nape to the dimples on her buttocks.

She reared and tried to throw him off. When her buttocks rose off the mattress, he slipped one arm beneath her, positioning her as he thrust into her moist center. His rocking became faster and faster. Holding her hips, he kept her from moving upward on the bed.

Though his lovemaking was enthusiastic, he was careful not to thrust to the hilt, fearing he would harm the bairn.

Their heavy breathing broke the silence in the room. He moved his hands to wrap her hair around and around them, tugging on them like the reins of a horse. She had never felt so vulnerable in her life.

"Release my hair! I am not some mare to be mounted!"

Graemme shook his head, though she could not see him behind her.

"Yer hair belongs to me, now, as ye do. I will do with it whatever pleasures me!"

He transferred her hair into one fist. Reaching between them, he rubbed his fingers over her swollen nub until she tensed and quivered, then climaxed.

He kept a steel control over his pleasure and didn't allow himself to release his seed. Now, more than ever, she had to know she belonged to him. He kept her head raised until her muscles stopped trying to drain his cock.

Afore she could catch her breath, he rolled to his back and pulled her to sit atop him. His cock was still stiff as a shaft, swollen and so red he feared it would burst afore long. She flipped her head so hard her beautiful hair flew around her face. He closed his eyes, reveling in the scent of heather and the feel of the silky strands caressing his body.

His teeth gritted together and his eyes closed tight. Never had he had such an exquisite feeling on his flesh as he did now when she leaned forward until all her hair enveloped his head. With slow, deliberate movements, she timed each downward thrust with her body with inching her hair down over him, until at the last stroke it covered his stomach and belly.

When she straightened and rocked until the bed ropes

creaked, he couldn't hold back any longer. When she reached her peak again, he didn't try to stifle his pleasure.

Strangely, she was silent until she moved up to his waist where she could come forward on her hands and knees. Again, she let her hair surround them as she was a hand's length from his face.

"Ye think even my hair belongs to ye, do ye?"

"Aye. It does."

"Then 'tis only right that all of ye belongs to me."

"It is not the way of a man. No man belongs to a woman."

"Well, then, other's may not, but ye do. If ever I dinna have all of ye, then ye'll not have all of me. This hair ye set such a value on will be beneath yer pillow."

"Do so and I will beat ye!"

"'Twill be the one and only time. Ye'll never lay a hand on me again, either in pleasure or anger."

She shoved herself off him and moved as far as she could to the edge of the bed. It was fortunate he kept his tongue behind his teeth.

She was ready to do battle.

CHAPTER 30

THE HUGE BLACK HORSE thundered toward the castle ruins in the distance. It stood atop Ben Clibrick on a cliff overlooking Loch Naver. To the west was Altnaharra. To the east was half a day's ride to Clibrick Castle.

The man leaned into the wind, the hood of his cloak whipped back revealing a face too beautiful for a mortal man. Blond hair streamed in the wind, but he didn't care. Anyone who saw him would think they saw a ghost. He was far from one. Fury made him strong as the god he should have been. He'd named his horse Thor, The God of War, so people would note his strength.

Months before, he'd gone to Clibrick to demand Magnus return Muriele. But first, he sought out a woman known to be a witch. She'd refined a potion and, using a vein from a pig, sucked a small amount into it and tied off both ends. He'd slit her throat for payment.

When he'd arrived outside Clibrick Castle with his father and warriors, he stored the potion between his teeth and cheek in his left jaw. Should the unbelievable happen and he lost the inevitable fight to come, he would crush it with his teeth. It would make him appear dead until the effects wore off. He didn't think he would ever have need of its use, but he had.

His father was about to put him in a shroud when he gasped and came out of a deep sleep. It had scared his father so badly his reddish-blonde beard turned white overnight. When he recovered from the shock, Chief Olaf banished him, saying he wouldna have a coward for a son.

After racing hard over the mountain, sweat covered Thor.

Fury at another failure had made Feradoch vicious with his whip. When he yanked on the reins and brought Thor to an abrupt stop, the horse reared with eyes rolling and mouth foaming, near unseating Feradoch. The man would have struck the horse again, but its rearing hooves near unseated him.

"Elspeth! Where are ye?"

His shout brought the woman waiting in the shadowed doorway out into the light. She was a fitting mate for him. Their coloring was so alike they could have been twins. They were also alike in temper. She had laughed as heartily as he when he spirited her away after her betrothal to Graemme. She had watched, hidden, when search parties combed the mountains and woods around. Elspeth's biggest triumph came when they'd found a young lass with blond hair who had wandered too far from her farm. After using her until her novelty wore off, it was easy enough to dress her in one of Elspeth's kirtles, kill her and leave her in a gully covered with snow. It was near two years afore they found her bones.

Feradoch charged toward Elspeth, ready to smash his fist into her face. She widened her stance and held up a well-honed sword. Hearing her snarl and her eyes light with a strange madness, his mood changed. For the first time, he was sorry he'd taught her how to use the sword. He shrugged and smiled. Later, he would discipline her with bed sport.

He enjoyed making her suffer. It excited Elspeth as much as it did him.

Magnus and Muriele may be lost to him, but there was still the weakling Graemme. Better yet, the woman with the glorious, dark hair would make interesting bed sport for him and Elspeth — and a lure for her husband.

CHAPTER 31

FOR THE NEXT SENNIGHT, Elyne avoided Graemme during the day. Once they were abed, she could not. But if he dared approach her intending on bed sport, when he was at his most amorous, she pulled away and promptly spewed what she'd eaten.

She didn't do it on purpose, though he thought she did. One night, Grunda scratched on the door just a heartbeat before Elyne needed her. By the time Elyne raised on her elbow, Grunda held the basin under her chin.

"How do ye always know when I am feeling my worst," gasped Elyne.

"By the look in Graemme's eyes when he escorts ye to bed."

"Old woman, do ye say Elyne is making herself sick on purpose so I willna touch her?"

Graemme scowled up at her as he held Elyne's forehead, supporting her.

"Nay. Some women have night sickness as well as early morn. The thought of bed sport when they feel queasy is enough to make them spew," Grunda said and handed him a cold cloth.

He frowned as he carefully wiped Elyne's face then lowered her back onto her pillow.

"Has yer sleep been filled with dreams, lass?" Grunda poured out a small portion of an elixir that soothed her stomach.

"Dreams, yes. But not about the black wolf. It is a large golden wolf. A woman rides astride him like he is a horse. They chase me through the woods until I take refuge in the ruins of an ancient castle. They find me. The woman shoves me into a cell and closes the iron bars. Though I can see the bars hasn't a lock, no matter how hard I try, I canna push them open."

Grunda frowned. She handed Graemme a long, thin piece of material. "'Tis best ye tie her ankle to yer own to keep her from walking the grounds. She may wander off into the forest or climb high again."

"Aye." Graemme gently tied one end onto Elyne's right ankle and the other to his left. "This should alert me should ye start to wander during the night."

Elyne wanted to protest, but was too tired to argue. She was always sleepy, day or night, and right now, all she wanted to do was crawl between the sheets and close her eyes.

The night before Ysabel and Colyne were to wed, Elyne tossed and thrashed about, awakening Graemme. He held her in his arms and murmured soothing sounds until he felt her body relaxing into a deep sleep. When dawn came, he was still awake and watchful. He heard the portcullis rise and the drawbridge lower earlier than usual. From the sounds of it, several horsemen came through into the bailey.

Careful not to awake her, he untied the cloth, dressed and went below. Colyne and Brian were waiting for him. Before long, the castle teamed with people laughing and looking forward to another day of feasting and revelry. He looked around for his father, but saw the closed door to his solar. Likely, he was with an old friend catching up on good times. They wouldn't want to be disturbed.

Elyne felt better than usual this morning. After Ada helped her to dress, they spent the morning aiding Ysabel. The bride was pale and uneasy, for she never expected to have more than a handful of people attend her wedding.

"I am the widow of the third son of a baron. My father was a knight, not a Chief," she whispered to Elyne.

"Ye are a friend, Ysabel," Elyne said and hugged her. "Besides, it is a wonderful reason to have a day of feasting and revelry."

The wedding itself was simple but lovely. When they returned from the church, Elyne noted several knights she hadn't seen before. One elderly knight put his head close to Chief Angus. When he finished whispering, Angus face turned white. He looked around until he spied Graemme.

Something was amiss. One minute, Graemme was talking and laughing with her, but when he looked up and saw the knight, he stopped in his tracks. His face tightened, his lips thinned and he forced a smile when the knight looked his way. So. He knew the man. But why was he upset? She wasn't surprised when his father beckoned to him.

"I'll join ye as soon as I find what Father wants, love," Graemme said and kissed her cheek.

Grunda came to walk beside her, as did Brian. He looked grim, also. Worried now, she frowned and looked at Colyne. He forced a smile, swung his bride in his arms and teased Ysabel that she, too, would soon be sick when the sun rose.

"What is it, Grunda? Is there a raiding party heading our way?"

"Now, how would I know about it? Do ye believe I am a warrior now?"

"Nay. But you do know what is going on."

"Yer husband will tell ye when he has the time."

The great hall bustled with people when the solar door opened and the three men came out. Chief Angus smiled at Colyne and Ysabel and led them to the seat of honor. Angus sat on Ysabel's left, and Elyne and Graemme sat at Colyne's right.

The mysterious knight wasn't as old as she had thought. What she took to be gray hair was the palest blond. He stood, watching the doorway uneasily. When he stiffened and stared, she looked to see the reason why.

Framed by the massive door stood the most beautiful girl Elyne had seen. Her hair was like silken sunshine. She had eyes the palest blue of the sky on a summer morn, and skin as smooth as a bairn's. Her plump lips didn't need berries to make them red. She was everything Elyne was not.

She was dainty from head to toe. Elyne felt long-limbed

and drab with her heavy dark hair. One glance at the grim set of Graemme's lips told her all.

His love, Elspeth, was not the dead woman they had found. She was very much alive. And it was obvious from the way she devoured Graemme with her eyes — she wanted him.

In her life.

In her bed.

Elyne felt the urge to spew but swallowed and wouldn't allow herself to be sick. What a horrible contrast it would make in Graemme's mind to see his wife heaving like a weakling compared to a woman as beautiful and delicate as a butterfly.

Hold yer dignity, girl. Lift yer chin high. He loves ye, not her.

'Twas Grunda's voice in her head, yet Grunda stood far away, her back against a tapestry picturing the castle with the mountains in the background. The old woman blended into the scene.

Elyne squared her shoulders and lifted her head high. Feeling Elspeth's blue eyes studying her, she stared back. Before she looked away, her lip curled with contempt, dismissing the woman as if she were no more than a slovenly servant. A glimpse of rage stared back. Mayhap she imagined it? She dismissed the woman from her mind and joined in the conversation.

The woman turned her attention to Graemme, constantly sending him soulful looks, and the pink tip of her tongue wetted her parted lips. 'Twas a clear invitation to Graemme. Elyne tightened her jaw, determined to ignore the both of them and concentrated on the entertainment instead.

Pipers were playing a lively tune. Men jumped up from the table and put their swords on the floor, one across another. They took turns doing a sword-dance until each dancer got dizzy and either cut himself or fell on the floor. Soon, men sprawled in the cleared area laughing as if they'd been in their cups since dawn.

Elspeth's laugh grated on Elyne's nerves. It tinkled and was melodic like she imagined a fairy would laugh. It made her conscious of her own laugh, for when she found humor, everyone looked at her and smiled, saying she was gleeful.

Soon it was time for the bride and groom to go above. As

she held Ysabel's hand and led her up the first steps, she glanced back at the room. Graemme stood next to Elspeth, his head lowered as he whispered in her ear.

The woman glanced up at Elyne, a triumphant smile on her face. Reaching up, she held his head as he pressed his lips to hers. The kiss seemed to go on and on. He certainly ground his mouth on hers, for his head would move back then return like he couldn't get enough of her taste. When Graemme finally pulled back and placed his hand on the small of her back, he near shoved her ahead of him in his eagerness. When they went through the doorway leading to the darkened hallway, she looked reluctant and shy.

There was naught Elyne could do now without ruining the night for Ysabel and Colyne. Anger boiled through her. Had she her short sword with her, he would be missing those precious stones her father had threatened.

"What the Hades are ye doing here, Elspeth? Ye disappeared years ago, so why did ye bother to come back now? We even found a body with yer clothing clinging to it."

She pursed her lips and wet them, trying to entice him. He didn't fall for it, but she had a radiant smile on her face as if he'd actually said he'd loved her!

"Did ye cry for me, love?"

"I cried for the woman who I thought loved me. I cried believing ye had died a fearful death! But after talking to yer father today, ye are no longer the woman I once knew and loved."

She reached up and locked her hands behind his head. When had she become so strong? She rose on her toes and started to kiss him as though she was ravenous. He tried to lift his head, but each time he did, she forced it back to her lips, grinding her mouth against his until he tasted blood on his teeth.

Finally, she stopped and smiled at the stairway. He glanced up and saw Elyne's stiff back disappearing as she led Ysabel up to her bridal bedchamber. Fury built in him for Elspeth pretended she was his lover to make Elyne suffer. He grabbed hold of the woman's shoulder and shoved her into the hallway.

"Ye little bitch! Ye were Feradoch's lover all those years when I worried about ye. Now he's dead, ye think to fool yer father and me into thinking ye were helpless!"

"Oh, but I was. Feradoch was such a powerful lover. I truly was helpless to leave him. Where ye were soft and reluctant, he was strong and forceful. He satisfied me in every way possible. Yer wife looks more your squire than a woman. If ye'd like, I will teach ye ways to pleasure yer gawky wife so she'd appear feminine to ye?"

"Gawky? Squire? She is a hundred times more the woman than ye. If ye dinna leave within a sennight, I will force ye to marry the most warty, ugliest warrior in Clibrick's army!"

He shouted so loud he feared the guests in the great hall would hear him.

"I don't think so," she said silkily. "Ye'd best look to yer own. I heard about her sleep walking. Maybe she's looking for a real man to pleasure her?"

"Stay away from her and from me. I want ye gone from this castle!"

Graemme turned and near fled her hateful presence. His hands kept clenching and unclenching, longing to have her tiny neck within them.

He shuddered thinking she had been Feradoch's leman all those years while he had mourned for her.

For the first time, he felt no remorse. He was truly glad Feradoch was dead.

He went back into the great hall in time to escort Colyne up to his bride. He tried to calm his breathing, but he knew from the tenseness in his neck that his face was red. The men looked at him and shook their heads. Did they, too, think he had swived the bitch?

He pasted a smile on his face when he went up to bang on the door. 'Twas his place to bring the groom to his bride.

"Yer husband is ready and eager, Ysabel! If ye make him

wait, he will split at the seams!"

The door swung open and the men burst into the room, pushed from those behind.

The bride looked as beautiful as any bride could. Her long wheat-colored hair curled around her shoulders and down across her breasts, hiding them beneath the thin smock she wore. He felt Elyne's eyes scorching his skin. She was far past angry. She was as furious as any woman could be. The others might not see it. But he knew. He could feel it radiate from her.

"Back yerselves out and return to the hall," Grunda said in her loudest voice, "or do ye want me to shrivel yer tarses to the size of a newborn?"

She flicked her hands at them as she came. They felt her force against them as surely as an army of shields. They near fell over their feet backing out of the room.

She held Graemme with her eyes. "Ye are a blind fool. Dinna try to explain this night. Wait until she sleeps afore ye come to yer room."

Graemme nodded, inwardly glad to put off having to explain to Elyne what had happened.

He doubted she would believe him!

"Let me brew ye a draught to help yer sleep," Grunda asked Elyne.

"Nay. I will sleep well enough. If Graemme's brain is as wise as a hare's, he will stay away from me this night. Ada will help me undress. Seek yer own bed."

Elyne reached out and hugged the old woman who looked so tired and worn.

"Ye will do nothing foolish if he appears?"

"Foolish? Like cutting his ballocks off to send to Father?" She shook her head. "Nay, too bloody. I'll do nothing so drastic. He will be safe enough."

Elyne kept her face still and tried to appear serene. When Grunda went through the doorway, Squat squeezed past her and came scurrying into the room. He must have escaped from Gille, who had taken such a liking for the little dog.

Jumping up on the bed, his beady eyes looked at Elyne,

studying her. He turned his head to the right, listened for a bit then flipped it over to the other side.

"Dinna try to figure me out, Squat. Ye are a male. Ye would need to be a bitch to understand."

"Sometimes I think the dog does understand everything," Ada said as she untied the ribbons on the sides of Elyne's red kirtle.

Once Elyne had her night smock on, she didn't get into bed. Ada stood there holding the blankets and sheet up for her to slide between, but Elyne lowered her hand. She went over and opened her clothing chest. She picked up a sheathed knife off the top wooden tray and brought it over. Ada gasped.

"Ye told Grunda ye wouldna do anything foolish!"

"I'm not. I want ye to help me. Remember when ye first saw Muriele's hair after it was cut?"

"Aye." She eyed her suspiciously.

"Help me, then."

Elyne walked over to the polished steel hanging over the wash basin. She grabbed a handful of hair at her shoulders and cut through it before Ada realized what she wanted. The poor girl gasped and backed away.

"By the Saints! What have ye done? Yer beautiful hair!"

"Looks terrible, doesn't it?" Elyne studied herself in the mirror. "Well, now, the only thing we can do is cut it the same length. Ye are better at trimming the men's hair than I am. This should be simple for ye."

She turned the handle toward Ada and waited until her friend's trembling hand accepted it. As she cut each hank, Elyne took it in her fist with the first one. Finally, she had to hold it with both hands.

"There are some ribbons on the tray. What do ye think? All in one bundle or two?"

Ada swallowed. "Two. It will be easier to tie."

It took longer than Elyne expected to tie the curly hair into two bundles. Lifting Graemme's pillow, she fashioned each bundle into a ring then replaced the pillow. Every footstep she heard, she prayed it wasn't Graemme.

Her head felt lighter. She stood back and fluffed it after Ada finished trimming. Freed of its length, it curled and bounced as she walked. One curl fell over her right eye. She stuck out her lower lip and blew at it, lifting it away.

" 'Tis a trick I learned from Muriele," she said then grinned.

After they'd picked up the stray pieces and threw them out the window, the room looked normal again.

"Thank, ye, Ada. Ye are a good friend. Dinna tell Graemme ye helped me. Go to yer lover now and relax for the night." She leaned over and hugged her friend.

After she climbed into bed, she realized how tired she was. Anger had drained her energy. It had also drained all other feelings from her, too. After the door closed, she yawned and was asleep.

When Graemme entered the bedchamber, he placed his feet carefully and dropped his clothing as he made his way to the bed. He was already snoring by the time his head hit the pillow.

CHAPTER 32

GRAEMME SLEPT ON HIS stomach, his face pressed against the end of his pillow. His nose twitched and disturbed his sleep enough to half awake him. When he tried to brush a hand over his nose, he realized he gripped heather scented hair in his right hand. Burying his face in it caused his sex to stir.

He tamped the feeling down, for if she was as angry now as she had been in Ysabel's room, she'd probably stop him with a whack to his nose. Instead, he gathered her hair and rubbed his face in it. Her hair had grown lately, from the feel of its abundance. Frowning, he rose up and squinted, trying to see her. If he pulled the hair too close, it would wake her.

Blinking, he could swear she was an arm's length away, close to the edge of the massive bed. Too much wine last night must have caused his eyes to misjudge the distance. But why did he not see the trail of hair between them. He got up on his knees and bent down, the better to see the handfuls of hair. His eyes cleared when he saw they led back to his pillow.

Graemme flipped the pillow onto the floor.

His bellow of rage was loud enough to wake the creatures of the night.

"Cursed Lucifer's... Satan's black...!"

His voice spluttered as he stared at the two bundles of dark, curly hair. Light from the fireplace flickered, showing the hair's fiery auburn lights. He threw the offending locks in her face.

He spluttered even more, trying to find words to satisfy his anger.

"Satan's windy arse!"

His screamed words echoed off the walls so loudly footsteps

raced toward their room and swords struck the walls as men ran to battle whoever was attacking Graemme.

He leapt across the bed and locked Elyne between his legs. She shook her head, sending the hair beside her on the pillow. Her brown eyes flashed fury up at him.

"Blessed Saints, Graemme, what have ye done!" Chief Angus yelled.

"Dinna tell me ye cut her lovely hair in spite," Colyne said.

"Why, he's trying to strangle her with it," Ysabel cried out as she ran and leapt onto Graemme's back.

Grunda quietly walked up to the bed and pried Ysabel off him.

"Nay, he isna trying to strangle her. 'Tis his own fault. Did Elyne not forewarn ye what she would do if ye wavered in yer marriage vows?"

She turned to Chief Angus and ordered him as if she was in charge of Clibrick.

"Send everyone back to their beds. This is a matter to be solved between these two alone."

Elyne was as angry as she had ever been. Here she was with all these naked people in her room staring at her as if she had four legs. Or were the women staring at Graemme's handsome arse? His blond leman was taking her time looking him over. Elyne didn't miss the passion which flared on Elspeth's face when Graemme's nested sex appeared as he rose on his left knee and swung his right leg off her. Elyne could finally take a full breath.

Elspeth licked her lips when Graemme snarled on spotting her. His expression was murderous, yet the woman became even more excited.

Well piss and shite! The bitch was nekid, too! Her nipples hardened as she kept her eyes on the joining of Graemme's legs.

"Get out of here, ye slut, else I'll push this fool off the bed and skewer ye instead!" Elyne pulled out a dagger from beneath her pillow as she struggled to get out of bed.

When Elspeth turned and swayed her beautiful, bare buttocks as she left the room, her tinkling laughter of triumph trailed her.

"Fool. I once told ye to take heed of two who say they love ye, for one is yer worst enemy. Did ye pick the wrong one to believe?" Grunda's gravelly voice asked.

She turned her eyes on the people still in the room and they scurried to leave afore she could lay a curse upon them.

The old woman shook her head and left once Elyne and Graemme were alone.

"I canna believe ye'd cut yer beautiful hair to spite me! Why did ye do such a sheep-witted thing?"

Elyne sat up in the bed and brushed the shorn hair from her lap.

"Why? Ye ask me why when ye near crawled into the mouth of that blond devil's spawn? In front of my very eyes and everyone in the hall? I saw the way ye watched her. Yer thoughts were clear enough for everyone to read."

"Whatever ye saw in my eyes, it wasna lust! I have not swived the girl, nor will I ever."

Graemme advanced on her, his lips thin, his dark eyes black with rage. His hands balled into fists then opened, again and again. Never had he been so enraged at a woman.

She didn't even cringe, but sat there with sparks flashing from her eyes.

"I told ye I would beat ye if ever ye took a knife to yer hair!"

"And I told ye I wouldna share any part of ye."

"I just told ye I didn't swive the girl!"

"Maybe not. But ye sure as Hades wanted to. Half the people in the hall expected ye to throw her on the banquet table! They saw the blood on yer lips from yer passion, ye horse's arse!"

Elyne rose to her knees and gripped her dagger in front of her. Firmly.

Graemme had never violently beaten a woman. He'd thought the threat would be enough to make Elyne obey him. He should have known she wouldn't pay heed to his words.

To keep himself from doing something despicable he'd regret for the rest of his life, he gathered his clothing from where he'd dropped them in his drunken stupor and dressed quickly. He avoided even going close to the bed and made a wide detour to collect his sword and weapons.

"Where are ye going?"

"I'll sleep elsewhere until ye come to yer senses."

"Dinna forget to take yer present with ye!"

Two soft objects hit his back, one after the other, and then slithered to the floor. 'Twas her beautiful locks. He looked over his shoulder to glare at her.

"There is nay talking to ye when ye're dafty as a half-plucked fowl!

He made his exit in the nick of time. No sooner had he closed the door than a hard object hit the inside panel. Whether the pitcher or the basin, the door would have a good-sized gash in the wood.

Or was it her dagger?

The tension in the keep for the next three days was enough to ignite a fireplace. The men were careful not to tweak Graemme's nose, after Brian's comment the first morning.

Bewildered as Graemme stalked away, Brian shook his head. He rubbed his jaw as he wobbled up from the middle of a mud puddle. He jiggled his legs to shake off the excess mud and looked at Colyne.

"All I did was ask if the kiss was worth it."

Each day, Elyne broke her fast after she had her stomach under control. There was no danger in running into Graemme late in the morning. At the noon meal, they were coldly polite to each other. Graemme took his last meal of the day elsewhere. He didn't come to their bed to sleep, either. It pricked Elyne's temper for Elspeth was also missing.

Ysabel pried it out of Colyne that Graemme had his meals sent to the soldier's barracks. He swore Graemme slept there, too, but Elyne doubted it. His cock was too lively to go without a good swiving every night since they'd married. She didn't believe he'd stop now.

Each day, someone told her how much they liked her hair, for her curls reached her shoulders. The women were tired of the long time it took to wash and brush it, much less the work to braid and twist it around their heads. They asked their husbands if they could cut their own hair, but the men were like Graemme and forbad it.

Grunda gave Elyne a light sleeping draught each night to keep her from walking the parapets. After the third night, the old woman thought it worked well enough Ada didn't have to sleep across the doorway.

Whenever her father, Sir Malcolm, was away, Elspeth blushed and acted coy when her gaze met Elyne's. Ada and Ysabel were constantly at Elyne's side so the sly hellion wouldn't try to prick Elyne's temper.

Even young Gille tried to bring a smile to her face when he'd bring Squat to spend some time with her. He'd been teaching the dog tricks, to make her laugh. Having his widened legs aided him to sit for the longest times. If she ignored him, Squat would hold up a paw and wave it, wanting her to reach out and grasp it. He fetched whatever Gille threw. If it was a stick much longer than the dog, he lifted his head high and pranced, trying to lift it off the ground.

Elyne smiled and pretended everything was normal, but she was sick at heart. She missed her verbal sparring with Graemme, missed his teasing and even her anger when he treated her like a simpering woman. Most of all, she missed his loving. A big lump formed in her chest when she saw his back disappear around a corner of the keep. He avoided any contact with her.

When night fell, she took her draught as usual. She slept peacefully. One night, she dreamt of walking through the darkened keep and going out into the orchard. Someone took her hand to lead her. 'Twas Muriele in a brown cloak. She knew it was her friend because blond hair blew from beneath the hood.

She didn't talk, just kept beckoning her on.

They came to a hole in the wall hidden from within by brush piled against it. Muriele pulled the brush back and pointed for her to go through. Someone called to her, but Muriele let her hand go and shoved her shoulders, telling her to run or the black wolf would tear out her throat. She scrambled through and ran for all she was worth. She tripped over a fallen log and heard his snarls close behind her. Glancing over her shoulder, she saw Muriele stab the wolf. With her heart pounding, she ran hand-in-hand with her friend. Finally, a ruined castle appeared ahead of them. As they came close, something struck her from behind.

Her dream ended.

Graemme awoke immediately when he heard something strike against the outside door to the men's tower. Not only did something hit once, but it kept a steady beating. And whining. Why, it sounded like a dog running at the door and leaping at it. What animal could be so crazy?

Squat! It had to be him. Graemme bolted up from his pallet and hurried to the door. He must have opened it when Squat had started his leap, for the door swung inward and Squat landed with all four paws smack in the middle of Graemme's belly. He grabbed the little rascal before he could fall to the floor and hurt himself.

"What the Hades is the matter with him?" Brian asked. His voice blurred with sleep.

"Bring a torch. Looks like he's injured himself. Blood. All over his chest." Graemme cradled him and moved close to the light Brian had fetched from outside the door.

"Poor little guy. He must have tangled with a bigger dog," Brian said.

Other warriors woke and crowded around, for they all liked the friendly little misshapen ball of fur.

"Looks like a knife wound to me," one man said as he pointed at blood welling from the dog's shoulder.

"Aye," Graemme grabbed his sheet and tore off a piece to

hold against the wound. "Grunda will know what to do."

Though all had stitched other warrior's wounds when they didn't have a healer handy, none had ever tended a dog afore. They didn't have far to go. Only to the door again, for Grunda appeared out of the darkness. Guards were lighting torches all over the wall walks and the bailey.

"Elyne is missing! I woke yer father. He's already started a search."

"Why did ye not come to me first!"

"Because, fool, he was closer within the keep like ye should have been.

"I will tend the dog. Not all is his blood. 'Tis also from someone else. Check first for Gille," she ordered.

"I just came from the postern gate," an out of breath guard said. "Someone has used a heavy blade to break a hole in the oldest part of the wall alongside the gate. 'Tis not very thick there to allow for the gate. They had it well-covered with brush, from the looks of it. Found this caught on a rough piece." He held up a small piece of thin fabric.

Graemme grabbed it and held it to his nose. Heather!

"Get yer weapons! Someone has taken my wife."

Graemme didn't bother with being neat. He wrapped his kilt around him like it was a blanket and held it there with his sword belt. Sitting on a cot, he stomped into both boots at the same time. By the time he took two breaths, he sheathed his sword, strapped a dagger onto his thigh and started for the door.

"Take Squat with ye." Grunda's voice was commanding. "The wily little dog isna cut deep. He must have shied away in time. He's come to lead ye to Gille and will help hunt for Elyne." Her eyes grew foggy and everyone stilled. They knew she was seeing something none of them could.

"Look for the ruins of a castle. One who was dead has returned to seek revenge. Hurry, for he will be enraged that perfection has been blemished."

Graemme didn't argue or ask for an explanation. Barking frantically, Squat ran out into the darkness.

Graemme and ten of his men followed behind.

CHAPTER 33

ELYNE'S HEAD HURT. WHEN she opened her eyes, she could hardly see. Everything looked dark. She was terribly uncomfortable, so she wasn't in her bed. Why, she was standing against a damp, cold wall! Devil take it! She'd been walking in her sleep. This time, she knew she was in deep danger and 'twas likely no one would find her in time.

A cold fist squeezed her heart, and her back felt as if a family of spiders crawled up it.

Her arms were above her head. When she tried to move them, chains clinked against a moldy stone wall. She felt someone's presence. And heard tinkling laughter.

The hated Elspeth! What was she doing here? For certs, she wouldn't be laughing if she, too, stood chained to a wall.

"Ye made it so easy for me."

Out of the shadows, the woman in the brown cloak came close. With a sweep of her hand, she threw back the hood and revealed the blond hair Elyne dreamed was Muriele's. She remembered wanting to get away from Graemme's painful presence in the keep and crawling through the hole in the wall at the woman's urging.

"There was no wolf chasing me, was there?"

"Nay. Only a young fool with hair as light as mine."

"Gille! Ye didna harm him, did ye?"

"If ye call plunging my dagger in him harmful, then yes, I did. With great satisfaction. He was trying to stop ye."

Elyne surged forward, until the chains jerked her to a halt. The shackles around her wrists cut into her skin.

Elspeth laughed again then put her finger on her chin and

tilted her head, pretending to think. "Oh, and the ugly creature ye're so fond of got in my way."

Elyne cried out in anguish for the loss of the young man and the dog. Both had shown her loyalty and love since she'd met them.

Before she could ask any other questions, someone carrying a torch descended the crumbling steps into the dungeon. He thrust the torch to Elspeth and came close. His hair was as light as Elspeth's and his face too comely for any man. Her mind went through all she knew of Magnus and Clibrick Castle. Her eyes widened in shock and she shook her head to make sure she was seeing aright.

"Ye're Feradoch. But ye were dead when ye left Clibrick. Ye had no heartbeat!"

"Does this feel like a dead man to ye?"

He came over and brought his face close to her. He grabbed her chin to hold her steady and plunged his tongue into her mouth. Elyne tried to pull away but couldn't. She gagged, for after Graemme's kisses, this was no kiss but a vulgar intrusion.

Feradoch's hand on her forehead slammed her head back against the wall.

"That's for not returning the greeting." He scowled in the dim light and reached out to touch her hair. "Bring the cursed light close!"

His pupils dilated when he grabbed her hair and felt over it, looking for braids. He grasped a handful and pulled her head down to see the back of it.

A crazed look came over his face. Veins in his neck stood out in livid ridges as he shrieked. He struck her across the face with such force her head slammed into her right shoulder.

"The bastard has cut yer hair to thwart me!" Grabbing her face again, he forced her to look at him.

"What did ye do to deserve it? Were ye so foolish to tup another man? Mayhap the pretty youth Elspeth killed?"

"I cut it myself! Mayhap ye'd best ask who yer leman has been tupping the last sennight!"

He snarled, turned and backhanded Elspeth across her

cheek. She held tight to the torch as she went flying against the far wall.

"Get back here with the light." He kicked out at her to hurry her. Elspeth pushed away from the wall and came close.

Elyne expected to see tears, hatred or some expression of horror at his striking her, but she had a rapturous look instead. Was the woman crazed?

"Hold the fire close. I will see what pleasure she will bring us." His voice changed from harsh to silky. He moved his feet restlessly. "Let us see if her hair is as dark and fiery around her slit as on her head."

When Elspeth held the torch close, Feradoch grasped Elyne's thin smock with both hands and ripped it from her body so swiftly it created a cold draft. To her shame, her nipples puckered.

"Ye are anxious for me," he gloated and reached out to cup both breasts and squeeze.

"Ye are as crazed as yer leman if ye think ye can take Graemme's place. Ye make my skin crawl."

Elyne gathered all the courage she could and spat at his face.

His fist hit her jaw. Though her ears rang so loud a thousand birds could be chirping in her ears, she imagined she heard a shout of rage.

She welcomed the blackness.

Graemme followed Squat, holding back his horse so the dog's little legs could keep ahead of him. When the dog veered off the path into the bushes, Graemme spotted Gille's body no more than 200 feet from the castle walls. Sliding off his horse, he was on his knees by the young man afore Brian or Colyne could join him.

Blood covered Gille's chest. He breathed a sigh of relief, thankful the blade had struck a rib and deflected it from entering the young man's lungs. His breathing sounded labored, but his eyelids flickered open.

"My Lord," he whispered, "I'm sorry. The small woman fought like a wild creature."

Squat came close and licked his face, causing his lips to twitch in a strained smile.

"I thought she'd killed the wee one."

"I'll have to leave ye, but the men will get ye to Grunda." Graemme pointed to two men who ran over. "Bind his wound. Take him up in front of one of ye and get him to the old woman. She'll have him aright in no time."

He forced a smile down at the young man. "Ye did a verra brave thing, lad. Yer lady will thank ye for it when I return with her."

He had his foot in a stirrup and was onto his mount by the time he finished speaking.

"Brian, let Squat go. He'll lead us to Elyne."

They rode as fast as the little dog could smell the tracks. Squat's legs were lagging when they came to a rise in a hill. Off to the right they saw the ruins of a castle. Only the outer walls of the keep and the lower part of a tower remained.

"Pick the dog up and dinna let him bark, Brian. Stay within the woods and go as quietly as ye can." He motioned to two men at the time, sending all eight to surround the ruins. Once they were in position in the woods, they got off their horses, drew their swords and quietly made their way into the ruins.

Graemme inched up the crumbled part of the tower. When he came to an opening leading beneath the earth and saw flickering light coming from it, he motioned to Colyne to follow. Never had he walked so stealthily when his body urged him to run, for he knew Elyne was below.

His lips twitched and a wave of acid welled up from his belly on hearing what could only be Feradoch's voice. Though it was soft and silky at first, it became harsh and filled with fury.

Below Graemme, a single torch held by Elspeth lit the small dungeon. Before he left this place of torture, he vowed to see her dead for what she was doing.

A few steps more and the scene below unfolded like a nightmare.

His beautiful Elyne hung from shackles against the moldy wall. Her cheeks flamed where Feradoch had struck her

He reached out to rip Elyne's smock from her body. When he cupped both her beautiful breasts and squeezed, only Colyne's hand on his shoulder held him back.

"Ye are anxious for me," Feradoch gloated.

Graemme's anguish at seeing the pain on his love's face near made him cry out. When she spoke, it was the first time he knew she truly loved him as much as he did her.

"Ye are crazed as yer leman if ye think ye can take Graemme's place. Ye make my skin crawl."

She spat in her tormentor's face. Feradoch's mouth contorted grotesquely. He balled his fist and struck her. Her head banged back against the wall then fell forward, her knees crumpled and her weight hung on the shackles around her wrists. Streaks of blood trickled down her arms from where they cut into her fine skin.

Graemme howled with rage as he leapt from the side of the stairwell. He landed close to the cell. Feradoch turned in surprise and ran toward him, screaming and drawing his sword.

"Lock the bars, bitch!" Feradoch hollered at Elspeth.

Colyne called out in his strongest voice, "To Graemme! To Graemme! The dungeon!" He too jumped down the last steps and ran to block Elspeth.

Afore Colyne could reach her, she used the fiery torch to keep him back as she locked the cell's iron door.

Over the years Feradoch lived within Clibrick Castle, Graemme had trained with him. Each knew the other's strength and weaknesses. Feradoch believed he was a superior fighter and could best anyone. He made sure he won, for faced with a loss, he resorted to every dirty trick he could. Graemme was familiar with those, too.

With both hands on their fighting swords, they circled the area until Feradoch struck out. Their swords clashed together, screeching as the blades struck and slid down their lengths. They twirled and struck again, but neither drew blood. They danced apart and studied each other, then flew together for another strike. Feradoch's blade came straight down in a hacking motion, but Gramme turned his blade horizontally to block him and surge upward, shoving Feradoch backward. They tumbled to the floor, shoved apart and sprang back to their feet.

Both blades were free and they attacked again. This time, Feradoch's blade swooshed through the air to behead Graemme. Graemme, expecting it, quickly ducked beneath the blade. As the blade sang in the air, Graemme felt his hair move. He swung his own sword and slashed the skin across Feradoch's thighs.

Feradoch screamed with fury and twirled out of reach. Graemme had time to see Colyne out of the corner of his eye. His friend was having a hard time keeping Elspeth from burning him with the torch. Only his blade kept her back enough so she couldn't reach him. It would be a mistake to make her drop it. Dead leaves and branches on the earth floor accumulated over the years would go up in flames.

Graemme heard the rest of the warriors arrive. He was even aware of Squat's frantic barking. He thanked God that Brian kept a good hold on him or, the wee dog might be injured.

Elyne slowly raised her head and blinked, trying to clear her blurry vision. What hurt the worst? The back of her head, her cheek and jaw, or her wrists that felt like something was trying to separate her hands from her arms?

Fuzzily, she realized 'twas her weight. She shuffled her feet closer to the wall and forced her legs to straighten. Where was that bastard Feradoch? And Elspeth? The woman was not right in the head to prefer the evil, comely blond to Graemme.

Finally, everything seemed to come together. She knew where she was and what was happening so close to her prison.

Saints help them! The crazy woman was trying to set Colyne afire! She was swinging the torch like a fiery sword. It lit even the corners of the room.

'Twas like her dream! Two wolves, one black haired the other blond, struck at each other with their claws. Her forehead wrinkled. She winced again. She must not move her head or face. It hurt too much.

Nay. 'Twas not claws. Swords. Though they snarled like beasts and their eyes clearly showed they intended to kill, they were not wolves but men.

The shrill ringing in her ears was steel striking steel.

Graemme had come for her! After she had shown him naught but scorn since they met — even more so in the past ten days! Yet, he cared enough to risk death to save her. When blood streaked across his chest, she kept herself from crying out. 'Twould distract him.

Elyne's legs wobbled. Widening them a bit, she leaned back against the wall for support.

As she watched, she caught her lower lip between her teeth.

The men fought until both dripped with blood. Graemme began to tire, but each time he glimpsed Elyne hanging in the cell, fury spurred him on. Finally, Feradoch snarled, anticipating a kill. Both their blades pointed to the ceiling, ready to swing down on an unprotected shoulder. Graemme felt a surge of relief. One day while Ranald was at Raptor, he had shown Graemme a new maneuver. He prayed it worked as well now as on the practice field with wooden swords.

When the blades clashed together, they slid down to the guarded hilt, forcing their hands down. By this time, their hilts were even with their stomachs. Graemme shoved forward until Feradoch jumped backward.

He came at Graemme, his sword point aimed to stab him in the heart. Graemme used all his strength to force the blade up over Graemme's head. Turning slightly to the side, Graemme used his elbow to push Feradoch's arm out and away, giving him space. With a rapid move, he brought his own sword up beneath Feradoch's chin and slashed it across his throat.

Feradoch's eyes widened in surprise. Blood spurted in rhythm, splattering Graemme. The dying man's arms dropped and his knees slowly folded until he crashed forward on the floor. The surge of blood slowed as his heartbeat weakened. Finally, it stopped.

Exhausted, Graemme fell to his knees. His head was down as he gasped for breath.

The men surged into the dungeon, now that they wouldn't

be in the way. He saw a flash of hair as Squat headed for his mistress' cell.

Elspeth evaded Colyne and ran with the torch's flame aimed for Graemme's face. Elyne screamed from her cell. He shook his head and looked up. His former love ran at him with a crazed look. He still had hold of his sword, though the tip rested on the floor. His lifted it to thrust the fiery torch out of the way. But he didn't have enough time. She came too quickly.

His blade was halfway up. Crazed, Elspeth didn't notice. Didn't stop.

With the fire still aimed at his face, she screamed incoherently. Squat swerved from his path and charged at the woman's legs. Just before she reached Graemme, the dog sank his teeth in her ankle and tripped her.

Still screaming, she fell onto Graemme's blade. As the sword stabbed through her belly, he heard the sickening sound as it scraped against her backbone on its way through.

The torch fell to the floor.

CHAPTER 34

As THE TORCH IGNITED the debris, the fires of Hades broke loose in the crumbling dungeon. The dog howled when a spark lit the hair on his crooked tail and men yelled and stamped at the floor.

The only quiet came from the two dead bodies.

And Elyne, for she had passed out.

Graemme gathered his senses and shoved himself off the floor. Brian grabbed the dog and swatted at its tail until the flame went out. Colyne and Graemme used their sword hilts to strike at the lock on the cell door. Finally, it broke open. The shackles were old. With one blow, they fell away. Graemme kept his arm around Elyne's waist to keep her from slumping to the filthy floor.

"Hurry, Graemme! We canna hold back the fire!"

"Get yerselves out! We're right behind ye," Graemme yelled.

He handed Colyne his sword and swung Elyne up in his arms. He prayed the bairn was unharmed. He ran, dodging the flames until he reached the stairway. He didn't know which of his men it was, but someone grabbed his waist from behind and shoved, keeping him from stumbling over the side of the ruined steps.

Those who had already escaped grabbed his shoulders and pulled him into the fresh air. Seeing his men were safely above, he glanced down as fire enveloped the dungeon.

They ran from the ruins until they were clear of the flames shooting up from the gaping hole.

"We didna take time to bring their bodies," one man said.

Colyne handed Graemme a blanket.

"Aye. 'Tis best they burn and are covered with rubble," Graemme said as he sat on the ground and tenderly covered Elyne's naked body on his lap.

She groaned and kept her eyes shut tight like a fearful bairn.

"Give her a drop of water," Colyne said as he handed his flask to Graemme. "She looks ready to pass out again."

Elyne had a dreadful ache in her head. Someone was kissing her. Though sloppily.

"Squat, not the lips, ye mangy cur." 'Twas Graemme's voice.

Someone had wet a cloth and washed over her face. It felt delightfully cool. Opening her eyes, she blinked. Obviously, 'twas Squat with the sloppy kisses, for he kept shoving at Graemme's hand holding the wet cloth.

Why was Graemme's chest so bloody? And his kilt?

She blinked again.

"Ye were injured!" She scrambled around and tried to get up, but he tightened his arms around her. "Let me go, ye dim-witted lout! Dinna ye know ye can bleed to death without someone tending to ye?"

She grabbed the sides of her head, for pain shot through it when she moved.

"Hm. Still calling me by delightful names are ye, my sweet talking wife?"

Epilogue

"WHY IS THE BAIRN afeared to show himself?" Graemme stopped pacing to stand in front of Ranald. Chief Angus grinned at his son. Magnus had the nerve to laugh aloud. They had all gathered in the bedchamber across from Graemme and Elyne's while Muriele and Catalin helped Grunda with the birthing.

"She has only been in labor since the midnight hour. The sun is just overhead. Birthing is hard work and takes time," Ranald answered.

"Waiting is hard work, too. She should be more considerate and not worry me so. I've a good mind to go back in there and tell her!"

"Brother, did a chalice striking yer forehead not give ye a clear message?" Magnus' eyes twinkled. "If I were ye, I wouldna go in there again."

Graemme didn't answer but marched over to the door and swung it open. He had not gone inside the birthing chamber more than three steps afore Elyne knew he was there.

"Ye misbegotten, randy goat of a man! I should have let Father pin yer balls to the barbican!"

She stopped to howl out in pain. Once it eased, she screamed at him again.

"Get a leman! Ye'll never swive me again!"

Muriele was standing near Elyne's head, holding it up for her to take a sip of water from a pewter cup. Then Catalin moved from behind Grunda, to see who had entered. He backed up. His eyes widened as he got a clear view of his wife's struggling body. He saw the bairn's head bulging, trying to force itself out of an opening clearly stretched so tight he envisioned her body splitting in two.

He turned to flee through the door. He nearly made it.

Elyne's aim was as good as it ever was, even though she was screaming obscenities at him he had never heard.

The pewter cup hit him squarely in the middle of his back.

Catalin giggled. "Best ye not come back for a while, Graemme. She's, uh, a little angry at ye now."

"Told ye so, brother," Magnus bent over laughing.

"Come, sit," Ranald patted the bench beside him.

Three huge gulps of his wine later, a blood-curdling scream near made Graemme pass out. He started to run to his wife, but Ranald's firm hand kept him seated.

"Tis the sound of the final labor pain. Be patient. Catalin or Muriele will appear soon to tell us whether ye have a son or a daughter."

Graemme slumped back on the chair when a sound like a small kitten sounded from the room.

Another howl of pain, every bit as loud as the previous one, made him straighten. He wanted to go in there in the worst way, but Ranald still held tight to his arm.

"Uh, that sounds familiar. But ye'd best wait and let them clean her up. Ye go in there now, and ye're liable to faint." Ranald smiled and slapped him on the back.

"He's right," Magnus added. "Birthing is a bloody business. She's pretty messy right now, too. She won't appreciate ye seeing her afore she's cleaned up."

Graemme gulped down another swallow of wine then put the chalice down to hold his head. He heard the door open and close and peeked between his fingers to see Ada carrying a bundle of sheets out of the room. Noting they were soaked with blood, he stifled a gag.

The next time the door opened, he didn't dare look for fear of seeing a bloody pallet or such. Instead, he heard steps coming toward him and a small sound.

He straightened and opened his eyes.

Catalin and Muriele stood before him, beaming. They each

held a bundle.

Each bundle squirmed.

"Ah, 'twas what I expected from Elyne!" Ranald said. "Twins!"

Catalin bent down to show Graemme a tiny red face. "Meet yer wee son, Graemme."

Muriele did the same beside her. "Meet yer wee daughter, Graemme."

Graemme promptly fainted face forward, on the floor.

Elyne waited impatiently for Graemme to return the bairns. Ada and Grunda had already bathed her, put a fresh night garment on her then propped her up on clean pillows and brushed her hair.

Finally, someone cautiously opened the door. Graemme peeked around the corner, wary of entering.

"Dinna throw yer soiled water at me or anything of that nature. I have my little army with me," he said with a look of intense pride.

Elyne's snort was as loud as any man's.

"Ye dimwit! Ye fainted like a dairy maid!"

"Humph! I fainted from exhaustion. Being an expectant father is stressful."

Graemme walked as though he was carrying something he feared he would crush. He stopped beside the bed and Elyne saw naught but gentleness in his face. How could she ever have believed he hid evilness in his soul? All because of some stupid dream of a ravening black wolf!

"Ye'd best get over here afore I snatch ye bald. Newborns need nursing, ye know."

"Ah, ye're still enticing me with love talk." Graemme grinned. "If ye think to lure me into swiving ye this night, I'd best confess I am way too tired from all the trouble ye've put me through to think of bed sport!"

He kissed each tiny red forehead afore bending down to lay the bairns in her arms.

"Lout! Ye're tired? Ye lazy Highlander." Her lips twitched

to keep from chuckling at his banter. "If I were not nursing my bairns, I would skewer ye."

"Ye must surrender yer fierce nature. And ye must never hit me now. Think of what it will do to our wee son and daughter to see their fierce mother being cruel to their loving father."

He stopped and rubbed the stubble on his face. His eyes lit. "Mayhap we can have bed sport on the morrow?"

She was busy getting the twins to nurse with Grunda's help, but he jumped back when he saw the look on her face.

"Get near me with a cockstand and I'll cut it off! I have my blade beneath my pillow, so be forewarned, ye unspeakable churl!"

"Grunda, is it natural for a mother to be so unloving after her husband has sacrificed his rest for many nights to give her two perfect bairns?"

Ada laughed so hard Grunda needed to raise her voice to speak.

"Lad, if I were ye, I wouldna come back unless ye have Ranald to hide behind."

He kissed Elyne's forehead and between her eyes then snuggled his head close to her neck to kiss her there.

"Thank ye, from the bottom of my heart for our beautiful family," he whispered.

"And thank ye, my darling, for being so patient. Kiss me properly now!"

He did. With as much fervor as she kissed him.

AUTHOR'S NOTE

Dear Readers,

No reading this before you finish the book! It'll ruin all your fun if you do.

Finally, Elyne has her own story. Surrender takes place at the same time as Ruthless. Ranald's little sister isn't so little any more. In the previous books, he often warned her that spying on men who bathed at the well would lead her to trouble.

I had a lot of fun using her paranormal gift of lucid dreams. In the previous novels, I referred to them as more of a curse than a gift. She was more than likely to misinterpret them than to recognize their true warning.

She'd awake in strange places. Sometimes sitting in the muck of a pigsty, in a horse stall or atop the tallest wall. Being beneath the apple tree was one of her most harmless places until Graemme's footsteps alerted her. Of course, where else could she go but up?'

She couldn't very well balance on the branch with her hands over her eyes, so she really wasn't spying on him, was she? And it was only natural that he thought the lass watching his, er, performance was a serving girl waiting to have a warm toss between the sheets.

Of course, everything had to go wrong. Poor wet, nekid Graemme. He didn't know when he pulled the trim ankle that a beautiful, near nekid lass would fall and send him to the ground with her atop him. Screaming. When Chief Broccin's very large feet appeared to near cradle Graemme's head, their fate was sealed.

They were both too hardheaded to give in easily. It was tremendous fun to write their sparring with each other, each determined to win. And Squat added to the fun.

Did you notice Chief Broccin really had a fondness for the little misshapen dog? You didn't? Pfft! Read the book again, this time between the lines!

He could have kicked Squat across the great hall when he peed on his boots, but he didn't. He could have had it thrown outside the outer gates to fend for itself. Nope. Instead, he tossed food to the dog. Maybe he was gruff because he didn't want anyone to know he had a soft spot? Heck, when he said if Elyne didn't take the dog with her, he'd toss it to the woodland creatures, I believe he was being gruff to hide the fact he'd miss the dog's antics when he was gone.

I knew Elyne couldn't cave in and marry Graemme without a fight. She was mean as a snake when the old crone didn't scare him off. He wasn't about to let Elyne escape him. After all, if the handsome warrior didn't marry her, the Chief promised to, er, take his knife to Graemme's most treasured secret parts and display them as warning to all. Even with the threat to his marvelous anatomy, he had a hard time keeping them secret when they sprang to life every time he thought of her.

The predicament that Graemme and Elyne were in tickled my funny bone. I couldn't help but have fun with their arguments. There's a serious side to the story, too. Graemme is as honorable as Magnus, and he vowed he'd marry Elyne. He had to overcome obstacles that would make a lesser man run for his life!

Oh, and I hope you liked the ending.

Let me know what you thought about this intensely sensual tale.

Brother Cadfael's Herb Garden by Talbot & Whiteman provided information on medieval plants and their uses. There's a wealth of information in this book.

As in the Blackthorn Trilogy and this Raptor Castle Series, please keep in mind that it is not always possible to use only words appropriate to the time. I kept the dialect down to few characters. If any word puzzles you, check The Glossary Pages in my web site at www.sophiajohnson.netor email me at julrig@bellsouth.net.

I'm always happy to answer any questions.

Sincerely,
Sophia

Look for these intriguing romances in
Sophia Johnson's Raptor Castle Series

Available Now
Book 1 *FORBIDDEN*

Brother Ranald of Raptor Castle, a scarred monk in Scotland's Kelso Abbey, has a fearsome temper that causes objects to fly about, turn still waters stormy and candles to light with but a look. In the peace of the abbey. He controls his rage and fights his forbidden desires, but what would he become in the secular world?

'Tis his greatest fear when his father arrives with an army to force Ranald to return to Raptor Castle and wed. This monk turned man must now become husband and warrior.

Book 2 *SEDUCED*

Letia of Seton Castle is as beautiful as she is capable. Famed for her skill at training archers and slingers, she is used to commanding the castles defenses when needful. Married to elderly Baron de Burgh, she has never birthed an heir.

She must protect her castle and people when Maud and Stephen's battles throw England into anarchy. She sacrifices all when her husband devises a plan to save Seton Castle from ruin when he dies.

'Twas a simple plan with very few steps to follow: Capture her enemy, seduce him, bear his child and save her people. But falling in love was not in the plan.

Book 3 *RUTHLESS*

The Morgan and Gunn clans in the Highlands of Scotland have been feuding for longer than anyone can remember, until the chiefs decided to foster their sons with each other.

Before Magnus of Clibrick Castle and Feradoch of Kinbrace Castle exchanged places when they reached their seventh year, their fathers ordered them to swear a blood oath that each would uphold the peace when they became men. Once they are grown and return to their own strongholds, should either man be felled by treachery, the other will seek vengeance for the deed.

Years later when the Gunn's call Magnus to honor the oath, he never expected to hunt down and hang Muriele of Blackbriar, a bewitching woman he captured and fell in love with when he besieged her castle.

Book 4 *SURRENDER*

In *The Taming of the Shrew*, Katharine met her match in Petruchio. She was fortunate not to be in Elyne of Raptor Castle's shoes. When Elyne goes toe to toe with Graemme of Clibrick Castle, he checkmates her every move!

Graemme is not the harsh man that Magnus is, but a vow made is also sacred to him. Elyne keeps one step ahead of him and leads him a merry and sometimes treacherous race before he gets the better of her.

But all is not laughter. Someone plots to kidnap Elyne, and when he tires of her, he will delight in killing her.

Coming Soon!
Book 5 *UNTAMED*

This will be Ysabel and Ranulf's story. Can you picture a beautiful woman, disheveled, wearing a lovely sleeveless smock standing on cobblestones with blood running between the stones? She's holding a bloody short sword, its shaft red and dripping. Her gaze is blank. Shoulders slumped.

Where is Colyne? Instead, a Crusader squats about five paces away, his face curious yet cautious, studying her. Ranald stands behind him, ready to protect her, should the need arise.

Why is she here? What has she done?

ABOUT THE AUTHOR

What can I tell you that won't bore you to bits. I'm a woman - you knew that because I write intense, sensual novels where there's a happy ending. I was born in and still live in Florida, so I know to be careful of the sun and bite my tongue when I see people trying to burn their skin to a crispy brown.

My husband and I are retired. I didn't start writing until 2000. I do historical romance with history as wallpaper - that means I don't bombard you with the politics but do let you know what is the most important thing going on at that time.

I research to use names and foods, medicines, clothing and language of the time. You'll not only picture a dining room table in the middle of a Great Hall when I'm writing but will get a feel for the way things were done at that time.

The names are the most fun to pick out. Especially for women. They used ungodly ugly names for women then, so I always search for one that will give you the picture of the lovely heroine I'm trying to tell you about. Men's names are easier because what male wouldn't like to be called Graemme or something similar. But Graemme wouldn't want to whisper sweet nothings in Wolfleda's ear. *gag* So she became Elyne. Much better isn't it?

Enough about books and a little more about me. My husband and I live with Jamie, our long-coat Chihuahua the neighbors call "The Terrorist," and a mischievous Papillon named Konner.

I write every day in my home office, in case the taxman asks you, and my husband plays golf three days a week and works in the yard the rest. Oh. And he cooks dinner every night.

Now, what could get more romantic than that?

My Tag Line is "Sensual Love through the
Ages," the theme of my novels.

www.sophiajohnson.net

READER REVIEWS

I have not added reviews of The Blackthorn Trilogy because there are so many on Amazon.com for *Always Mine, Midnight's Bride and Risk Everything.* Kensington Zebra didn't advertise the books as a trilogy because they came out with the last one first. But I named it The Blackthorn Trilogy because a trilogy is what it was. The first book, *Always Mine*, sets the whole trilogy into motion.

The Raptor Castle Series should be read in the proper order, because you'll learn the secondary characters from one book and follow him/her to the next.

FORBIDDEN

Janet "bsmrk" *****
"I didn't think that this was possible to surpass *Always Mine (Zebra Historical Romance)* an intense love story or *Midnight's Bride* a love story of delightful innocence or even *Risk Everything (Zebra Debut)* but with Forbidden, the first of the Raptor Series, Sophia Johnson has out done herself. From the first Forbidden grabs you and doesn't let you go until the end which in itself segues into Seduced so well and leaves you so anxious to read this next book."

Stacy *****
"I am a lover of medieval historical romance books and came upon Sophia Johnson's Blackthorn Trilogy.... . Sophia blew me away and took me far away to a medieval castle with some very sexy and sensitive warrior leading men and their feisty heroines! I loved the Blackthorn Trilogy and couldn't wait to

get more of what Sophia delivers: entertaining, amusing and downright sexy books! The first book in the Raptor Castle series *Forbidden* sizzles!"

Brenda Ollis *****
"If you have read any of Sophia's books, you know that she is an exceptional historical romance author. I read the three books in the Blackthorn trilogy and loved them. . . . I didn't think she could top the last three. Well, have no fear!! I read *Forbidden* and could not put it down. Sophia has outdone herself with this first book."

Suzanne Canada *****
"I love her characters - strong, handsome, sexy men and lovely, adventurous, brave ladies all interwoven in a story with twists and turns, ensuring I couldn't put her books down. This first in her new Raptor Castle series, *Forbidden*, certainly did not disappoint! The handsome and mysterious Ranald and his lady Catalin, along with the other intriguing characters in the story, again kept me ignoring housework and family!"

Lauren "llwotb" *****
"I love the writing that Sophia Johnson creates. I have read the Blackthorn series and have just finished *Forbidden* for the second time. Her characters are strong and I wanted more. Hopefully her next books will be out sooner than later."

SEDUCED

Captured by Raptor
BooksRfriends2 *****
"Seduced is the second book in the Raptor Castle Series. If you read book one (*Forbidden*), this continues with Raik's story. Warin De Burgh, the Baron of Seton Castle, is ill and his time is limited... . The Baron has a plan that includes Raik of Raptor Castle, but his beloved wife must agree. It will not be easy to convince her since Letia and Raik do not like each other. If you like historical romances you will want to add this series to your library."

SEDUCED
Cigram33 *****
"Amazing read. So entertaining and informative of the times that the story was set in. I am looking forward to the next offering. CJM"

Wonderful
Tisha *****
"I love this book along with all Sophia's other book. She is by far my favorite author of Medieval romance novels. I can't say enough about them."

A Mesmerizing, Sexy Seduction
Stacy *****
"Sophia has outdone herself with SEDUCED! I LOVED IT!! … A great and entertaining read full of humor and the perfect, feisty seductress."

RUTHLESS

Love, Love, Love this Series
Yolanda *****
"I read the first two in no time *Forbidden* and *Seduced* and had to wait for this to be released. Ruthless was well worth the wait…. . The sexual tension and the fighting between her (Muriele) and Magnus was great, you felt like you were right there with them. I Can't say enough if you haven't read you are missing out on a very good series."

This series just keeps getting better and better and hotter!
Jacqueline "beachpoet" *****
"The Raptor Castle series is a tapestry that weaves itself through time and space, slowly but richly developing a saga of rugged realities, wounded spirits, delicate hearts, silent hopes and ultimate redemption. Each character is given her full attention and is carefully nurtured and developed throughout the series and it is a pleasure to meet them again and again. Her plot lines are skillfully woven, giving small hints here and there, but

never giving themselves away completely, allowing the reader to discover and savor the tension as the stories unfold. All of this is set within lush descriptive period settings and beautifully researched historical detail.

In addition, her "romantic" scenes are fabulous. Few authors can handle sex scenes with her ability to balance romance, sexual tension, sensuality, emotion and eroticism, blending each element into the other to create something the reader can believe in."

www.ingramcontent.com/pod-product-compliance
Lightning Source LLC
La Vergne TN
LVHW041151080426
835511LV00006B/551

* 9 7 8 0 6 1 5 9 8 0 4 6 1 *